No. 2654
$19.95

The Complete COMPUTER CAREER GUIDE

JUDITH NORBACK, Ph.D

TAB BOOKS Inc.
Blue Ridge Summit, PA

dedicated to my Craig Thomas

FIRST EDITION
SECOND PRINTING

Copyright © 1987 by TAB BOOKS Inc.
Printed in the United States of America

Library of Congress Cataloging in Publication Data

Norback, Judith.
The complete computer career guide.

Includes index.
1. Computers—Vocational guidance. I. Title
QA76.25.N67   1986   004'.023   86-5726

ISBN 0-8306-9554-0
ISBN 0-8306-2654-9 (pbk.)

TAB BOOKS Inc. offers software for
sale. For information and a catalog,
please contact TAB Software Department,
Blue Ridge Summit, PA 17294-0850.

Questions regarding the content of this book
should be addressed to:

Reader Inquiry Branch
Editorial Department
TAB BOOKS Inc.
Blue Ridge Summit, PA 17294-0214

Contents

6   Computer Careers of the Future
79

7   Computer Employment Agencies
111

8   Computer Professionals: What Are They Like?
142

9   The Future
158

10   How to Get Your First Computer Job
164

11   Long-Range Computer Career Planning
170

Acknowledgments

I would like to thank the following individuals and organizations for their assistance with *The Complete Computer Career Guide*: Pamela Destaffaney; Peter G. Norback of Rapid Graphics; Pat Walsh of the Bureau of Labor Statistics; Honeywell, Inc.; Apple Computer, Inc.; Sperry Corporation; Applied Data Research, Inc.; the Education Department of the Society of Manufacturing Engineers; the National Association of Personnel Consultants; Schenley Industries; Secretary of the Air Force, Office of Public Affairs; Department of the Army, Headquarters TRADOC; United States Marine Corps Computer Sciences School, Education Center, Marine Corps Development and Education Command; Department of the Navy, Chief of Naval Education and Training, Public Affairs Office; the National Home Study Council, and the National Association of Trade and Technical Schools.

Introduction

The Complete Computer Career Guide is a comprehensive, easy-to-use book that provides current information of vital interest to persons already in computer careers and individuals wanting to work with computers. This book will save you the trouble of consulting many different sources for information about computer careers; for the first time, all the relevant information appears in one place.

The Complete Computer Career Guide will give you fast answers to questions such as these:

- ☐ How hard is it to get a position in computers today?
- ☐ What types of benefits will I experience once I have worked in a computer job for a year?
- ☐ What is involved in a switch to a computer career, and how can I tell if computers are for me?
- ☐ Where can I get the training I need to advance from my present position?
- ☐ What other computer careers are open to me once I have some experience working in a computer job?
- ☐ Which computer careers pay the best and offer the best opportunity for advancement?
- ☐ Should I seek the help of a computer employment agency?
- ☐ What are the latest developments which will lead to major computer careers of the future?
- ☐ How do I get started in finding my first computer job?
- ☐ What are the people like who are now working in computers?

Because you have accurate answers to these and hundreds of other important questions right at your fingertips, you will not have to research each question separately. The *Complete Guide* has been carefully constructed to provide in concise, easy-to-read language information regarding computer careers. Whether you are interested in switching to a computer career, looking for a job in computers, or already working in a computer career, you stand to benefit.

The Complete Computer Career Guide, which is based on 1 1/2 years of research, is a unique, time-saving book that will be your most important reference about computer careers for years to come.

Chapter 1

Working in Computers Today

"The demand for computers and related equipment such as data storage devices, printers, calculators, and similar items is projected to continue to boom through the 1990s. Computer process control and computer-assisted design and manufacture will be widespread. Purchases of computer equipment will represent about one-fifth of all capital expenditures by businesses, by far their largest item of durable equipment spending. The value of domestic production of computers and peripheral equipment is projected to post a 6.9 percent yearly growth rate, ranking it among the top five output gainers.

"Employment in computer manufacturing is projected to grow 3.8 percent a year. Productivity gains have typically been very rapid in this industry, and this will continue."[1]

Projections of the growth of the computer industry into the 1990s, such as the one above, are widespread. In fact, computer applications have ex-panded greatly over the last two decades, and they are expected to continue to expand through the next 10 or 15 years.

The number of workers engaged in developing computer-based systems and in operating these systems is projected to increase substantially by 1995. The number of computer systems analysts, for example, is projected to grow 69 percent between now and 1995, adding more than 212,000 jobs. This occupation will benefit from the rise in new computer applications. The number of computer programmers is also expected to increase 72 percent by 1995 or by 245,000 jobs over this period. The mounting number of new computer applications and the need to modify existing systems should bring about rapid employment growth for computer programmers, despite the increasing efficiency of programming methods and the availability of software packages.

Computer operators should continue their healthy employment growth, increasing 46 percent, or by 111,000 jobs, between now and 1995. This increase is expected to occur as more small and

---

[1]From Monthly Labor Review, U.S. Department of Labor, Bureau of Labor Statistics, "The Job Outlook through 1995: Industry Output and Employment Projections."

1

medium size firms introduce more comprehensive computer systems.

The number of data processing equipment repairs is projected to increase about 56 percent, adding 28,000 jobs by 1995. Many workers will be needed to service the more mechanical computer-related equipment, such as disk and tape drives and printers, in addition to computers. Computers have become increasingly modular in construction, leading to greater ease of repair, but the number of computers is expected to increase rapidly enough to require the services of numerous data processing equipment repairers.

These are just a few examples of computer occupations which will expand a great deal by 1995. More specifics regarding all of the major computer jobs are discussed in Chapter 5.

Despite the overall picture of continued growth, there is one computer career, data entry, which is not expected to grow. The technology for data entry is changing so quickly that fewer keypunch operators are needed. These employees are being replaced by terminal operators, many of whom do this work only incidentally to their main functions—for example, airline ticket agents, cashiers, and so forth. Optical character recognition equipment and direct sensing equipment are other ways of inputting data which are increasing in usage.

Although for most computer careers, the outlook for the next decade is rosy, two major trends, which are expected to continue, have developed in the industry over the last few years. First, the need for experienced computer professionals is very high, but the number of entry-level opportunities has decreased, making it harder to break into a computer career than it has been in the past. For specific advice, whether you are just completing your education or just about to switch into a computer career, read Chapter 5 thoroughly and be sure to consult Chapter 2, "Should You Work in Computers," Chapter 4, "Changing Your Career to a Computer Career," and Chapter 10, "How to Get Your First Job in Computers." Although breaking into the field takes a great deal of persistence and energy, the payoffs as early as a year later will be substantial.

The second major trend is the hiring of more renaissance people or liberal arts graduates for computer jobs. For some computer careers, a technical education such as a bachelor's degree with a major in computer science is a necessity. For other positions, however, people with a more general background, such as a degree in liberal arts with some computer course credits are in demand. Some companies prefer to train the individual for the particular job, knowing that that person is more likely to be promotable to a management position than a person with a highly technical background. A broader education is generally taken to indicate a higher level of communication skills and the ability to get along well with people.

The computer industry, then, is still experiencing substantial growth, which is expected to continue. Entry-level jobs are harder to find, but do exist, and the demand for experienced personnel is high and on the increase in almost every computer career. For some jobs, the emphasis on formal training is gradually changing from a narrow, highly technical approach to a broader orientation.

Chapter 2

Should You Work in Computers?

Whether or not you really want to work in computers depends to a large part on your personality as well as your interests and aptitudes. Be sure to read the paragraph on personality requirements for each of the computer careers described in Chapter 5. You will see that the remarkable variety of computer careers that exist allows for different types of people to find satisfaction in a computer career (Fig. 2-1.) Overall, people working in computer jobs must have the ability to reason logically, a strong sense of responsibility, good communications skills (both oral and written), and an interest in being challenged in their work. Often persons with good mathematical skills do well in computer careers, and an aptitude for music or philosophy is also a plus. For a more complete description of the personality traits of people working in computers, see Chapter 8.

To help you decide whether or not you would be happy in a computer career, do the following:

☐ Read several introductory computer books.

☐ Visit some computer installations in your area.

☐ Ask for a demonstration or two at some of your local computer stores.

☐ Look through the course catalogs from colleges in your area with programs that relate to computing (for more information, see Chapter 11 on Training and Education). They are available in your local library or can be obtained by writing to each college. Visit several classes.

☐ Enroll in one or two courses on computer programming.

☐ If possible, arrange to take a programmer aptitude test. These half-day examinations are sometimes given by large companies or universities to programming position applicants.

☐ Prepare for and arrange to take the Institute for Certification of Computer Professionals' examination for beginning or junior programmers (see Chapter 3).

Fig. 2-1. There are a variety of ways to find out in advance if you would be happy in a computer career. (Photograph courtesy of Applied Data Research, Inc., Princeton, NJ 08540.)

☐ Visit the local chapter of some professional societies relating to computing, for example, the Data Processing Management Association (DPMA), among others. See Appendix A for the names and addresses of other professional societies.

☐ Visit local meetings of user groups for various types of microcomputers. Often users' groups are formed based on the hardware or hardware vendor, so there may be an Apple/Macintosh Users' Group or an IBM PC Users' Group in your area. The best way to find out about meetings, other than word-of-mouth, is to call a local computer store or check the local newspaper.

☐ If possible, you may want to look into using a computer program that is specifically written to help people with their career choices. For more information about these programs, one of which is the System of Interactive Guidance and Information (SIGI), developed by the Educational Testing Service in Princeton, New Jersey, contact your high school guidance counselor or the computer department of a college near you.

You may want to do only some of the things suggested above to help you decide whether a computer career will be rewarding for you. Each of the ten recommendations will help you find out more about your interests and talent as they relate to a computer career.

Chapter 3

Certification

Some companies encourage their employees to acquire certification within a certain area, while others are not as interested in certification as in other qualifications.

Certification in four different areas relating to computing is available from the Institute for Certification of Computer Professionals (ICCP), 2200 East Devon Avenue, Suite 268, Des Plaines, IL 60018, (312) 299-4227. The Institute was founded in 1973 as a nonprofit umbrella organization by eight computer societies: The Association for Computing Machinery (ACM), The Association for Educational Data System (AEDS), Automation One Association (A1A), The Canadian Information Processing Society (CIPS), Data Processing Management Association (DPMA), Computer Society of the Institute of Electrical and Electronic Engineers (IEEE), the Association for Systems Management (ASM), and Office Automation Society International (OASI). Today, the eight societies are joined by a ninth, the Association of the Institute for Certification of Computer Professionals (AICCP). The goal of ICCP is to ensure the professionalism of the computer industry, and in accord with this goal, it has certified over 29,000 computing professionals since its inception.

In order to be certified, a computer professional must take an examination, which is offered twice each year, and agree to subscribe to the ICCP Code of Ethics, Conduct, and Good Practice.

WHO CAN BE CERTIFIED?

As of 1986, individuals working in four different areas can be certified by ICCP. Certification in Data Processing (CDP) is meant for individuals knowledgeable about the management of computer systems. Certification in Computer Programming (CCP) was developed for senior programmers. The two new certification programs are Certified Systems Professional (CSP), which is intended for high-level systems analysts and system managers, and Associate Computer Professional (ACP), which is available to qualifying junior programmers and entry-level programmers.

Each half-day examination is reviewed annually and updated as needed, so it reflects the rapid changes in computer technology. The tests are given each year in May and December at various sites across the country and abroad.

CERTIFICATION IN DATA PROCESSING (CDP)

The application fee for first-time registrants for the CDP examination is $35, although this one fee extends through four testings. (The testing fee is $25 plus $16 per section.) To take the examination, the applicant must have the equivalent of five years of computing work experience. The typical candidate for the CDP exam is a systems analyst or a business programmer. The exam itself consists of five sections which must be completed successfully (70 percent of each section answered correctly) in order for a candidate to be certified. The five sections are data processing equipment, computer programming and software, principles of management, accounting and quantitative methods, and systems. A second prerequisite of certification is the agreement to abide by the ICCP Code of Ethics, Conduct, and Good Practice.

As of 1986, in order to continue to be certified, an individual with Certification in Data Processing must, every three years, either pass another CDP examination or complete 120 hours of course work.

An official CDP Study Guide, which includes sample questions that actually appeared on the CDP examination several years earlier, is available from the ICCP for $14 ($12.50 plus $1.50 for postage and handling). Also available free of charge is the Certificate in Data Processing Examination Announcement, which includes a list of the test sites; an application; a description of the exam content; a copy of the ICCP Codes of Ethics, Conduct, and Good Practice; and a bibliography.

CERTIFICATION IN COMPUTER PROGRAMMING

The testing fee for the CCP examination is $105. No specific level of experience is required for applicants, although, as noted above, the examination is intended for senior-level programmers or programmers with quite a breadth of experience. The exam is made up of six sections. Each candidate must take the first five sections, which cover data and file organization, principles and techniques of programming, interaction with hardware and software, interaction with people, and associated techniques. For the sixth section of the test, each candidate can choose one of three specializations: business programming, scientific programming, or systems programming. All six sections of the CCP examination must be successfully completed in a single testing session, and the individual must agree to abide by the ICCP Code of Ethics, Conduct, and Good Practice for certification to be awarded.

As of 1986, in order to maintain his or her certification, a person with CCP status must, every three years, either successfully complete another CCP examination or take 120 hours of relevant courses.

An official CCP study guide, which contains sample questions used on previous CCP examinations, can be ordered for $14 ($12.50 plus $1.50 postage and handling) from the ICCP. Also available is the CCP Examination Announcement, which includes a list of the test sites; an application; a description of the contents of the test; a copy of the ICCP Codes of Ethics, Conduct, and Good Practice; and a bibliography.

CERTIFIED SYSTEMS PROFESSIONAL (CSP) AND ASSOCIATE COMPUTER PROFESSIONAL (ACP)

As mentioned previously, the Certified Systems Professional program and the Associate Computer program both began in 1986. Information on testing fees for the CSP and ACP examinations and on the renewal of certification for the two programs is available from the ICCP. Study guides, as well as CSP and ASP examination announcements, can be ordered from the ICCP. The price of each guide is expected to be similar to the guide prices for the CDP or CCP examinations.

Chapter 4

Changing Your Career to a Computer Career

Career changing has become a wide-spread phenomenon in recent years. One recent estimate suggests that 80 percent of all working Americans think they are in the wrong job. Another indicates that up to a third are dissatisfied with their current job. Some job counselors say that the average American now has three careers in a lifetime (Fig. 4-1).

Why are millions of Americans changing careers? Many reasons are cited for the phenomenon. Individuals today feel less loyalty to the company and are looking for more fulfillment and challenge in their jobs. Some also switch careers for monetary reasons. Changing careers has become acceptable instead of being the stigma it was a generation ago.

Many who change careers have chosen their first career for the wrong reasons. Often they "fall into" a career just out of college because of family expectations or because of the excitement, high salary, or status that they feel the job will offer them. They do not always consider their actual interests and abilities.

Usually, career changes stem from unhappiness and often from lifestyle considerations—a Wall Street broker, for example, may start dreaming of spending more time in the country.

Many people, of course, consider changing careers but do not actually carry out their plans. Their financial obligations sometimes prevent them from doing so. The majority of career changers either have a spouse with a paycheck or are single and have fewer financial responsibilities. Other people never make a career switch because the actual process of switching is difficult. And, instead of being dissatisfied with his or her career, a person in a new career trades dissatisfaction for anxiety. Usually, it takes an entire year for most individuals to feel comfortable with the changes they have made.

Other individuals, however, consider the potential benefits of the switch worth the trouble. Sometimes even a lower financial payoff is an acceptable trade-off to a person who will be enjoying his or her work.

Once a person has decided to try to make a ca-

Fig. 4-1. One of the most important parts of a career switch into computers is getting started. Many programmers later move into other computer positions. (Photograph courtesy of Sperry Corp.)

reer change, though, he or she usually stays with his or her new occupation. Experts estimate that between 70 and 80 percent of people who try to change their career succeed—that is, they remain in their new vocation.

TIPS ON MAKING THE CHANGE

Some amount of introspection or self-analysis is helpful before switching to a computer career. Consider what you want out of your career and what aspects of a job are the most important for you. One job counselor recommends pretending to write your own obituary as a means of helping you to decide just what kind of work you want to be doing. "Joe Smith, best known as _____, passed away yesterday at the age of 119 . . ." The recommendation seems pretty drastic but can be effective in helping you to see what you consider most

important in life. Many career changes are made at midlife, partly because the individual becomes aware of the imminence of death.

Instead of imagining your obituary, you could think about what it is that you have done in the past (part-time job, full-time job or hobby) that you have liked. What activities do you enjoy even when you are not paid to do them? Think about why you want to make a career change and what attributes of a job are the most important for you. Monetary reward is important but, as industrial psychologists have known for some time, it is not the sole determinant of job satisfaction for most people. Work environment, the opportunity to advance, the amount of travel required, the amount of hours in a normal work week, and the amount of communication between supervisor and employee are among the many variables that affect whether or not a person is satisfied with his or her job. Make a list of the things you dislike about your present career, and then put them in order of importance. Make a second list of the things you feel will be important to your liking your new career, and then prioritize this list. Be sure to review and modify these lists often, so what you are looking for in your new career will be very clear to you.

Many aspects of the major computer careers are described in Chapters 5 and 6. Read them very carefully. Additional specifics on deciding whether or not a computer career is for you are discussed in Chapter 2.

Be sure to keep your present job while you are attempting to change to a new career. Doing so will make you more marketable; a person who is presently employed, even if in another profession, is more readily hired than an individual who is unemployed or "between jobs." Do not quit your job to allow more time for your job hunt, because the disadvantages will outweigh the advantages.

Keeping your current position is also important because it will allow you to make small changes, where possible, before you make drastic or major changes. For example, get work experience in the computer field before you drop all ties to your old job. There's no substitute for experience when it comes to finding out what the job will really be like. If, after reading about particular computer careers and after reading Chapter 2 on "Should You Work in Computers?," there are two or three computer careers that seem to fit your abilities and interests, work part-time in all three positions before making a permanent leap. Although it will be possible to change later from one computer career to another, it is easier to make a career switch into computers if you really enjoy your new work.

If you cannot keep your present position while you are job-hunting, your next best alternative is to have a part-time job related to your new area of interest.

Be patient and persistent. Changing careers takes almost as much time per week as working at a full-time job. And with today's job market (see Chapter 1), it will be much easier for you to move up the ladder once you've worked with computers

for a while than it will be to get your first full-time computer job. You will need to follow the recommendations in Chapter 10 on "How to Get Your First Job in Computers."

Besides patience and persistence, many experts mention motivation and courage as essential to switching to a computer career. The transition will not be easy, but when you have completed this book, at least you will be well-informed regarding what to expect.

JOB HUNTING

When I decided to switch to a computer career from teaching almost five years ago, I started by getting a part-time job working as an assistant in a data processing training department. At the same time, I enrolled in an introductory COBOL course at a nearby community college. I had decided to switch to computers partly because I had enjoyed working with the computer as a user while running statistical tests for my masters and doctoral theses. I had also enjoyed math all through high school and part of college (at which time I stopped taking it because I did not want to teach it). Also important to me was a steady 12-month job (unlike nine-month teaching jobs), and I wanted to work in a field which offered more opportunity for advancement than did teaching. I enjoyed my COBOL class, partly because I have always liked working on and finishing projects, and each program was like a small project. It was gratifying for me to work on a task, see it finished, and know the job was well done, because the program did the work it needed to do.

I interviewed at various companies near where I lived for three or four months. The list of companies to which I sent my resume included companies listed in the local Chamber of Commerce booklet under "Data Processing" as well as other companies of which I had heard on my part-time job. I also sent my resume to companies which had ads for computer position openings in several local newspapers. A few days after submitting my resume, whether it was sent in response to an actual opening or not, I called each company and asked for an interview. At one company in particular, I remember having to call the personnel manager at 7:30 a.m. His assistant had suggested my calling back at that time because I had been unable to reach him for the past few days. Even though my persistence was beginning to give out, I did talk with him that day at 7:30 and, after several more phone conversations, he agreed to interview me. Meanwhile, I had been making inquiries at other companies.

I had hoped to start in computers as a programmer, but I felt that getting a full-time job in computers—to get started—would be better than remaining in my part-time position. I interviewed at two other companies for computer positions that were at a lower level than programming. In a second interview, the personnel manager to whom I had talked at 7:30 a.m. mentioned that his company was presently discussing the possibility of having some systems programmer trainee openings. He had me come back to be interviewed by two people in the systems programming/software development department: the manager and a supervisor.

The two most important points of my interview were that the supervisor asked me if I wanted to be an applications programmer or a systems programmer. I honestly admitted that I didn't know the difference, and he then explained them to me (Chapter 5). I answered that I definitely wanted to be a systems programmer, because the work sounded more challenging. When the manager interviewed me, he said the final decision on whether to hire trainees had not yet been made, but that he would get back to me. I mentioned that I was interviewing at two other companies with openings for computer positions. He looked surprised when I said I would accept one of their offers if they made them first. He asked if that were the case even if I would be working in a much lower-level position.

I replied yes, that I wanted to start.

A few days later, I was offered the job, and a week later started working as a systems programmer trainee.

I've described my experience changing careers from college teaching to systems programmer trainee because it illustrates several of the points discussed earlier. Persistence is very important during a career transition. Even if you've determined that a change will bring you innumerable benefits, the switch does take time. It is important to continue to work while you are investigating a change of occupations. Keeping your present job is highly recommended; otherwise a part-time job related to your new career area is a good idea. Do not spend all of your time job-hunting; a part-time job demonstrates your interest, as does enrollment in a course in an area related to your new career.

My experience also demonstrates that in making a change in careers, it is important to be willing to prove yourself and to be willing to start in a lower-level position, if necessary. In my case, things worked out so I could avoid this. Even if an individual has to accept a lower salary as part of a career change, however, the salary level will be only temporary. It is well-known within the computer industry that it is easier to make a job change (to another job within the area of computers) or be promoted with a year's experience in computing than it is to try to break into the field. Although I recommended earlier trying to find an opening regarding your favorite type of work (or what you expect to be your favorite) when you are switching into computers, it may be necessary to compromise in order to get started. Once you have started, a number of opportunities and alternatives will be available to you.

Chapter 5

Computer Careers

The computer-related positions described in this chapter offer a wide range of career options. Each position is followed by a complete job description listing its environment and related responsibilities, educational requirements, benefits and drawbacks, and an outlook on the future of that particular career.

APPLICATIONS PROGRAMMER

No computer can do any work on its own, but it can follow step-by-step instructions in special languages which tell it exactly how to perform a particular task. *Applications programmers* write these step-by-step instructions, called *programs* or *software*, that guide the operation of the computer (Fig. 5-1). The programmers basically fill in the sketch provided by the analyst's specifications. They describe the task in one of a variety of programming languages in which, unlike English, each phrase is very specific and has only one meaning.

Business applications programmers work on business-oriented projects, while *engineering* and *scientific applications programmers* are concerned with scientific and/or engineering computer programs and with business programs which are mathematical in nature. The specific tasks that programmers want the computer to accomplish vary a great deal. For example, some programs analyze traffic congestion, while others process car loan payments or telephone bill payments. Processing payroll checks and controlling warehouse inventory are other tasks that are done by programs. Computer software is used to arrange the flight patterns of thousands of airplanes at major airports, to predict the amount of stress that will be felt by the parts of a building during a hurricane, and even to land astronauts on the moon. Every day, people in America and around the world are devising new ways to use the computer to perform even more jobs.

Many individuals enter the field of computers by finding applications programming work, although it is no longer quite as easy to break into the field this way as it used to be. Because today's employers are especially interested in hiring ex-

Fig. 5-1. Applications programmers write step-by-step instructions that guide the operation of the computer. (Photograph courtesy of Applied Data Research, Inc., Princeton, NJ 08540.)

13

perienced programmers, sometimes it is necessary to work part-time before working full-time. For more information, see the paragraphs below regarding "Training and Background (or Experience) Required," and "Outlook for the Future."

Newly hired and relatively inexperienced applications programmers spend their first several weeks attending training seminars and classes. During the next several months, the programmer usually works under the close and direct guidance of a more experienced programmer. Throughout his or her career, an applications programmer keeps abreast of changes in technology by going to seminars or workshops offered by vendors or their own employers. Usually, the programmer's employer foots the bill for training directly related to the programmer's responsibilities.

Applications programmers perform seven different functions: examination of the system analyst's specifications, program design, coding or writing the program, testing and debugging the program, documenting the procedures related to the program, implementing the program, and maintaining or supporting the program. Different positions will place more emphasis on one activity than another, but usually each function is part of an applications programmer's job. The seven functions will be described below, after which variations from the norm and general points will be discussed.

The programmer usually begins a new project by taking the time to review and understand the systems analyst's specifications. He or she will check to see exactly how the data is expected to be processed and what the results of the program are expected to be. Often, the programmer's examination of the analyst's specifications will reveal some inconsistencies or some points which have been overlooked.

Once the programmer has a thorough understanding of what is needed, he or she meticulously plans or designs the program. To do this, the programmer gathers further information about the project. For example, if the program will be taking an inventory of the parts in an auto parts warehouse, before designing the program, the programmer must know how many different auto parts there are in the warehouse, how each part is ordered, where the parts are located and how they are identified, how the warehouse clerks know when a particular part is out of stock, and many other things. Then the programmer uses this information to design the program or to plan out all of the logical steps that the program must include in order for the computer to do the correct job. Most programmers prepare a *flow chart*, or a diagram of the *logic flow* or each of the steps that are required for the program. The flow chart must indicate all the possibilities. For example, at a decision point where the question "Is this part out of stock?" is checked, the flow chart must indicate what processing will occur if the answer to the question is "yes" and what processing will be done if the answer to the question is "no."

Many programming managers emphasize the importance of spending time in meticulous program design. Some managers feel that, ideally, a programmer should spend more time on this step than on any other. If a program is not well-planned, the programmer can spend days or weeks in the testing and debugging stage, which will be described shortly.

A third programming function is the actual coding or writing of the step-by-step instructions. The programmer translates each part of the flow chart into very precise instructions, which cause the processor or computer to execute one of its operations—for example, storing data, comparing digits, or printing out information or displaying it on VDTs. Although there are a number of different programming languages used by applications programmers, four of the languages are used frequently. The most popular is *COBOL*, the Common Business-Oriented Language, which is used for most business applications that do not run on microcomputers. *FORTRAN*, which is an acronym for Formula Translation, is used primarily for mathematical, scientific, and/or engineering problems. The programming language that is now used widely on microcomputers, although it was designed for use by beginners, is called *BASIC*, Beginners' All-Purpose Symbolic Instruction Code. One language which has gained in popularity recently is *RPG*, Report Program Generator, which is utilized when producing reports.

During this stage of programming, which involves the basic task of translating the flow chart into lines of code, the programmer must be extremely meticulous and pay very close attention to the order of the instructions and their syntax.

The most time-consuming of all the programming stages is usually the *testing* and *debugging* stage. During this step, sample data is used to test almost every logical function of the program (time usually does not permit the testing of every branch in the code, but this is clearly the ideal). Programmers almost always find a mistake or "bug" in some part or parts of their programs; the program "blows up" or ceases to process at some point. Errors of this type are almost inevitable because so many instructions are included in the program, and there are so many different ways in which they can be combined. Some senior programmers, however, have enough experience and spend enough time in program design to minimize this stage. When the program encounters an error, it produces a *memory dump* or a map of the computer's memory at the point in time when processing halted. Often, the dumps amount to huge stacks of computer paper. The programmer reads the dump to see if he or she can locate the problem; he or she can locate the exact instruction that is in error as well as a great deal of other information. Dump-reading is a skill that is usually taught to beginning programmers, and their skill improves by actually reading dumps.

Once the problem or bug is located, the programmer must correct it and test the program to be sure that the error has been fixed. Then he or she continues with his or her testing until he or she is confident that the program has been completely debugged—contains no mistakes—and is therefore ready for use.

The testing and debugging process is critical because companies can lose enormous amounts of money if a program is not processing correctly. It is the programmer's responsibility to check the program thoroughly enough to know that it is performing all of its functions or calculations properly.

Documenting the program, or writing a description in English of what the program does, is the next stage of programming. It is the least favorite stage of most applications programmers, who sometimes skip this stage so they can progress more quickly to working on a new project. Documentation, however, is very useful to the computer operators, the system or program users, and to other programmers who modify the program in the future.

The *implementation* stage involves making the program available to users for their day-to-day tasks. Minor modifications may be made in the program at this time, and part of the program may be automated according to the company's standards. The programmer sometimes discusses the program with the analyst one more time.

The last function of programming is one of the most important functions: *maintenance*. Periodically, due to a change in the hardware configuration or because of a new function that is needed, the program is checked and modified. Before the modification is made, the programmer must look through the code until he or she understands the design of the whole system. This may be a lengthy process, especially if inadequate documentation has been provided by the program's original author. Then the programmer must code his or her changes with care, so the added functions will not affect the program's present functions. After adding the code, the programmer will need to test and debug it, just as if he or she were writing the program from scratch.

It has been estimated that three out of four programmers are involved with maintenance work. The initial development of a program, according to some sources, costs about 40 percent of the total costs that will be required during the life of the program. The other 60 percent is required for maintenance.

Despite the fact that so many programmers are involved with at least some maintenance work, most programmers definitely prefer to work on new, more exciting projects. For this reason, inexperienced or beginning programmers are often assigned to maintenance work. The work of a *maintenance applications programmer* differs from that of a development applications programmer in a number of ways. Development programmers usually code only a section of the program, because they often work in teams. They do not need to fully understand in detail the overall design of the program, while maintenance programmers do. Development programmers normally work on only one project at a time, while maintenance programmers often work on modifying more than one project at once. And while development programmers experience a great deal of pressure when they are approaching a deadline, maintenance programmers often get calls in the middle of the night regarding a system malfunction that must be fixed right away.

Senior programmers may have other responsibilities in addition to the above seven functions of all programmers. They may help coordinate the programming department's work with the work that is being done in other DP departments. They may frequently discuss projects with systems analysts, and they sometimes help solve difficult programming problems. Sometimes, they serve as the head programmer on a team of programmers who are coding a large program. As the team leader, they supervise the work of the four to six programmers who are each working on different segments of the program. The team approach has proven quite successful in the writing of very large programs. Team members solve difficult problems together and discuss ideas with each other. They also help keep each other motivated until they finish the lengthy project.

One issue that has been a concern of programming managers for a number of years is the question of standardizing program code. Each programmer tends to write programs very different from every other programmer. If these differences could be minimized, then it would be easier for a programmer to modify another programmer's code. The use of *structured programming* and *application development software* has increased in an effort to help solve this problem. For example, when structured programming techniques are used, a large program can be split into parts, coded by separate programmers, and then fitted together.

This approach lends itself to the team programming approach. Application development software are programs that can be used to develop other programs more quickly and effectively. Instead of writing programs from scratch, programmers can fill in the blanks and then string together pieces of programs into larger programs. The use of applications development tools helps to standardize the code written or generated by programmers, and it also helps to speed up the programming development process, thereby saving the company quite a bit of money.

Cutting the costs of programming is important because companies invest thousands and sometimes millions of dollars annually on programming. According to one estimate, each debugged program costs about $10 per line, and most programs consist of thousands of lines.

It is not unusual for there to be an enormous backlog of applications that users have requested but that the programming department has been unable to work on. Irregardless of the tremendous demand within companies for applications programming, sometimes management decides to drop large programming projects that have been worked on for several years. There are a number of reasons this type of decision is made, including simply a change of guard at the upper levels of a company.

Programming work can be methodical and boring, and it can be fascinating. The results of a programmer's efforts are quite tangible—he or she can watch the computer do what he or she has instructed it to do, such as produce a report or perform some calculations. Programmers normally work about 40 hours per week, although their hours are not always from 9 to 5. Once or twice weekly, programmers usually need to go in early or work late in order to get test time on the computer or to move systems into production. Weekend hours are required at times, in particular when an important deadline is approaching. When new programs are being tested, it is not uncommon for programmers to be called at any hour by the operators for advice.

Job Environment

An applications programmer spends most of his or her day seated at a desk in a semi-private or private office. The programmer's office is usually located near the data center, and most application programmers have their own terminal (VDT) or microcomputer. When the programmer is not working on the terminal, he or she may be talking with end users or the systems analyst about his or her present project.

Alternate Titles

Applications programmers are sometimes called *computer programmers*, or commercial or business programmers. Related careers that are described in this section are: *database programmer, minicomputer and microcomputer programmer, systems programmer* and *telecommunications programmer*. Programmers are sometimes referred to as *programmers/analysts,* as mentioned above, if their responsibilities include systems analysis functions as well as programming.

Training and Background (or Experience) Required

Some employers believe that the area or discipline in which an individual is trained is not as important to his or her success in applications programming as whether or not he or she has an aptitude for programming. Therefore, a number of companies—especially large ones—have applicants for trainee or junior programming positions take aptitude tests, which usually last half a day. The scores on the tests are used to cut down the pool of applications; individuals who made the cut are interviewed. If an applicant does not score well on the aptitude test, then he or she may end up with a programming job in a smaller company that does not have as rigid a selection procedure. There is, though, quite a bit of skepticism on the part of people who work in computer careers as to whether scores on aptitude tests actually reflect how good a programmer a particular person will be.

There is, in fact, no universal training requirement for applications programmers, because employers' needs vary. Most people now working as programmers have two years of college or vocational school training, although computer science is taught in some high schools, many vocational schools, community and junior colleges, and universities.

Recently, more and more employers prefer to hire men or women with a college degree as applications programmers. Having a B.S. in computer science or a related field is especially important for an individual who expects to progress up the DP management ladder. Scientific or engineering programmers are expected to have a B.S. in engineering, computer science, math, or a related area.

One indication of expertise in the field of programming is the acquiring of certification. For an individual to obtain a Certificate in Computer Programming, he or she must take and pass the Institute for Certification of Computer Professional's extensive examination. In addition, he or she has to agree to subscribe to the ICCP Code of Ethics. For detailed information on certification, see Chapter 3.

The job of applications programmer is an entry-level position, but most companies prefer to hire a person with at least some part-time experience. As recently as five years ago, companies were in such desperate need of programmers that most of them were willing to train programmers themselves. Today, because there are more programmers with experience than ever before, fewer companies have their own training programs, and it is harder to break into programming with no experience than it has been in the past. As soon as programmers have at least one year of experience, however, especially in COBOL programming, they find themselves very much in demand. One computer employment agency estimates that senior programmers (those with more than three years of experience) stay at a job for an average of less than two years.

Benefits and Drawbacks

Salary. As with other computer careers, an

applications programmer's salary depends upon his or her level of experience as well as the size and location of the firm for which he or she works. Generally, annual salaries range from $22,000 to $37,000 for commercial or business programmers and slightly higher for engineering or scientific programmers. Large companies tend to pay higher salaries because they often need more complicated programs which require more technical expertise.

Opportunity to Advance. An applications programmer's opportunity to advance is usually very good, regardless of the size of his or her employer. Many applications programmers move into systems programming positions, especially if they enjoy the technical aspects of their work. Programmers who enjoy their work but prefer more interpersonal interaction often become systems analysts. DP management positions such as project leader or programming manager are also jobs into which applications programmers can progress. Some seasoned programmers start consulting businesses of their own or work for consulting firms. Read the descriptions of these careers in the following sections for a more detailed account.

Travel. The amount of travel that an applications programmer does depends on his or her specific responsibilities. For example, many programmers travel very little, mostly to attend seminars or trade shows. Other programmers, however, need to implement their programs at many different user locations, which may be located as close as a nearby city or as far away as another country.

Other Considerations. There are many disadvantages and many advantages to the job of applications programming. The major drawback is the pressure to complete programs by a certain date. Although the pressure is generally not as intense as that felt by systems programmers, there are times when it can be almost relentless. Of course, more important projects have more important deadlines, so as a programmer progresses from a junior level to a senior level, he or she will feel the tension in his or her position increase. Secondly, programmers are sometimes required to work in the evenings, early mornings, or on weekends, es-

pecially during the testing of major systems. And they are not always directly compensated for extra hours. During the testing and the implementation stage of their projects, programmers often get calls late at night or very early in the morning due to the presence of some errors or bugs in their programs.

The exhilaration that most programmers feel after successfully implementing their system, however, is one advantage of this type of work. Many programmers feel a real sense of accomplishment because their work is so challenging. The challenge itself—of finding the exact sequence of instructions that will tell the computer to do just what the programmer wants it to do—is enjoyable to most people working in this field. As mentioned above, a keen sense of intellectual satisfaction is often felt by individuals developing systems that many people will use and that will save their employers money. One final advantage to the career of applications programming is the respect that the position is given in the business world.

Personality Required

An applications programmer must be logical, organized, and analytical. He or she needs to be able to work with a high degree of accuracy and have the ability to think through long complicated problems. The ability to communicate both verbally and in writing is also required of today's programmers, who find themselves interacting with other people as well as working on the terminal or microcomputer. But working alone still constitutes a major portion of the programmer's day, so a programmer should enjoy working in solitude.

Successful programmers are persistent, patient, and even-tempered. In order to solve new problems, they need to be creative and independent thinkers. And because, by some estimates, job skills in the computer industry are outdated every three years, programmers need to be individuals who enjoy constantly learning how to do new things.

In his book *The Psychology of Computer Programming,* Gerald Weinberg discussed the six traits which he believed to be essential to computer programming. These traits, which are discussed in more detail in the chapter on "Computer Professionals: What Are They Like?," include the ability to tolerate stressful situations, adaptability to change, neatness and orderliness in work, humility, assertiveness, and a sense of humor.

Outlook for the Future

Several years ago, the Bureau of Labor Statistics estimated that the demand for computer programmers would increase by 77 percent from 1980 to 1990. Recently, the Bureau predicted that the demand for programmers would increase from 1984 to 1995 by 72 percent. So, although the field is not expanding quite as quickly as it used to be, there will be many opportunities for programmers in the near future. Demand for experienced programmers is now exceptionally high and is expected to remain high over the next few years.

Two trends will have a substantial impact on the future demand for programmers. First, as office automation spreads—as more processes that were done manually become automated—more programmers will be needed to support and maintain the programs that are being used. Some feel, however, that the increasing use of user-friendly software packages may decrease the need for the applications programmer in the future. Companies will come to rely on packages bought or leased from vendors instead of depending on programs that were developed by their own programmers.

Realistically, the second trend is not expected to exert a substantial influence in the marketplace for years to come. Companies have invested millions of dollars in programs written in COBOL, which is now the language in greatest demand. These programs need to be supported and maintained. Because the cost of replacing an existing system is quite high, and because the cost of replacing a large system is enormously high, most companies will not be phasing out their COBOL programs for many years. This will be true even if, once the vendor's package were installed, costs would decrease. In summary, most companies have so much money invested in COBOL programs, and the cost of converting a system is so high, that they will continue to use those programs in the near future.

Where to Find Openings

Companies with large computer installations, particularly the headquarters of large businesses that are located in or near major cities, usually have dozens and sometimes hundreds of applications programmers on staff. Examples of these organizations include banks, insurance companies, government agencies, manufacturing firms, and companies that deal in wholesale marketing. Computer service firms, which provide services for a fee, are also major employers of applications programmers. Companies with medium-sized or small computer installations also employ applications programmers. These organizations often make good starting points for inexperienced programmers because their entry requirements are sometimes less rigid and because a programmer working in a smaller company often has broader responsibilities and therefore gets valuable experience.

COMPUTER CONSULTANTS

Computer consultants perform a wide variety of tasks, depending on the particular situation. Often they give companies advice regarding the purchase and installation of new computer equipment. They check to see if the system the company plans to acquire will definitely fulfill the company's needs. Consultants advise both large and small companies as well as individuals, such as doctors, who are interested in computerizing their offices, but who do not have the time to decide on the equipment and purchase or develop the appropriate system.

Consultants also design systems for client companies. Their work ranges from running feasibility studies and advising company employees on the design of the software for a particular system to working with hardware designers to create the hardware that will meet the company's needs.

Sometimes consultants write computer programs or make coding modifications to existing systems. A consultant is hired to help with programming when the company is experiencing a peak workload for example, or when the company has been unable to hire a full-time employee with the programming skills required for a certain project.

Some companies hire consultants to teach some of what they know to company employees. The consultant will share his or her expertise at a seminar or a series of workshops held at the company. Once in a while, and usually only in a very large client company, a consultant will supervise or manage other programmers. Although about four-fifths of a computer consultant's work is highly technical in nature, about one-fifth involves the preparation of documentation, written material, charts, and working manuals.

The exact conditions of a computer consultant's work varies with the project upon which he or she is working. The consultant usually works under the supervision of a technical manager. The project on which he or she is working may be completed in a week, a month, or a year or two. And consultants sometimes work on several different projects—for several different clients—simultaneously. When working under such an arrangement, the consultant will usually spend two or three days a week working at one customer's site and the rest of each week working at another customer's location.

There are many different types of clients, and they have a wide variety of reasons for hiring consultants. A small company, an individual with an office, or a company whose business is done in an area unrelated to computing (for example, retailing) will hire a computer consultant to advise them on their office automation because they do not have the interest or the time to do the work themselves. They would need to take the time to learn new skills that they may need only rarely in the future, and meanwhile, their attention would be diverted from their primary money-making activity. At times, large companies will hire consultants to work on a project with a very tight deadline, when their DP department is already backlogged. Besides the need for expertise, companies also hire consultants to get a new perspective or an objective viewpoint on a system that is in development.

Consultants either work for a *consulting firm* or for themselves. If they work for a firm, they are basically full-time employees of the company. They receive an annual salary and benefits; the company absorbs the cost of their salaries even when the consultants are in-between assignments. In contrast, an *independent consultant* does not receive fringe benefits from anyone, and when he or she is not working on an assignment, he or she does not have a steady income. An independent consultant contracts to work for a consulting firm or a client company on a project-by-project basis. When working for a consulting firm, the independent or free-lance consultant is basically a subcontractor. He or she works on projects just as the consulting firm's full-time employees do, but he or she receives either a daily rate or a fee for the specific services performed. The responsibilities of a self-employed computer consultant are broad and include bookkeeping, advertising and promotion, and accounting (billing and collections).

The advantages and disadvantages of working as an independent consultant versus a full-time employee of a consulting firm are discussed below under benefits and drawbacks. The fact is that because the demand for more diverse and more exact consulting expertise is on the rise, many computer consulting firms engage independent consultants as well as full-time salaried consultants. Sometimes, client companies are not aware of exactly for whom their consultant works.

Job Environment

The computer consultant works in an office, but because the office may be a temporary one, it may not be very comfortable. He or she usually works at the client company for the duration of his or her assignment there.

Training and Background
(or Experience) Required

Most computer consultants have a bachelor's degree and many individuals' degrees are in computer science or a related area. An advanced degree, an M.B.A. for example, is desirable, although not required.

Experience in programming and systems analysis is normally a prerequisite to becoming a computer consultant, although people working in training or in management consulting sometimes move into computer consulting. The length of experience varies with the individual, but usually persons have from six to nine years of experience before they work as consultants. Individuals with a technical and a business background who have a great deal of firsthand experience with computer applications will do better in this field.

Benefits and Drawbacks

Salary. A computer consultant's salary normally ranges from $28,000 to $50,000, although some consultants earn as much as $100,000 annually. Salary depends on the person's level of experience, the demand for the area of expertise, and on the reputation of the individual and of the firm for which he or she works. Independent consultants earn more than full-time salaried consultants; one estimate indicated that free-lance consultants, on the average, earn in a little over half a year what salaried consultants earn in a year.

Opportunity to Advance. Computer consultants who enjoy their work are usually not interested in their opportunity to advance; the idea does not really apply to them. After a period of time spent as a consultant, however, and because of the broad experience he or she has acquired, a consultant can join a company as a full-time employee at a very good salary.

Travel. Consistent travel is required of computer consultants. They travel to each client company's site for the duration of their assignment with the company, and then they travel to the location of their next assignment. Sometimes the opportunity for a well-paid project takes a consultant far enough from home that he or she has the time to return home only on weekends. Computer consultants tend to relocate frequently to avoid long daily commutes.

Other Considerations. Computer consultants must withstand a great deal of pressure. Their work is fast-paced. The travel required may be a burden to some individuals, because, as noted above, part of each day may be spent in a long commute to the site of a present assignment, and often relocation is required in order to accept the best projects.

One of the advantages of computer consulting work, however (other than the financial reward), is the exposure to a wide diversity of projects and companies, which increases an individual's well-roundedness. Many people get a lot of personal satisfaction from doing the work they know and like very much. In a sense, consultants solve the problem of whether to progress into management or remain technical by getting the best of both worlds; they are able to stay up with the latest technological advances and continue their technical work while earning a very big income.

As discussed previously, some computer consultants work on a full-time basis for consulting firms, and others work independently and sign contracts with consulting firms only for specific projects. The advantages and disadvantages of each mode of working are numerous and will become clear by discussing the plusses and minuses of working as an independent computer consultant.

The major disadvantage of working as an independent consultant is the number of additional responsibilities involved. First of all, the consultant must assume the costs of the benefits he or she would receive if he or she were a full-time salaried employee. Benefit costs include medical insurance, vacation time, and any training costs that he or she needs to stay current in his or her area of expertise. Second, the independent consultant must assume the risk of time between assignments. A third responsibility of an independent consultant who does not subcontract is meeting the sometimes rigid qualifications of the client companies, for example, detailed financial statements, reference checks, and liability insurance. Fourth, if the independent consultant does not subcontract, he or she may not have enough client company contacts to keep himself or herself booked. And if he or she does, he or she will have to spend time marketing his or her services. Often marketing ability is not among a consultant's strong points. Fifth, the independent consultant has to handle bookkeeping and billing in addition to the work he or she has contracted to do. A sixth responsibility involved in the position if an independent consultant does subcontract is the careful review of his or her own contract with the consulting firm as well as the *master agreement* that the firm has with the client company. The master agreement includes paragraphs indicating whether or not the consultant will be paid if performance issues arise. And, of course, a management fee is charged by the consulting company who represents the independent consultant. The higher the consultant's billing rate, the greater the management fee, which is generally around 30 percent. (The management fee helps pay for the overhead experienced by the consulting firm and also increases its profit.)

Despite these six major disadvantages to working as an independent consultant, there are a number of substantial advantages. First, the independent consultant works for himself or herself—he or she really has no other boss. Second, because the independent consultant is his or her own boss, he or she controls his or her own hours. Third, individuals with an entrepreneurial spirit get a lot of personal satisfaction from working independently. Fourth, an independent consultant's job has more status than a full-time salaried consultant's job. And fifth, independent consultants earn more money than their full-time salaried counterparts.

It is clear that there are many advantages and disadvantages to working as an independent consultant as opposed to working as a salaried employee of a consulting firm. A number of individuals make the choice they do because one or two of the above points are much more important than the others. For example, not assuming risk for the time in between assignments may be more important than any of the potential payoffs of the position of independent computer consultant.

Personality Required

Interpersonal skills and the ability to work well with all kinds of people in a wide variety of circumstances are essential to becoming a successful computer consultant. The individual who works in consulting must be flexible, stable, adaptive, and independent. He or she must also be able to handle pressure well. To be a computer consultant, a person should be creative, patient, and thorough.

Outlook for the Future

The demand for computer consultants is expected to remain high in the near future because companies are expected to continue to have the needs discussed earlier in this section.

Where to Find Openings

Most companies which hire computer consultants are located in or near urban areas. Computer consultants are engaged by insurance companies, manufacturing companies, banks, and companies dealing in retail and wholesale trade, as well as other firms which have very big computer installations.

COMPUTER OPERATORS

No company can have a computer without having the personnel required to operate it. The exact responsibilities of a computer operator vary with the employer, but basically, a computer operator is responsible for the smooth day-to-day functioning of the mainframe computer (Fig. 5-2). He or she monitors the computer's processing by watching the *central console,* which used to be a board of switches and lights but is now a VDT (*video display terminal*). For each job that is processed by the computer, a message or a number of messages appear on the system's central console. Requests by the job for input and output devices sometimes also appear. The operator watches the console for any messages that may indicate some kind of error. When he or she sees an error message, it is his or her job to locate and solve the problem or else terminate the program. To do this, the operator usually consults message manuals (which are written by the computer system's manufacturer), other more senior computer operators, and sometimes other technical personnel such as systems programmers.

Because many different types of errors can occur and no two are every exactly alike, the com-

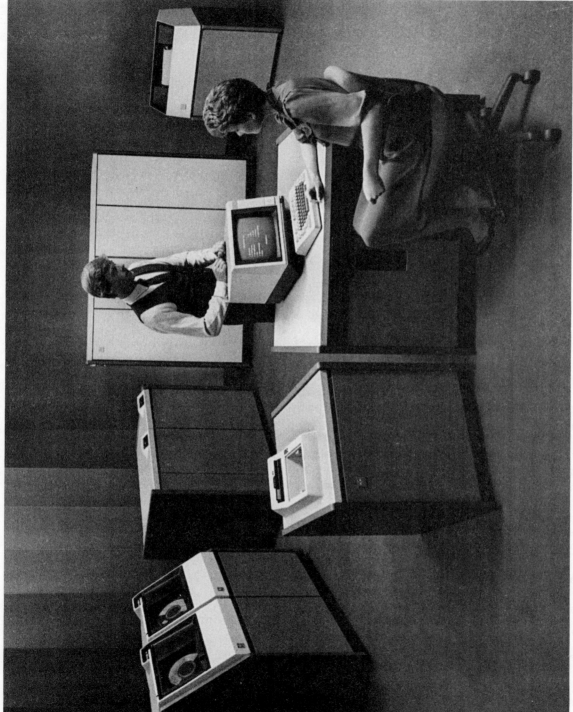

Fig. 5-2. A computer operator is responsible for the smooth day-to-day functioning of the mainframe computer. Photograph courtesy of Sperry Corp.

23

puter operator must be resourceful in solving the problems which arise. He or she may need to enter system commands at the central console in order to cancel the job or correct the problem. Or the operator may find that the instructions for a certain operations procedure have to be changed. In some cases, the systems programmer will need to make a change to his or her code which modifies the operating system; in other cases, the problem will be located in the applications program that was running at the time or in its JCL (*job control language*, a basic programming language that provides information to the operating system about how and when each job should be processed). Sometimes, the problem is located in the hardware, in which case the computer operator will need to call a *hardware service technician* (see a later section of this chapter).

The computer operator keeps a record of problems which occur, of machine performance, and of exactly which special jobs or programs were submitted for execution at what time.

As mentioned before, the operator's duties vary from employer to employer. They also vary according to the size of the computer installation in which he or she is working. If the shop is small, a computer operator may operate all of the peripheral equipment in addition to watching the console. He or she may need to check the printer to be sure it has enough paper and periodically remove its output and distribute it to users' bins. The operator may also be responsible for finding the appropriate tape in the tape library, mounting it on a tape drive when a message appears on the console indicating a need for the tape, and then removing the tape when the program has completed its processing. In this type of situation, the title "computer operator" is really used to describe a person who performs a broad range of functions—who does more than simply enter data but less than programming.

In a larger shop, the operator's duties tend to be more specialized. Usually, he or she will concentrate on the central console. In some cases, more than one operator will be assigned to a console.

There is a central console for each mainframe or computer that is running, so a large shop may have three or four central consoles. Because so many programs will be running at the same time and because troubleshooting errors is sometimes a very difficult task, the job of an operator who is responsible for monitoring the central console is not simple. In a large installation, usually peripheral equipment operators are in charge of the printers, tapes, and other equipment.

Although the work of a computer operator is critical to the smooth functioning of the system, the job is not a very prestigious one. This may be due to the fact that, when the system is running without problems, the operator may appear to be doing very little. Monitoring the console may become quite tedious in hours like these. On the other hand, if an error appears, and the operator is in the middle of following up on it, then because he or she is asking questions it may somehow be felt that he or she is responsible for the problem, which of course most of the time is not the case. This reputation could be due to the fact that partly because the job is not glamorous and allows for little opportunity to advance (which will be discussed shortly), there is often a sizable amount of turnover on the operations staff. Many operations staff members, then, are relatively new and are in the process of being trained on the job. They may be somewhat unfamiliar with the system console commands or the process of troubleshooting.

Because the computers in most installations are run around the clock, computer operators work in shifts. Recently, the most popular arrangement seems to be the three-day week, with an operator working 12 hours a day. The schedule is rotated every few months. Operators are usually required to work a night shift some of the time, especially when they are new to the job.

Job Environment

Most of an operator's time is spent in the computer room, which is well-ventilated but usually noisy. As mentioned above, evening or night shifts are sometimes required of a computer operator.

Training and Background (or Experience) Required

A high school diploma is required for the job of computer operator. Many employers prefer their operators to have some trade or vocational school training or junior or community college training as well. Several months of on-the-job training is provided by most firms to new computer operators, because they must become sufficiently familiar with the computer to be able to identify the possible causes of equipment failures. The new operators also need to learn the system commands or operator commands that they will eventually be entering at the central console.

No experience is required for a person to work as a computer operator; the position is an entry-level one. Even if an operator has extensive experience, however, he or she will require retraining if his or her current employer's hardware or equipment is made by a different manufacturer than the machines with which he or she previously worked.

Benefits and Drawbacks

Salary. The computer operator's annual salary ranges from $18,000 to $27,000.

Opportunity for Advancement. There really is limited opportunity for advancement from a computer operator's position without additional training or education. Without this training, most operators can progress upward only through the operations staff. Some companies are so dependent on experienced operators that they tend to keep those individuals working in operations. When an operator with experience looks into changing companies, he or she will find that his or her experience is machine-specific.

Some companies, however, have a specific career path and training program for individuals new to the company who want to progress to a management career in computers. These people are often started in operations and are given a substantial amount of in-house training. If a person is not part of such an extensive training program, he or she can still move into a programming position with more training, enrolling, for example, in programming courses at a junior or community college or trade school.

Travel. Usually no travel is required of computer operators.

Other Considerations. One substantial drawback to the job of computer operator is the evening or night shifts which are required part of the time. Also, the job environment tends to be quite noisy, though usually well-ventilated. Working as a computer operator is one way to gain experience with computers which, when combined with trade school or junior college classes, can lead to a programming position.

Personality Required

A computer operator must be alert and enjoy working with machines. He or she should also be able to communicate well with many different types of people, including programmers, managers, and hardware service technicians. The ability to deal with more than one thing at a time and a high frustration tolerance are important to success in this job. In addition, computer operators should be good problem solvers, and it is helpful if they are flexible about their working hours.

Outlook for the Future

From 1980 to 1990, the U.S. Bureau of Labor Statistics expected the demand for computer operators to increase by a startling 92 percent. In the most recent estimate available, demand is predicted to increase by 46 percent between 1984 and 1994. Although the employment picture for operators is not quite as rosy as it was three or four years ago, the increase in demand that is expected for the next decade is still more than three times as great as the expected overall growth for all occupations.

Strong demand is expected to continue partly because of the number of jobs which are becoming available in smaller companies that are buying computers for the first time.

Where to Find Openings

Computer operators are employed in almost every

industry and in small and large firms which have one or more large computers. Most work in manufacturing firms (in particular computer manufacturing firms), banks, insurance companies, colleges and universities, wholesale and retail trade establishments, government agencies, hospitals, and computer service firms that provide computer services for a fee. Many of these companies and organizations are located in large cities.

COMPUTER SCIENTIST

To some people, the title of a *computer scientist* differs from the title of an electronics or electrical engineer because computer scientists are familiar with computer and programming theory—that is, the theoretical side of computers. Sometimes, the job of a computer scientist will involve more software design than the job of an electrical engineer. For example, sometimes computer scientists are more apt to design operating systems. In many cases, however, the two titles are used to describe jobs which are quite similar. For example, either job can involve the design and development of computers and/or peripheral equipment. Often the work includes some report writing on schedules and cost estimates for tentative projects.

Job Environment

The computer scientist's time is spent in his or her office or laboratory or in a plant. How much time is required in each setting depends on his or her specific responsibilities.

Alternate Titles

The title of *computer engineer* is sometimes used in place of either computer scientist or electrical engineer.

Training and Background (or Experience) Required

A bachelor's degree in computer science is required for a person to work as a computer scientist. Electrical engineering courses may or may not have been taken as part of the undergraduate curriculum. A master's or doctoral degree in computer science is expected by some employers.

Some individuals work part-time while they are still in school, but experience is not usually required for beginning jobs.

Benefits and Drawbacks

Salary. The salary of a computer scientist depends on the size and location of his or her company and his or her experience and education. Individuals with doctoral degrees make substantially more than those with master's degrees, and they, of course, are paid better than persons with no graduate education. Computer scientists' salaries range from about $28,000 to over $45,000.

Opportunity to Advance. If a computer scientist finds that he or she enjoys technical work much more than working with people, he or she may reach a position from which the opportunity to advance is limited. There is, however, substantial opportunity to advance between starting position and that of a person with extensive experience.

Travel. Some computer scientists spend up to one-fifth of their time at work traveling to seminars through which they update their computer information.

Other Considerations. Because of the regular deadlines with which they must contend, computer scientists sometimes are required to work overtime. The mental stress of this concentrated technical work is felt by some individuals.

The work of a computer scientist can be very challenging and exciting, however, because the work often involves state-of-the-art computer technology. The position of computer scientist is highly respected.

Personality Required

Interest in and an aptitude for working with computer technology are clearly essential to being a computer scientist. To do well as a computer scientist, a person must also be very thorough and logical and capable of working without supervision, when necessary.

Outlook for the Future

With the new technological developments that are rapidly occurring, the substantial demand for computer scientists is expected to increase even further.

Where to Find Openings

Computer scientists often are employed at the research and development centers of very large computer manufacturers.

COMPUTER SECURITY SPECIALIST

Everyone is familiar with computer crime, because it has received such widespread coverage by the media and has even inspired several movies. *Computer security specialists* work to prevent computer crime, which includes the distortion or falsification of computer files, the stealing and selling of information contained in computer records, the changing of computer files to cover illegal withdrawals or deposits of money, and the possession and distribution of confidential information by unauthorized personnel. The security specialist is responsible for protecting the company's hardware—its computers—and its data from unauthorized individuals. To this end, he or she works with the EDP auditor to design controls to prevent fraud. The security specialist works with other personnel to set up television surveillance or install controlled-access doorways in the computer center. Other activities with which he or she can be involved are the use of special controls within programs which are devised to trip up unauthorized users, and the transmission of *scrambled, encrypted,* or secretly *encoded* communications signals.

In some companies, the computer security specialist is also responsible for devising a *disaster recovery plan*, which would take effect if or when a natural disaster ruined part or all of the computer system.

Except when problems arise, the job of security specialist is relatively low-key, although he or she is responsible for keeping abreast of the latest advances in security measures and for continually devising new and more effective safeguards and protective procedures. If a problem occurs, the security specialist is responsible for following up on it and resolving it.

Job Environment

The computer security specialist works in an office in or near the company's data center.

Alternate Titles

The computer security specialist is sometimes referred to as a *computer security analyst.* If his or her position includes the responsibility of managing other security staff members, such as guards, then sometimes he or she is known as a *computer security administrator.*

Training and Background (or Experience) Required

Many computer security specialists have a bachelor's degree; a B.S. with some computer science is preferred. The position is not entry level but requires experience either as a computer operator, a programmer, a systems analyst, or a combination of the above. Sometimes, individuals who become computer security specialists have worked as long as six years in other computer careers.

In addition to being knowledgeable in many areas of computing, a security specialist is expected to have advanced training in the latest security measures and techniques.

Benefits and Drawbacks

Salary. A computer security specialist is usually paid from $28,000 to $37,000 annually, depending on his or her experience and responsibilities.

Opportunity to Advance. A computer security specialist needs additional training in order to advance into other positions of greater responsibility. If a security specialist does an excellent job, however, upper management will usually take note.

Travel. In order to stay abreast of current security techniques, sometimes a computer security specialist travels up to 20 percent of the time.

Other Considerations. One drawback of

computer security work is the necessity of unremitting attention to detail. The constant monitoring of security is an important part of effective security techniques.

Many people, however, consider the challenge of devising new and better security measures both interesting and rewarding. Also, computer security specialists often enjoy working with state-of-the-art protection devices.

Personality Required

A computer security specialist must, of course, be honest and responsible. It is also important for him or her to be thorough and a good observer.

Outlook for the Future

Computer systems are becoming more complex and computer usage is increasing. Security problems and reports of computer crime are becoming more and more frequent. For these reasons, the demand for computer security specialists will continue to grow.

Where to Find Openings

The larger the company with a computer installation, the more apt it is to have a computer security specialist on its payroll, especially if it is a credit company, a bank, or a consulting firm which specializes in security. Most companies employing security specialists are located in major urban areas.

COMPUTING SYSTEMS DIRECTOR

The *computing systems director* is responsible for all of the computer processing at his or her organization (Fig. 5-3). It is his or her job to ensure the smooth day-to-day operation of the computing or data center and to see that its work is completed on schedule. The director needs to have a detailed understanding of the current and future computing needs of his or her company, because he or she decides what project will be done by the computing center. He or she is a generalist with a technical background who manages the technical specialists or their supervisors.

In most companies, the computing systems director reports to a vice president or the chief executive officer (CEO) of the company. In smaller organizations, the director is more involved with the daily functioning of systems and applications programmers, systems analysts, operators, and sometimes individuals with other technical responsibilities. In larger companies, the managers or supervisors of these people report to the computing system director. Hundreds of employees can report indirectly to him or her.

Computing systems directors are involved in a wide range of activities, including the purchase of hardware and software, the hiring and firing of employees, the assignment of individuals to various projects, the setting of work standards, and the planning of annual budgets for all of the computing departments. The director also works with managers of other departments and users to decide on future projects and, as part of this function, he or she usually reviews feasibility studies. A computing systems director is expected to continually educate himself or herself with respect to current developments in the field.

Job Environment

The computing systems director works in an office located in the company's computing or data center.

Alternate Titles

The computing systems director is sometimes called the *information systems director,* the *DP manager,* or the *MIS (management information systems) manager.*

Training and Background (or Experience) Required

A B.S. in computer science or related field is required for the position of computing systems director, and an M.B.A. (Master of Business Administration) degree is preferred by many employers.

A prospective computing systems director must have business as well as technical ability, including leadership skills and an interest in and ability

Fig. 5-3. A computing systems director must have business as well as technical ability, including leadership skills and an ability to work with and motivate people. (Photograph courtesy of Honeywell, Inc.)

to work with and motivate people. These characteristics are sometimes more important than the amount of experience an individual has had. Most companies, though, look for work experience in several areas, for example, programming, systems analysis, and operations. Some supervisory or management experience is also a necessity, in particular for a person interested in working for a big organization. The exception to this rule: a small business installing a computer system for the first time may hire an individual for the position of computing systems director or DP manager who does not have a great deal of management experience and who might have been working as a project leader or a senior systems analyst.

Benefits and Drawbacks

Salary. The annual salary of computing systems directors varies with their experience and the location and size of their firm. The typical range is from about $45,000 to about $75,000.

Opportunity to Advance. A natural progression for a computing systems director would seem to be movement into general management. Some studies predict good prospects for this in the future due to the increasing importance of the role of computing systems director or DP manager. Presently, however, it is difficult for the director to move into these positions, partly because his or her technical background is not seen as broad enough for general management. As a result, some computing systems directors turn to consulting.

Travel. Usually, a computing systems director travels about one-third of the time to seminars, demonstrations of new products, and to the company's other data centers, if all the computer processing is not done at the central location.

Other Considerations. One drawback of the computing systems director's job in a company with an independent computing or data center is pressure resulting from the emphasis on profit and loss. In a number of other companies, the computing departments' budgets are treated as overhead. In general, though, the position of DP manager involves as much or more pressure than most other computer careers. The manager has to keep his subordinates, his boss, and the users happy even if they make extremely high demands on him. Most computing systems directors put in a great deal of overtime.

On the other hand, the position of computing systems director brings with it power, status, and close interaction with top management on a regular basis. Directors are very well paid.

Personality Required

The computing systems director needs to have good technical skills in order to be able to understand the computing needs of his or her organization. He or she also must have good management and communications skills. Managers need to be leaders who are able to motivate others. One study found that effective computing systems directors are more democratic, less formal, more intellectu-

ally flexible, and better planners than effective managers not working in DP.

The directors must also have excellent verbal and written communications skills and the ability to deal with users who are unfamiliar with computers but who rely heavily on them. More and more companies are presently emphasizing the communication skills of the director over his or her technical knowledge. Finally, computing systems directors should be poised and able to work well under pressure.

Outlook for the Future

There is still a short supply of individuals who have both technical and managerial ability, so the demand for computing systems directors is strong. It is expected to remain fairly stable as more and more companies of all sizes computerize their operations.

Where to Find Openings

Most computing systems directors work in companies or organizations with big computer installations, many of which are found in urban areas. Opportunity for a first job as a computing systems director can also be found in small companies which are just becoming computerized. The major employers of DP managers are banks, hospitals, insurance companies, government agencies, manufacturing companies, wholesale and retail trade establishments, and computer service companies (which provide services for a fee).

DATA ENTRY OPERATOR

Data entry is the actual entering of data into the computer. Although new methods of entering data are continually being developed (see the section entitled "Outlook for the Future"), a sizeable amount of data that is used by programs today is being entered by *data entry operators*. A common example of such a program is a payroll program that requires specific information including employees' names, addresses, social security numbers, salary levels, gross salaries, and number of exemptions, in order to process the company payroll and print out the employees' paychecks.

In the past, data entry operators used *keypunch machines* to punch information onto cards, which were then used as computer input at a later date. Keypunch machines are today mostly obsolete, having been replaced with microcomputer system keyboards or keyboard terminals through which the data can be directly transmitted to the main computer.

The duties of a data entry operator vary according to the experience level of the operator. Junior or lower level operators spend their entire day entering data at the keyboard, but higher level operators help to train new employees and often assist with scheduling various data entry projects. Departmental supervisors oversee personnel and their data entry activities.

In the past, many companies had centralized data entry departments which were linked with the DP department and which serviced all of the business departments of the company. Today, however, the data entry function is beginning to be spread throughout the company and become a part of a number of different computer jobs. In "Outlook for the Future," this trend will be discussed in more depth.

Job Environment

Data entry clerks or operators work in an office setting. Usually a number of operators work in the same large office.

Alternate Titles

Data entry operators or clerks are often referred to as *junior data entry operators, senior data entry operators,* or *lead data entry operators,* according to the level of their responsibilities.

Training and Background (or Experience) Required

A high school education is required for the job of data entry clerk, as well as minimum typing skills of 50 to 60 words per minute. Accuracy is very important. Some companies offer on-the-job training, which usually lasts less than one week, but training is also available from vocational schools, business schools, and community colleges.

Certification for data entry managers is available from the Data Entry Management Association, P.O. Box 16711, Stamford, CT 06905, (203) 967-3500. The certification program, referred to simply as *Certification in Data Management* or *CDM,* is relatively new. It involves the evaluation of a manager's knowledge in the following seven areas: forms design, equipment selection, interviewing, programming and documentation, scheduling and control, training, and employee motivation. More information on the program can be obtained from DEMA at the address shown above.

No experience is required to become a data entry operator. Data entry supervisors or managers, however, usually are expected to have from three to five years of experience working as a data entry operator.

Benefits and Drawbacks

Salary. The annual salary for data entry operators starts at about $14,000 and increases to about $19,000 for a manager's position.

Opportunity to Advance. Opportunity to advance is limited in some companies. Data entry operators are sometimes viewed as unambitious, and often they are unable to progress up a career ladder within the company. Sometimes, however, they are able to increase their supervisory responsibilities. With training they are often expected to get on their own, sometimes they can move into word processing (see a later section of this chapter).

Travel. No travel is involved in a data entry operator's job.

Other Considerations. Data entry operators often feel that their jobs do not give them the opportunity to demonstrate the level of their intelligence. Some operators also complain that they are treated more as extensions of machines than as humans. As a result of these and other problems, the number of data entry operators who are joining unions is on the rise.

The job itself is not very challenging or very creative, but instead is quite monotonous. It can be very stressful, especially when productivity is closely tied to pay. In some companies, for example, data entry operators are given daily quotas that they are expected to meet.

Presently, a controversy surrounds the effect of VDT or CRT use by data entry workers. They use terminals more than any other computer workers. At this time, there is no hard evidence that heavy VDT usage has detrimental effects on a person's health, but as is discussed more thoroughly in Chapter 9, the final verdict is not yet in. It will probably depend on research that is being done now and that is planned for the future. Regardless of the fact that the results are unclear at this time, because some evidence suggests that continual VDT usage may have an adverse effect on an individual's health, frequent breaks (of about 15 minutes every few hours) have been recommended for data entry operators. Recently, more emphasis has been placed on proper lighting in the work area and the availability of chairs which can be adjusted to offer each individual maximum back support. In addition, unions have convinced some companies to adopt policies regarding pregnant women, allowing them to switch to another job during their pregnancies, despite any seniority issues.

For more detailed information regarding the VDT controversy, consult Chapter 9.

Personality Required

A data entry operator must be an alert individual who is capable of functioning well under considerable pressure at times. The person should be able to follow oral and written directions and should have good finger dexterity.

Outlook for the Future

The size of the data entry work force has been decreasing at a moderate rate for the last few years and is expected to continue to decrease steadily through 1995. In place of central data entry departments, more data entry is being done at separate sites by employees who perform the function as only one part of their job.

The look of data entry is changing rapidly, as new equipment, such as *optical scanners*, is being introduced on the market. *Speech recognition systems* are also greatly increasing the speed of data entry. The amount of money spent on speech recognition systems by companies in the U.S. is expected to double in the next five years. New software that is becoming available is giving data entry managers more options than ever before in processing and formatting data.

Clearly, the world of data entry is in transition at this time. It is important to note that the decrease in demand for data entry operators is expected to continue, although it is hard to predict when the position itself will no longer exist.

Where to Find Openings

Data entry operators are often employed in large urban areas. They work in a variety of firms, including insurance companies, banks, government agencies, manufacturing firms, and companies which specialize in wholesale and retail trade.

DATABASE ADMINISTRATOR

A *database* is basically a collection of data files cross-referenced for easy retrieval. Usually, a database is accessed by a number of different application programs. A bank, for example, may have a database of information on its customers that is regularly accessed by a car loan application program, a Christmas Club application program, a savings application program, and a checking applications program, among others. A university might have a central database with information on its faculty, staff, and alumni, which would be accessed by annual giving programs, payroll programs, and programs with other purposes. The database software is sometimes referred to as *DMBS* or a *database management system*. Sometimes, the DBMSs are written by the user company's programmers, but often the DBMS is purchased or leased from a software vendor.

A *database administrator* performs many different functions. First of all, he or she is responsible for the design of the database. Writing specifications and drawing charts are often steps that are required as part of the organizing of a collection of information into a database. The database administrator decides what data should appear in which files, how the database should be organized, and which programs should use which database files. The design stage must also include planning on how to avoid unnecessary duplication.

Second, a database administrator is in charge of the creation or development of the database. For example, he or she oversees the work of applications programmers who are writing the database program.

Finally, he or she is responsible for the operation of the database and therefore must monitor the database's day-to-day functioning. The database administrator must be sure that proper security measures are implemented to protect sensitive data, but he or she must also see that easy access to the database is provided to individuals who need it. The administrator is responsible for data recovery, so that if the computer or another piece of hardware malfunctions, the data can be restored from a current backup tape or disk.

In addition to handling the design, development, and day-to-day operation of a complex software system, database administrators establish the standards for the database and see that documentation is written for the database and its functions. The administrators also work with people from many different departments within the company in an effort to coordinate their activities and needs.

Usually, a database administrator has at least several database programmers reporting to him or her (see the next section of this chapter for a description of the career of database programmers). Although in theory one database administrator can manage all of the applications which access a database, often database administrators are responsible for only one or several of the applications—that is, usually there are a number of different database administrators for a single database. One reason for this is the decentralization of power and responsibility.

Job Environment

The database administrator usually has his or her own office but spends a great deal of time in meetings in a variety of different offices.

Alternate Titles

In some companies, database administrators are known as *database managers*.

Training and Background (or Experience) Required

In order to work as a database administrator, an individual is usually expected to have a college degree. A B.S. in computer science is desirable, but most college curricula do not include courses on database programming or administration. In fact, database courses are usually available only from vendors, with each vendor offering classes specializing in their own package. This type of training, as well as being highly specialized, is usually available to company employees who are presently working with databases or are about to work with databases.

The job of database administrator is not an entry-level position. Most people who work in database administration have at least five years of experience working with computers, usually in programming and systems analysis. They have had a chance to develop both technical and business skills, and they often move into database administration directly from a position in database programming (see the next section of this chapter).

Benefits and Drawbacks

Salary. The salary of a database administrator can vary with the amount of responsibility he or she has (for example, the size of the database for which he or she is responsible or the number of databases which he or she manages). Generally, annual salaries range from $30,000 to $48,000.

Opportunity to Advance. A database administrator or manager has an excellent opportunity to advance. This is mostly because, as is the case with information center positions, the individual develops many contacts in many different departments just by fulfilling his or her day-to-day responsibilities. As mentioned previously, requests regarding database usage are submitted from most of the company's departments. Because database administration has such high visibility within the company, an administrator's next step is often into higher management.

Travel. A database administrator travels only about one-tenth of the time, usually for seminars on new products and meetings with clients.

Other Considerations. As with other computer careers, mental stress is part of the database administrator's job. He or she must work to get his or her programmers to meet specific daily deadlines. Partly because of this day-to-day tension, however, a sense of satisfaction is often derived from the timely completion of a project according to specifications.

Personality Required

The database administrator must have two sets of skills—he or she has to be technically oriented but also must have quite a bit of management ability. Technically, the database manager needs the ability to translate specific departmental needs into database design. He or she will need to conceptualize the whole as the sum of its parts. A manager needs enough technical expertise to be able to decide how best to organize the information into the database. The individual should also be meticulous enough to ensure that adequate documentation for the database exists, because a nondocumented database is difficult to use.

The second set of skills that a database administrator must have is interpersonal skills. He or she should enjoy working with people and should have the ability to lead and motivate others. Because of the variety of people with which the administrator works, it is important for him or her to be able to explain technical terms in plain English. Interfacing with almost every department in the company also requires good organization and communicative skills, including the ability to negotiate and compromise.

Outlook for the Future

Databases are expected to continue to be one of the major growth areas in computers for the near fu-

ture. Computer professionals with experience in this area and with some understanding of distribution systems and telecommunications are and will be in especially high demand.

Where to Find Openings

Openings for database administrators are likely to be found in large companies and institutions, which are located in or near large cities. Consulting and service companies in particular are major employers of database administrators.

DATABASE PROGRAMMER

A *database programmer* is an applications or systems programmer who specializes in working with *databases*, which are storehouses of well-organized and cross-referenced files. The files are accessed by a variety of end users through different application programs. For example, a bank may have a database of information on its customers that can be accessed and added to by individuals in different departments. The database software is sometimes called a *DBMS* or *database management system*.

Applications programmers who are database programmers spend time developing the actual database program. For example, they are involved with chart drawing and with preparing or designing the layout of each file in the database. They actually write the program in some cases.

Today, more and more database programmers are *systems programmers* rather than applications programmers. Because companies are finding that it is more cost-effective to buy software packages from vendors than to have the software developed in-house (by the company's own programmers), database programmers often find that they are responsible for working with a DBMS package. Before a DBMS package is purchased or leased, the programmer may run feasibility studies to see which package would most adequately meet the company's needs. Then the programmer installs the package and integrates it with the rest of the department's software. This step usually includes working with systems programmers specializing in other areas. Finally, the database programmer is responsible for debugging any problems which arise with the DBMS system.

Job Environment

The database programmer works in an office setting, usually with a terminal, in or near the data center.

Alternate Titles

There are no alternate titles for the job of database programmer, although sometimes the level of the position is reflected in the title, such as "junior database programmer" or "senior database programmer." A related title and job is that of *database administrator* (see previous section of this chapter).

Training and Background (or Experience) Required

A database programmer is expected to have a four-year college degree. Having a B.S. in computer science is a significant advantage in the marketplace. Often, programmers who are hired to work on a database system are sent by their employer to classes specializing in the DBMS. Usually these classes are offered by the system's vendor.

Persons who move into database programming typically have at least two or three years of experience in either applications or systems programming. Normally, the job of database programmer is not an entry level position.

Benefits and Drawbacks

Salary. The annual salary of a database programmer varies depending on the size and location of the company and the amount of experience the individual has. The range is about $25,000 to $37,000. Database programmers who are systems programmers usually earn more than their counterparts who are applications programmers.

Opportunity to Advance. A database programmer can advance to the position of systems analyst or project leader. The most common next step, however, is the position of database administrator, in which the individual is drawing upon his

or her experience in working with databases.

Travel. The database programmer travels very little—usually only to vendor classes specializing in the database system with which he or she is working.

Other Considerations. A database programmer works alone and on the terminal much of the time. Also, database programmers who are systems programmers must contend with the pressure to resolve problems with the database management system by a set deadline. Sometimes a major problem with the system will occur, and a number of users will not be able to access the system until the programmer finds and fixes the problem. Database programmers who are applications programmers usually have a lower-pressure job that has a steadier pace, although they have specific deadlines to meet, also.

Database programmers—especially systems programmers—enjoy responsibility. Individuals working in this area also tend to get a lot of intellectual satisfaction from their job.

Personality Required

Database programmers who are applications programmers need to be able to reason logically and carefully. They should be able to work with a high degree of accuracy, with persistence and patience. Database programmers working with applications should enjoy a challenge, and they should not mind working within a set schedule.

Database programmers who are systems programmers must have the personality characteristics required of a systems programmer. Because the individual will spend a great deal of time working alone, the programmer should enjoy working in solitude. The person should also be logical and interested in how things work, and he or she is expected to be technically oriented. A high frustration tolerance and a great deal of persistence are also necessary traits of a successful database systems programmer.

Gerald M. Weinberg, in *The Psychology of Computer Programming*, discussed some characteristics essential to both applications and systems programmers. He mentioned that programmers must be able to tolerate stressful situations, because the work often involves rigid deadlines. Adaptability to change and neatness in one's work are important. A programmer needs to have a certain type of humility that will lead him or her to look through the entire program for similar errors once he or she has found an error of a certain type, instead of only fixing the first error of that type and then assuming the rest of the program will be correct. A programmer must also be assertive or self-confident enough to get things done. Finally, a programmer needs a sense of humor or an ability to laugh at himself or herself.

Outlook for the Future

The database area is one of the hottest new areas in computing today, and it is expected to remain so for the near future. Demand for database programmers is high, and demand for experienced database programmers is very high.

Where to Find Openings

The companies which are most apt to have openings for database programmers are firms with large computer installations and, in particular, big software companies.

EDP AUDITOR

An *EDP auditor (electronic data processing auditor)* is responsible for analyzing and monitoring a company's computer systems. He or she works to increase the reliability, accuracy, efficiency, and security of the computer systems. The EDP auditor reviews in detail both systems now in use and new systems being proposed. He or she also checks the operational procedures of the company's data center or data processing department. For example, an EDP auditor may check that a proper amount of documentation exists for a certain system. He or she might look into whether or not the proper controls are established to ensure financially sound record-keeping. He or she would question whether present data center procedures are cost-effective.

The EDP auditor sometimes participates in the development of new computer systems. In these instances, the auditor will check to make sure all alternatives have been taken into account in the program that will become the central part of the new system, and he or she will ensure that the proper auditing tools are built into it. The EDP auditor often works with the computer security specialist regarding security issues to design controls that will prevent fraud. He or she also reviews other existing controls to be sure that they are in order by, for instance, looking into exactly who has access to or the ability to authorize changes to the systems which exist. The prevention of fraud is becoming a more important part of the EDP auditor's work because companies lose billions of dollars annually to crime or incorrect computer practices.

The EDP auditor analyzes some sample computer systems every year or so to ensure that money is not being wasted and that the company's policies are being applied.

The EDP auditor's position within the company is important because of the amount of money invested in computer systems. After collecting information and evaluating the functioning of a system or procedure, the auditor writes a report for top management that describes his or her findings and recommendations.

The auditor will often then work with various managers within the company to implement the recommendations which were accepted.

Job Environment

The EDP auditor works in an office, but the exact location of his or her office will vary depending on his or her function and individual company. Some companies prefer to base their EDP auditors' offices in their accounting or finance departments. If an EDP auditor is responsible for monitoring the post-implementation stage of a computer system, his or her office may be located in or near the company's data center.

Alternate Titles

EDP auditors are sometimes referred to as *infor-*

mation systems auditors. Many companies distinguish between an EDP auditor trainee, a junior EDP auditor, and a senior EDP auditor.

Training and Background
(or Experience) Required

The recommended training for EDP auditors is a four-year college degree in accounting, finance, or computer science. If an individual majors in a field other than computer science, he or she should take some computer science courses. Often, EDP auditors have a master's degree in business administration or are Certified Public Accountants.

In order to become a CPA, an individual must go through a special certification process before qualifying for a license that reflects both his or her education and amount of experience. The specific requirements vary from state to state. The educational requirements are often met by a bachelor's degree with an accounting major. An exam, which is prepared and graded by the American Institute of Certified Public Accountants, must be passed, and the individual must accumulate from one to three years' experience.

Some EDP auditors are certified. The EDP Auditors Association, Inc. has implemented a program of certification for competent EDP auditors, or information systems auditors. To be eligible to become a *Certified Information Systems Auditor,* an individual must pass an exam which covers 11 areas: application systems control reviews, data integrity reviews, systems development life cycle reviews, application systems development reviews, general operational procedure controls reviews, security reviews, systems software reviews, maintenance reviews, acquisition reviews, data processing resource management reviews, and information systems audit management. The exam is given every April at exam sites around the world, and it consists of two three-hour sessions given in the morning and afternoon of the same day. The cost of taking the test is $185. A study guide and review manual for the exam is available from the EDP Auditors Association at a cost of $20 each, and sample tests can be ordered for $7.50 each.

In order to qualify for certification, an individual must also have five years of experience in EDP auditing. However, 60 college credits can be substituted for one year of experience, or 120 credits can be substituted for two years. One year of either auditing or computing experience can be substituted for one year of EDP auditing experience.

Continuing professional education is essential to maintaining a CISA designation. Within every three years, a Certified Information Systems Auditor must undertake 120 hours of educational activity or take the current exam, which is periodically updated as required by changes in the field.

For further information, write to or call the EDP Auditors Association, Inc., Administrative Offices, 373 S. Schmale Road, Carol Stream, IL 60187, (312) 682-1200.

Most employers expect a person they hire as an EDP auditor to have at least two years of experience in either programming and systems design or general accounting and finance. Also important is the exposure to many different types of computer systems and applications. An EDP auditor needs to have a blend of auditing skills and technical or computer skills. Some large accounting firms have training programs for accountants who want to specialize in electronic data processing.

Benefits and Drawbacks

Salary. An EDP auditor's salary will vary based on his or her experience and the size of the firm for which he or she works. EDP auditors are well-paid; their salaries range from $25,000 to $45,000.

Opportunity to Advance. An EDP auditor has excellent opportunity to advance. The two potential career moves for an EDP auditor are either the move into a corporate management position or the move into consulting. He or she is well-positioned for a move into management because of the broad exposure he or she has had to the company and because of the number of contacts he or she has in top management.

Because of its great growth potential, a move into EDP auditing for senior programmers or analysis is recommended.

Travel. The amount of travel required for the job varies but often amounts to 20 or 25 percent.

Other Considerations. One major drawback of working as an EDP auditor is the mental stress an auditor usually experiences. An EDP auditor essentially works alone in gathering and analyzing information, and sometimes the information is only available from individuals who are reluctant to divulge it. When he or she has submitted a report to top management, the auditor must convince a group of executives that the recommendations included in the report are valid and worth implementing, even if other company employees disagree with the suggestions.

One major advantage to an EDP auditor's position is the personal satisfaction derived from helping to make the company's operations more efficient and saving the company time and money.

Personality Required

An EDP auditor must have excellent communications skills. He or she must be able to talk with and listen to both technical people such as programmers and end users. He or she will need interviewing skills, because the EDP auditor has to gather information by asking the right questions of the right people. The auditor's written skills are important because his or her reports usually go to higher levels of management. The EDP auditor must be able to discuss his or her recommendations convincingly, so the individual will need to be persuasive and confident. In order to function effectively, the EDP auditor must be able to go against popular opinion but do so politely. Sometimes, the DPers will resent his or her recommendations because the implementation of controls can mean more work and more overhead for a department.

An EDP auditor basically works alone much of the time, so he or she must be conscientious. Because of the sensitive nature of the information with which he or she works, a high level of integrity is important to the job. Being organized, thorough, and inquisitive by nature are also personality traits belonging to successful EDP auditors.

Outlook for the Future

Demand for EDP auditors is on the rise. As more and more organizations and companies use computers to handle their financial record-keeping, the demand for EDP auditors will continue to grow. The increasing demand is also due to the growing concern with computer fraud and the increase in the complexity and the size of computer systems. Therefore, EDP auditors are expected to be in great demand for some time to come.

Where to Find Openings

Some of the best places to find openings for EDP auditors are at banks, insurance companies, accounting firms, and other large companies, mostly in urban areas. Consulting and public accounting firms are also good prospects, because they are often called in by other companies to review their computer systems.

ENGINEERS IN THE COMPUTER INDUSTRY

Electronics or *electrical engineers, mechanical engineers, chemical engineers*, and *industrial engineers* are all employed in the computer industry (Fig. 5-4). Job responsibilities vary from designing computer equipment to developing the strategy for the most efficient use of people, materials, and machines in the computer manufacturing process. Specific job descriptions are given below. In all four cases, however, engineers have duties over and above their technical work. For example, they usually write reports, help draft schedules, consult with and sometimes supervise other engineers, and keep up with the recent developments in their field by reading manuals and attending seminars.

Electronics or *electrical engineers* are the most common of the four types of engineers employed in the computer industry. They design or develop computers and/or peripheral equipment. Often electrical engineers use computers to test tentative designs for performance and other variables before the company commits money and time to the actual construction of a product. The types of design activities in which engineers are involved varies.

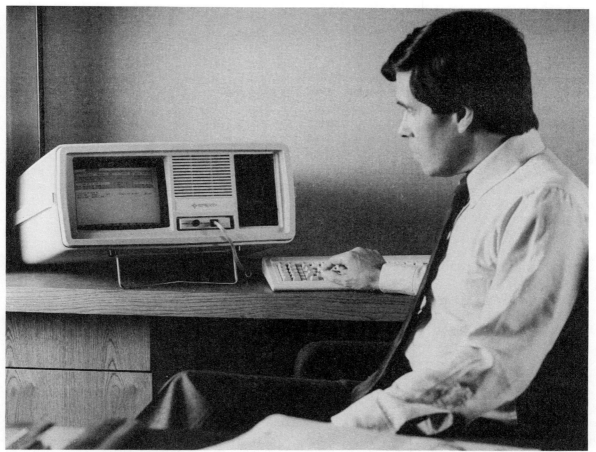

Fig. 5-4. Job responsibilities for engineers working in the computer industry vary a great deal, but are usually challenging. (Photograph courtesy of Sperry Corp.)

For example, they develop new types of printers and disk drives and design new microchips, they alter the design of circuit boards for new types of computers, and they come up with the *architecture* or form of the new hardware's electronics system. Electrical engineers also spend time working on various electrical problems that arise during the development of new computer products and which must be solved before the product can be introduced on the market.

Experienced electrical or electronics engineers are familiar with design processes and are knowledgeable about complex testing procedures.

In addition to their design and development work, electrical engineers write reports indicating the approximate cost of tentative projects and set up schedules for approved projects.

Mechanical engineers sometimes work on the development of new computer products also, but usually they are more concerned with the product itself than with its design process. In addition, they focus on the operation of the equipment used to manufacture the new product. Mechanical engineers who are familiar with *computer-aided manufacturing (CAM)* are becoming more and more in demand. For an explanation of CAM, see Chapter 6 on Computer Careers of the Future.

Chemical engineers employed in the computer

39

industry work with chemists on the production of semiconductors. They are also involved in the processes used to make a variety of other parts of computer systems.

Industrial engineers are more concerned with people and methods of organization than any of the other types of engineers described above. Their job is to develop the most efficient method of utilizing the individuals, materials, and machines employed in the production of new computer products. They often run studies to determine the most effective of several methods. Industrial engineers are also responsible for locating potential production problems and suggesting ways to correct or avoid the problems.

Job Environment

The engineer's time is spent in his or her office or laboratory or in the plant. The amount of time in each place depends upon the type of engineer and his or her exact duties.

Alternate Titles

Two fairly broad titles that are sometimes applied to engineers working in the computer business are *test engineer* and *computer engineer*. The latter is sometimes also applied to computer scientists.

Training and Background
(or Experience) Required

A bachelor's degree is required to work as an engineer in the computer industry. The preferred degree is in engineering but includes credits in computer science or computer technology. A master's or doctoral degree is expected by some employers; some engineers get a master's degree in business administration (an M.B.A.) or a related field in order to progress more quickly into management.

Some individuals work part-time while they are still in school, but experience is not usually required for beginning jobs. Experienced engineers, however, are in very high demand and are usually called regularly by recruiters.

Benefits and Drawbacks

Salary. An engineer's salary depends on the size and location of his or her company and his or her experience and education. Persons with doctoral degrees make substantially more than those with master's degrees, and they, of course, are paid better than individuals with no graduate education. The median annual salaries for engineers working for manufacturers of electronics and computer equipment are slightly higher than the median salaries for all engineers. According to the Engineering Manpower Commission, in 1985, the median starting salary for engineers in the United States was $27,300; the median starting salary for engineers working for computer manufacturers was $27,950. The median annual salary for all engineers with 10 years of experience was $39,850, and again, the computer engineers had a higher median salary of $43,350.

Opportunity to Advance. Engineers have a good opportunity to advance if they can communicate well with people. It is easier for them to progress into management if they have an M.B.A. or a master's in a related area. Some engineers eventually move into consulting work.

Travel. Depending on the particular job, engineers can travel up to about one-fifth of the time to attend classes and learn about new hardware components.

Other Considerations. Because of the regular deadlines with which they must contend, engineers sometimes need to work overtime. The mental stress of the concentrated technical work that they do is felt by some individuals.

The job is very challenging and exciting, however, especially for electrical engineers, many of whom work on state-of-the-art computer technology. Engineering positions can be very satisfying and usually carry quite a bit of status within the company. Because the demand for engineers is so high, persons working in this area have a choice of where they will work.

Personality Required

Engineers working in the computer industry must,

of course, have quite a bit of interest in and aptitude for working with machines and computer technology. They need to be logical and thorough individuals who can work well without supervision, when necessary. Finding enjoyment in working with other people is as important to success in this career as being able to work alone.

Outlook for the Future

Demand for electronics, mechanical, chemical, and industrial engineers in the computer business is high and is expected to increase during the near future. Supply is not presently keeping up with demand, and a great increase in the number of college engineering graduates is not predicted. Of the four types of engineers, most job opportunities now exist for electronics engineers, especially those with an understanding of *lasers*, *fiber optics*, *computer architecture*, and also *robotics* (see Chapter 6 on Computer Careers of the Future). Also now increasing in demand are chemical engineers familiar with CAM or computer-aided manufacturing (see Chapter 6).

Where to Find Openings

Engineers working in the computer industry are employed at the research and development centers of very large computer manufacturers.

HARDWARE DESIGNER

A *hardware designer* works to create a *prototype* or model of a new hardware product, for example, a new computer system. A great deal of time is invested in research and in the testing of the new circuit construction and logic design. Once the prototype has been created, all the different aspects of the system are tested and retested until they are all functioning correctly. About four-fifths of a hardware designer's time involves the designing activity described above. Carefully documenting the design requires the remaining one-fifth of his or her time.

The hardware designer usually works with minimal supervision, and the pace of his or her work is fairly steady.

Job Environment

A hardware designer usually works in an office setting and in a laboratory.

Training and Background (or Experience) Required

A B.S. in computer science or engineering is the minimum education required for individuals who want to work as hardware designers. A master's degree in engineering is highly desirable and will lead to greater opportunities.

At least two years of experience as a *hardware service technician* (see next section of this chapter), wiring, testing and repairing equipment, is useful to individuals who want to become hardware designers.

Benefits and Drawbacks

Salary. The salary of a hardware designer can vary greatly with the individual's amount of experience as well as the size and location of the company for which he or she works. The low end of the salary range is about $25,000 annually; the high end of the range is determined by the three factors mentioned above.

Opportunity to Advance. There are basically two avenues of advancement for a hardware designer. He or she can become a consultant, or he or she can advance within the research and development department of his or her own company or another company. There may be project manager positions in the R&D department, or the individual may move into the R&D manager's position. To make the move directly into management, though, sometimes further education, like a master's degree in business administration (an M.B.A.), is required.

Travel. A hardware designer usually travels very little.

Other Considerations. The major drawback of hardware design is the mental pressure experienced when a person is continually involved with concentrated technical work.

The job can be exciting and a challenge for a creative person who is technically oriented, however. Many hardware designers find their work very satisfying partly because they work under minimal supervision.

Personality Required

A hardware designer must be an individual who is creative but who also has technical talent. He or she needs to be logical and very thorough. There are long periods of time during which a hardware designer works alone, so he or she should be able to work in solitude and enjoy it. A hardware designer must be able to deal well with the mental stress resulting from a highly concentrated technical effort.

Outlook for the Future

The demand for hardware designers is not great at this time, but large companies that develop hardware sometimes have substantial needs for designers. In these companies, there are periods during which thousands of hardware designers are working on a major new project or product.

Where to Find Openings

Openings for hardware designers are often difficult to find. Most designers are employed by large firms that develop hardware.

HARDWARE SERVICE TECHNICIAN

The *hardware service technician* is involved with installing new computer equipment and is responsible for maintaining the equipment so that it will perform at its greatest efficiency levels (Fig. 5-5). Also, when a computer breaks down, the hardware service technician finds the cause of the breakdown and corrects it.

As part of the installation of new computer equipment, hardware service technicians often lay cables and hook up the electrical connections between different pieces of equipment. They thoroughly test new machines and peripherals— terminals or printers, for example—by running spe-

cial test programs and checking for any defective machine parts and any evidence of damage due to shipping. They correct any problems they find before the customer uses the machine.

Another part of the hardware service technician's job is *preventive maintenance*, which is scheduled at regular intervals. The purpose of maintenance is to prolong the life of the computer, to decrease the possibility of a computer breakdown, and to keep the machines or systems operating at peak performance. At this time, the technician sometimes analyzes the equipment performance records to see if there is evidence of any potential problem. He or she will also routinely adjust, oil, and clean the mechanical and electromechanical parts of the machine. The technician will check the electronic equipment for loose connections and defective components or circuits. Routine testing also includes the running of some test programs, for example, a program simulating a very heavy workload for the computer. By simulating actual events, problems can sometimes be identified and corrected before they cause the computer to fail.

When the computer does fail, the most critical function of the hardware service technician comes into play. When a company's computer is down, hundreds of workers cannot finish their tasks, and all of the manager's attention is focused on the complicated hardware upon which the company is so dependent. In larger installations, sometimes hundreds of thousands of dollars are lost whenever the computer fails for a substantial period of time. In these cases, the hardware service technician is responsible for diagnosing and correcting the machine's malfunction as quickly as possible. Of course, determining where in the system the problem has occurred is the hardest part of the technician's job.

Breakdowns can occur in the computer or central processing unit itself, in the peripheral equipment, in minicomputers that are connected to the central unit, or in the cables or data communications hookups that connect the machines. To locate the cause of electronic failure, technicians use several kinds of tools, including *oscilloscopes, digi-*

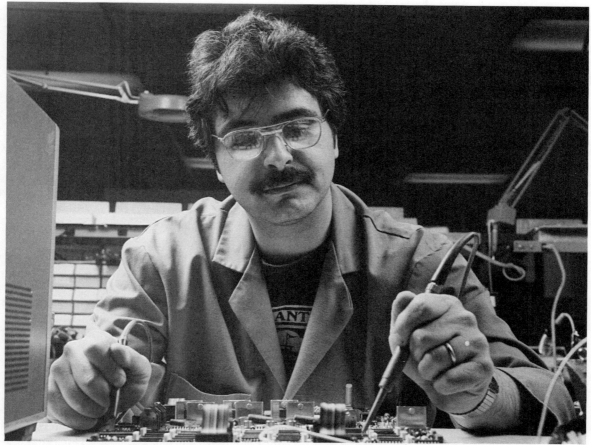

Fig. 5-5. To work as a hardware service technician, a person must be patient and very organized. (Photograph courtesy of Honeywell, Inc.)

tal voltmeters, and *ohmmeters*. They run *diagnostic programs* to help pinpoint certain malfunctions. Although it may take several hours to locate a problem, especially if it is an intermittent one, fixing the equipment may take just a few minutes. To replace a faulty circuit board, solder a broken connection, or repair a mechanical part, technicians use a variety of handtools, including needle-nosed pliers, wirestrippers, and soldering equipment. (The technician's employer provides the tools and test equipment, but the technician is responsible for keeping them in good working order.)

Because of the amount of money lost by a company when its central computer or even one of its minicomputers is down, the hardware service technician is under intense pressure to solve the specific problem quickly when it occurs. A technician will sometimes find that the problem is so difficult to diagnose that he or she requires assistance from his or her home office. In that case, a specialist or a more experienced technician will be dispatched from the office, and the two technicians will work together to solve the problem.

Sometimes, it is not clear whether the problem lies in the hardware or the software—the operating system program that is running the machine. While hardware technicians work to pinpoint any malfunction with the equipment, systems programmers may be asked to run special programs, such as *slip traps*, which will look for problems with the code. There are times when a malfunction is caused by both hardware and software. When the malfunctions are this complex, they sometimes take days rather than hours to resolve.

Larger computer installations generally run around the clock, and, as mentioned above, working time lost because of a breakdown can be very expensive. For this reason, technicians must be available to make emergency repairs at any time, day or night. Although the normal workweek is 40 hours, overtime of at least 10 and up to 30 hours a week is commonplace. The method of assigning overtime varies by employer. Some technicians are on call 24 hours a day, while others work rotating shifts—days one week, nights the next. Scheduling for emergency repairs is usually done by company dispatchers through the use of telephones as well as radio alert systems (beepers).

Although hardware service technicians can spend substantial amounts of time working on machine problems by themselves, they work with computer personnel of all different levels, also. The most important communicating they do regards the malfunction itself. The technician must listen to the customer's complaints and any description of what is known about the problem so far. Then, given what he or she knows about the problem at that time, the technician must let the manager in charge know that he or she is working on the problem and give the manager an estimate of the time that will be required to find the cause of the trouble and fix it. Because the situation is usually very tense, substantial communicative skills are required of the technician in order to keep the situation in hand. Of course, the technician has to have the ability to think clearly and logically under stress.

The hardware service technician sometimes offers customers technical advice on ways to keep equipment in good condition. In addition, experienced technicians often help train new technicians by working with them on the job for several months.

As another part of their job, hardware service technicians keep a meticulous record of preventive maintenance and repairs on each machine they service. This information helps with troubleshooting

in the future and is sometimes used as a basis by the technician's employer for deciding how much a company's annual service contract should cost. Technicians also fill out time and expense reports, keep an inventory of the spare parts available at each site, and order parts.

About 70 percent of a hardware service technician's time is spent with preventive maintenance, repair, and installation. The rest of the time, the technician has to learn and review various maintenance, repair, and installation procedures by reading the technical and repair manuals that are periodically revised and updated by computer manufacturers. Because each manufacturer has technical information for its own machines or equipment, the hardware service technician often specializes in handling the equipment of one manufacturer. For example, if a problem involves a system in which the machines of several manufacturers are networked together, hardware service technicians familiar with each type of equipment may need to work together to get the equipment up and running smoothly again.

Besides being responsible for knowing the contents of the most current technical manual regarding the machines they specialize in servicing, technicians usually spend one to three weeks annually in training courses regarding equipment and programming changes. The courses are offered by the equipment manufacturer and are paid for by the technician's employer.

Although some bending and lifting are part of the technician's job, the job is not strenuous. Work hazards are limited mainly to minor burns and electric shock, but these can be avoided if safety practices are followed.

Job Environment

Hardware service technicians are usually given a desk at their home office, but they spend only a few hours a week in that office—for a meeting with their boss or to replenish some spare parts that are needed for the inventory at one of the clients' locations. Most technicians are assigned several clients, depending on the technician's specialty and the type of equipment the user has. Individuals with several accounts must travel from place to place to maintain and service the systems and to make emergency repairs. In some cases, more than one technician will share an account and service different parts of a system. In other cases, an experienced technician may be assigned to work full-time at one client's installation to maintain all phases of that operation. So the technician's job environment, other than the desk at his home office, will vary depending on the number of clients with whom he or she works. In every case, the technician spends most of his or her time at the site of the computers and equipment for which he or she is responsible.

Alternate Titles

Hardware service technicians are also known by a host of other titles: *customer engineer*, *field service engineer*, *field engineer*, *service engineer*, *computer service technician*, and *computer maintenance specialist*. If a hardware service technician specializes in maintaining and repairing microcomputers, he or she may be called a *microcomputer service engineer* or technician.

Training and Background (or Experience) Required

A college degree is not required for a person to work as a hardware service technician, but it will give him or her an advantage over the competition. A high school degree and one to two years of formal training in basic electronics or its equivalent is expected. People expecting to begin work as hardware service technicians often get an associate's degree from a trade or technical school or a community or junior college (see Chapter 12 on Education and Training). Basic electronics training offered by the Armed Forces and by some vocational high schools also is acceptable preparation for some technician jobs. Some of the courses taken by individuals interested in working in this field focus on computer repair and maintenance, so when they complete their education they have an understanding of both the theoretical and the practical sides of electricity and electronics.

Newly hired technicians usually receive from three to six months of basic training from their employer. They may study elementary computer theory and circuitry theory in addition to expanding their knowledge of basic electronics. This training includes hands-on experience with computer equipment, doing basic maintenance, and using test equipment to locate malfunctions. As mentioned in the job description above, a technician's on-the-job training never stops. The training includes some classroom instruction each year as well as the responsibility for reading all of the most recent technical manuals for the equipment in which the technician is specializing.

No experience is required for the entry-level job of hardware service technician. Hobbies that involve electronics, however, such as operating ham radios or building stereo equipment, are relevant. Because no experience is necessary in addition to the formal instruction and basic training mentioned above, many hardware service technician "trainees" must complete six months to two years of on-the-job training. At first, they work closely with experienced technicians, learning to maintain machines that are relatively simple but that have the basic mechanical and electronic features of more complex equipment. As they become more experienced and learn to maintain more complicated computers and machines, they are assigned to specific maintenance and repair jobs and eventually to their own clients.

Benefits and Drawbacks

Salary. Hardware service technicians normally supplement their annual salary with paid overtime. At least 10 and up to 30 hours of overtime weekly is not uncommon, and the rate paid for overtime is either one and one-half or twice the normal rate. A technician who is willing to put in quite a bit of overtime can substantially increase his or her income. In addition, employers always pay all job-related expenses and sometimes provide a company car to technicians who travel a great deal. A technician's annual salary varies with experience but generally ranges from $17,000 to $38,000.

Opportunity to Advance. Technicians may find it difficult to transfer between companies that maintain different brands of equipment, because machines built by different companies are often unique in design and construction even though they operate on the same basic principles.

Within the same company, a hardware service technician can usually move up to the position of *service manager* based on experience, although it is easier if the individual has a bachelor's degree. Eventually, an individual with enough interest and motivation can open his or her own independent repair service. The services he or she offers would then have to compete, of course, in cost and quality with those offered by the larger third-party maintenance companies (see "Where to Find Openings" later in this section).

A hardware service technician with experience and a B.S. in computer science or engineering will be able to progress to working as a *hardware designer* (see previous section of this chapter), although there are a limited number of openings in the field of hardware design.

Technicians with four-year college degrees can also move into other computer careers, such as programming and systems analysis, and equipment sales or marketing, depending on their individual aptitudes and interests.

Travel. Some hardware service technicians are assigned to work full-time at one client's installation, and so the travel required as part of the job is relatively small and would amount to one or two trips a week between the client's site and the technician's home office. Most hardware service technicians are assigned to a number of clients, however, so a sizeable amount of travel is commonplace.

Usually travel is local; technicians are not away from home overnight. Employers pay for travel expenses, including job-related uses of the technician's car. Sometimes the employer provides a car for the technician's use. Hardware service technicians who work for a nationwide organization may be required to travel between states and must sometimes transfer to another city or state.

The amount of travel varies with the particular position and the size of the technician's employer, but generally a great deal of travel is required of hardware service technicians.

Other Considerations. The largest drawback of the hardware service technician's job is the mental strain experienced while working to solve a complex problem as soon as possible. It is also hard to change employers if another employer offers service for a different type of computer or machinery. Overtime is very common.

Despite these drawbacks, many technicians derive personal satisfaction from knowing that many people are depending on them to find and fix a problem so they can resume work. They regard each problem as an exciting challenge. Hardware service technicians enjoy the freedom of working without direct supervision.

Personality Required

To work as a hardware service technician, a person must be patient and very organized. He or she needs to have a logical, analytical mind and enjoy solving problems. A mechanical interest and aptitude is important, as well as the ability to work with people. As with many other computer careers, communications ability is central to an individual's success as a technician. In particular, a technician must be a good listener and should be good at explaining the problem as he or she understands it. The ability to work on one's own without close supervision is also necessary for hardware service technicians.

Outlook for the Future

The outlook for the future of hardware service technicians is very good. Although the increase in the need for technicians is not expected to grow as fast as in some other computer careers (for example, systems analysts), the demand for technicians is expected to remain strong. This is partly due to the increase in the number of microcomputers being used in business. The Bureau of Labor Statistics predicts that between 1984 and 1995 the number of hardware service technicians in the United States will increase by 56 percent.

Where to Find Openings

Openings for hardware service technicians are more common near large urban areas, where computer equipment is concentrated. Some companies with very large computer installations employ full-time technicians, but most technicians work for three kinds of companies: manufacturers, retailers, and independent maintenance firms.

Most hardware manufacturers repair only their own hardware and will not handle systems that include hardware from a variety of manufacturers (sometimes referred to as *mixed-manufacturer systems*). Breakdowns in this type of system are often difficult to fix. Many retailers are also in the repair business, but with mixed results. Some retailers find offering maintenance contracts and services for a fee profitable, and some do not. By far the most rapidly expanding type of company that employs hardware service technicians is the *independent maintenance firm,* also known as a *third-party main-* tenance company (the manufacturer is the first party and the retailer the second party). The major third-party maintenance firms are very large, but the size ranges down to small owner-operated repair shops that handle local jobs. Regardless of size, these companies specialize in computer repair and provide maintenance services for a set cost. Larger firms are likely to have more openings for hardware service technicians primarily because they employ a greater number of technicians.

INFORMATION CENTER POSITIONS

The concept of the *information center* was first introduced by IBM. The original idea involved making those computer tools available to end users which would allow them to do some of their own computing, instead of relying on the more technical departments for all their computing needs. Today, there exists a wide variety of departments all referred to as information centers but which vary

Fig. 5-6. Most information centers fulfill the two basic end user needs of education and training, and consultation. (Photograph courtesy of Sperry Corp.)

considerably by company.

The information center is basically the department to which end-users can go when they encounter a computing problem. The center is the link in many companies between the end-users and the DP department.

Most information centers fulfill the basic end-user needs of education, training, and consultation (Fig. 5-6). Trainers within the information center help users learn enough about computer software and equipment to be able to use it by themselves. Sometimes the training is formal and involves a certain number of classes arranged for a particular time, and sometimes the training is informal. Many information center personnel encourage users to drop by to get their questions answered or to get guided hands-on experience. Usually, the information center personnel do not become permanently involved in long-term projects, but instead are used as *resource people*. For example, people in information center positions may help users configure their microcomputer applications, such as database and spreadsheet applications.

Information centers also usually serve end-users in a consulting function. Advice will be given to users regarding the evaluation and selection of a computer product to meet their specific needs. Occasionally, consultants also assist users in buying hardware and peripherals. The information center is often the focal point for the demonstration of new computer products and capabilities. Information center personnel get all kinds of questions from users, ranging from topics such as electronic mail and network file transfers to questions regarding the usage of software packages that have been recommended by the information center. Basic questions often can be answered immediately by people working in the information center; more complex questions are referred to other more technical groups or are researched by the information center staff.

If these basic functions—education, training, and consultation—are fulfilled by a company's information center, an improved relationship between the end-users and the DP department can result. Users who had felt the technical department was totally inflexible gain an understanding regarding what is actually involved in developing a computer application. And technical personnel who had viewed users as unrealistically demanding and unaware of the complexities involved in developing software are able to communicate better with users via information center personnel.

There are several other needs that some companies' information centers meet. Some information centers are responsible for office automation and the use of personal computers in the company; some have different microcomputers available to loan to users for a trial period or for use during a temporary peak of demand for micro services. In some companies, the information center undertakes the work of developing regular reports for user departments. When this is done, the more complex requests are referred to more technical departments. Helping with the simpler projects can alleviate the backlog of user requests.

There is usually a director of the information center, who coordinates all the center's activities and is familiar with the newest developments in business computing. Other information center personnel have varying duties: sometimes they are assigned their responsibilities as questions and needs for certain services arise; in other cases, they are in charge of users' needs for particular hardware or software products. The exact job of a person working in an information center will differ from company to company and from month to month and often from day to day.

Job Environment

Persons working in an information center work in an office setting. They are either located in the information center or in the office of the user whose needs they are serving.

Alternate Titles

In some organizations, the information center is referred to as *decision support services, technical support,* or *user support.* But "information center" is the more current title for these groups.

Training and Background
(or Experience) Required

The education required for a person working in an information center position is a bachelor's degree, preferably in computer science or a related field. The individual is expected to have some experience in interacting with users in some capacity and enough of a technical background to be able to understand, research (if necessary), and respond to users' needs.

A move into an information center position is common for technicians who are interested in working with computing questions that are more closely related to general business.

Benefits and Drawbacks

Salary. The salary of a person working in an information center varies a great deal with his or her level of experience and particular responsibilities. Generally, salaries range from about $28,000 annually to about $37,000 annually.

Opportunity to Advance. As is the case with a database administrator (see a previous section of this chapter), a person working in an information center will meet many people from many different departments within the company. Because of these contacts, individuals in information center positions have a great deal of opportunity to advance.

Travel. Information center personnel can travel up to about 30 percent of the time, usually to attend training seminars on hardware or software products that they will be supporting.

Other Considerations. A major advantage of an information center position is the amazing variety of responsibilities that are involved. The job offers a combination of opportunities regarding working with people and also the chance to learn new technical skills.

A person in this position is constantly being interrupted, and so he or she must have the type of personality that allows for adjustment to a change in the focus of concentration. For example, a person may be in the middle of working on a report that one user needs the following week when another user calls about a question that is holding up a project due the next day. The information center staffer is often required to change the relative priority of his or her projects as the day or week progresses.

Personality Required

Individuals who are employed in information center positions must have a great deal of patience and the ability to deal with interruptions and a constant reprioritizing of their work. They should be able to communicate effectively both with technical personnel and with nontechnical end-users. Strong analytic and organizational skills are important to information center work, as well. Good business sense and an understanding of the company's business is regarded as an asset in a person working in an information center.

Outlook for the Future

Currently, there is a great deal of demand for persons working in information centers. This demand is partly a result of the increased business usage of computer products. As time goes on, however, the demand for personnel in this area will gradually decrease, although it is hard to predict how much it will lessen. In many companies in which the size of the information center is now growing, the center is expected to stabilize in size with a relatively small number of people. In one company, eight information center personnel are expected to be able to meet the needs of hundreds of users. Whether this expectation is realistic only the future can tell.

Where to Find Openings

Information center openings are more commonly found in companies with very big computer installations or in large organizations located in urban areas.

JOURNALISTS

Journalists specializing in the computer field work for a variety of different types of magazines, journals, and newspapers, including consumer-oriented trade publications, technical trade publications, and general interest publications which have a special technology section. They write articles and sometimes a column on topics of interest to their readers—major computer users in a certain geographical area, for example. Trends in the computer marketplace and events that will in some way affect the publication's readership are also covered.

In recent years, there has been first a proliferation of magazines and journals specializing in computer topics, and then an industry shakeout which resulted in many of the publications going out of business. It is now generally felt that the major impact of the shakeout has passed, and the technology publications industry is expected to remain more stable.

Journalists work on either a free-lance basis, submitting articles to one or more publications and being paid for each article that is printed, or a salaried basis, working as a staff member of a publication.

Job Environment

Salaried journalists work in the main office or one of the regional offices of their publication. If they work in a regional office, it is often their responsibility to cover computer events and companies in their area. A journalist working in a regional office near New York City, for instance, will cover that area for a publication whose main office is near Boston.

Alternate Titles

There are no alternate titles for the career of journalist. A closely related career, however, is the career of *technical writer* (see a later section of this chapter).

Background and Training
(or Experience) Required

A four-year college degree with a major in journalism is expected of persons interested in pursuing this career, but individuals with a liberal arts degree and the ability to write can also find work in this area, although at first they may have to work as free-lance writers.

Experience in writing for a magazine, journal, or another type of publication gives an individual a distinct advantage in the job market, especially if the writing focused on technology or technological issues. Sometimes, in order to break into the field, an individual has to start by writing articles on a free-lance basis. Once a person's ability to write articles about computer topics has been established, his or her writing will be in much greater demand.

Benefits and Drawbacks

Salary. A journalist's salary will vary according to his or her experience and depending on the particular publication for which he or she is working. Generally, annual salaries range from about $18,000 to about $35,000.

Opportunity to Advance. Journalists have the opportunity to advance to higher level management positions in their company or at other magazines, journals, or newspapers. For example, they can become bureau chiefs, with reporters working for them.

Travel. There is often a substantial amount of local travel involved in a journalist's job. A correspondent whose regional office is in the suburbs will spend quite a bit of his or her time in New York City when covering a story there.

Other Considerations. One major drawback of the career of journalist is the dearth of opportunities to advance. Also, the job can be mentally taxing when the reporter is searching for exactly the right words to tell his or her story. Most journalists find the job very intellectually satisfying, however. Completing a number of well-written and interesting articles can give an individual a real sense of accomplishment.

Personality Required

A journalist covering technology or the computer field needs to have a genuine interest in and curiosity about technology and computers. He or she should be inquisitive and persistent, because sometimes an article that is about a recent trend in the industry may require quite a few telephone and personal interviews in addition to some library research. Good interviewing skills and the ability to communicate well, both in person and in writing, are also important to being a successful journalist.

Outlook for the Future

As discussed previously, many publications specializing in technology have gone out of business over the past few years, but the publications that still exist are stable, and there is now a strong demand for journalists at these companies. The high demand is thought to be due in part to the many journalists who opted for other careers during the shakeout. Therefore, demand is expected to decrease somewhat in the future.

Where to Find Openings

Many journalists who cover the computer industry work for consumer-oriented or technical trade publications. For a list of the publications, see Appendix B. The main offices of the publications are usually in large urban areas, but regional offices are spread throughout the country. Some journalists writing on technology work for general interest publications that have a special technology section. For a list of all the newspapers in the United States, consult the *Editor and Publisher International Yearbook*, published by Editor and Publisher, 11 West 19th Street, New York, NY, 10011, and available in the reference section of your local library.

MINICOMPUTER AND MICROCOMPUTER PROGRAMMERS

Minicomputer and *microcomputer programmers* write and implement programs for users or manufacturers (Fig. 5-7). There are many more microcomputer programmers in the work force today than there were just five years ago due to the proliferation of microcomputers for business use. Microcom-

Fig. 5-7. Microcomputer or minicomputer programmers may work with applications programs or they may make modifications to the operating system. (Photograph courtesy of Sperry Corp.)

puter programmers can be involved in a number of different projects. They sometimes work with telecommunications programmers to solve problems arising when the microcomputers are networked together, the *uploading* of files from the microcomputers to a mainframe or minicomputer, and the *downloading* of files from the mainframe or minicomputer to the microcomputers. They can also be involved in putting up a database application which people can access via their microcomputers. Or they may work on upgrading a vendor package, such as *Yterm*, which was specifically designed for use on microcomputers.

Microcomputer or minicomputer programmers may work with applications programs, and in that case, they are a special kind of applications programmer. They may make modifications to the operating system or install various products, in which case the work they do is *systems programming* work.

The applications type of work may involve a variety of different areas, depending on the type of company for which the programmer works. He or she may program an electronic game, an inventory, or record-keeping system. The work may be done in one of a variety of higher level languages, such as Pascal or BASIC.

Minicomputer or microcomputer programmers involved in systems work may code the interface necessary for a micro user to utilize a certain software package or a certain piece of hardware, such as a particular type of printer. He or she may also install and test various software products available for use on computers. Programmers involved in systems work do their coding in *Basic Assembly Language (or BAL)*.

Job Environment

A minicomputer or microcomputer programmer works in an office, either on a terminal connected to the minicomputer or on a microcomputer that may be connected to the mainframe computer or a minicomputer. Exactly where his or her office is located depends on the company for which he or she works, as well as the type of projects on which he or she is working.

Alternate Titles

Sometimes individuals working in these positions are referred to either as *applications programmers* or *systems programmers*.

Training and Background (or Experience) Required

Minicomputer and microcomputer programmers working with applications are usually expected to have a four-year college degree, which includes some programming and computer science courses.

Although a person aspiring to be a minicomputer or microcomputer programmer may have the required education for the job, he or she will probably find it difficult to get his or her first job because the strongest demand at this time is for experienced programmers in these areas. Experience of some kind is a necessity. Work completed on your own micro at home will be helpful, but a part-time job working in this area during your college education will give you an advantage in the job market. It may be necessary to accept a part-time position in this field before you can get an offer for full-time work. But your patience will pay off; once you are working as a programmer you will be gaining experience which will be viewed by your employer as extremely valuable.

Minicomputer and microcomputer programmers working with systems are expected to have a similar education. They are, however, expected to have more experience than their counterparts who work with applications. Often minicomputer and microcomputer programmers begin by working with applications for at least a year before they work with systems. In order to advance to systems work, a mini or micro programmer may also need special training in Basic Assembly Language (BAL).

Benefits and Drawbacks

Salary. A minicomputer or microcomputer programmer's salary varies with his or her level of experience and increases as he or she does more system-related work. Annual salaries range from $28,000 to $40,000.

Opportunity to Advance. Minicomputer and microcomputer programmers have a number of opportunities to advance. As discussed earlier, a programmer who is working mostly with applications can progress to systems work. Or a minicomputer or microcomputer programmer can become a project leader (see a later section) or a systems analyst (see a later section). These two career paths represent the choice that advancement in many computer careers offers: a move into a more technical position or a switch to more of a managerial position.

Travel. Minimal travel is usually required of minicomputer and microcomputer programmers. Most of their travel is for specialized training seminars or classes.

Other Considerations. The largest drawback of a minicomputer or microcomputer programmer's job is the constant stress due to continual deadlines. Microcomputer programmers and often minicomputer programmers enjoy working with state-of-the-art equipment, however.

Personality Required

The same personality traits that are necessary for applications programmers are essential for successful minicomputer and microcomputer applications programming work. These programmers need to be able to work with a high degree of accuracy and have the ability to think through long complicated problems. The ability to communicate both verbally and in writing is required, and mini and micro applications programmers need to be persistent, even-tempered, and patient.

A minicomputer or microcomputer programmer who works with systems would need to have the personality characteristics required of a systems programmer as well as the traits mentioned above. Because he or she may work alone a great deal of the time, the programmer must enjoy working in solitude. The individual should also be very technically oriented and very curious about how things work. In addition, minicomputer or microcomputer systems programmers should have a high frustration tolerance.

Outlook for the Future

Although the demand for microcomputer programmers in particular is not as outstanding as it was several years ago, it is expected to remain strong in the near future. Individuals with an understanding of graphics and telecommunications will be in especially high demand.

The need for minicomputer programmers has increased slightly in the last year or two, along with the increase in minicomputer sales. To date, the demand has not reached the level of need for microcomputer programmers.

Where to Find Openings

Openings for microcomputer or minicomputer programmers can be found in large companies, in or near urban areas, which are utilizing microcomputers and/or minicomputers in addition to a mainframe. There are also a variety of other companies, including computer manufacturing companies and microcomputer software producers or vendors, which employ microcomputer and minicomputer programmers.

OFFICE AUTOMATION SPECIALISTS

For information on *office automation*, see the sections on Data Entry and Word Processing.

OPERATIONS MANAGER

The *operations manager* is responsible for all the activity that occurs in operations. He or she controls, schedules, and organizes the daily operation of the company's computer(s) and peripheral equipment such as printers, scanners, and disk and tape drives (Fig. 5-8). All of the computer operators report to the operations manager, who is responsible for hiring new employees and assigning specific duties to the operators. He or she also reviews the equipment records kept by the operators. Scheduling the installation of new equipment, the use of present equipment, and preventive maintenance on all equipment is handled by the operations manager. Often, the manager is involved in security planning for the computer room, which usually houses mil-

53

Fig. 5-8. The operations manager is responsible for all the activity that occurs in operations. (Photograph courtesy of Sperry Corp.)

lions of dollars of equipment. The operations manager in some companies reports periodically on the efficiency of the computer operation to the *computing system director*.

Job Environment

The operations manager usually has his or her own office. It is located near the computer room, where he or she spends a substantial amount of time. The computer room is ventilated very well but is noisy when the equipment is running.

Alternate Titles

There are no alternate titles for the position of oper-

ations manager. *Operations supervisors*, who report to the manager, are often assigned to a particular shift and are responsible for the computer operators working during that time period.

Training and Background (or Experience) Required

A college degree is required for operations managers, but the amount of experience required depends upon the particular employer. Some managers worked first as an operator for several years and then as an operations supervisor for two or three years. Others move from operations to work as an applications or systems programmer. In either case, the operations manager is expected to have a good understanding of both hardware and software.

Benefits and Drawbacks

Salary. The manager's annual salary varies with his or her amount of experience and the size of the installation in which he or she works. In larger companies, more people report to the operations manager, so he or she is paid more. Annual salaries typically range from $32,000 to $48,000.

Opportunity to Advance. The operations manager's opportunity to advance depends a great deal on the breadth of his or her experience and the amount of training he or she has had. An operations manager with prior experience working as an applications or systems programmer has a better chance of moving up the DP ladder to another management position than an operations manager without as broad a background. An operations manager who has kept up with the latest advances in technology through continued education will be viewed more favorably than one who has not. There is, however, no typical career path that is followed by operations managers. How a manager progresses is determined by his or her interests and abilities.

Travel. Virtually no travel is required of operations managers.

Other Considerations. There are periods during which a substantial amount of overtime is required of operations managers, for example, when a new mainframe is being installed. The installation is usually scheduled for the weekend and installation and testing may take all day Saturday and Sunday.

Managing operations, however, is fulfilling to individuals who enjoy working with many kinds of people in a fast-paced, always changing setting.

Personality Required

There are three characteristics that are important to being a successful operations manager. The first is the ability to communicate well with individuals on all levels. The second is the understanding of the technical aspects of hardware and software, and the third is creative problem-solving ability. An operations manager needs to be creative in order to help solve problems confronting his or her operations staff, and he or she must also think creatively about how to most efficiently utilize his or her equipment and his or her personnel.

Outlook for the Future

The demand for operations managers is expected to remain strong in the near future. The position is expected to continue to be upgraded in salary level as the hardware and software for which the operations manager is responsible become more complicated. The managers most in demand will be those with exposure to large database or telecommunications oriented systems.

Where to Find Openings

Operations managers work in almost every industry and for small, medium, or large companies with one or more mainframes or large computers. Most managers work for computer manufacturing firms, banks, insurance companies, schools, hospitals, government agencies, wholesale and retail trade establishments, and computer service companies which offer computer services for a fee.

PROJECT LEADER

In many companies, programmers and systems analysts work on projects in teams; the *project leader* is usually the person who heads the team. He or she may be appointed project leader only for the duration of one project, which can range from several weeks to one or two years. Or he or she may be permanently made a project leader, and when one project is completed, he or she will start to work on another one.

The exact responsibilities of a project leader vary widely from company to company. As mentioned above, the leader oversees the team effort on a project, which is often the development of a software system or a hardware product. He or she discusses with the end-users the information necessary to the completion of the project and drafts instructions describing how the job is to be done. The leader delegates specific parts of the project to the programmers and system analysts on his or her team, then supervises the efforts of his or her team members, checks the quality of their work, and makes sure that the work is progressing on schedule. There are several things that project leaders cannot do. In most companies, they cannot hire or fire employees, and usually they do not have budgetary responsibilities.

Project leaders either report to the project manager or the computing systems director. In smaller companies, their functions are performed by senior or lead systems analysts (see a later section of this chapter). Continued training to keep up with the latest technological developments is expected of project leaders, so they spend some time attending seminars and presentations.

Job Environment

The work of a project leader is done in an office setting. A major portion of the day is spent in meetings and on the telephone.

Alternate Titles

In some companies, a *project manager* is one level above a project leader, and the leader works for the manager. In other organizations, the two titles are used to describe the same position. A third title that is sometimes used for the job is *project director*.

Training and Background
(or Experience) Required

A bachelor's degree in computer science or a related area is required for the position of project leader. An M.B.A. (master's degree in business administration) is desirable.

A project leader must have enough experience to thoroughly comprehend programming and systems analysis or design, and he or she must also have management skills. Usually, employers expect at least two years of experience in programming and/or systems analysis or design.

Benefits and Drawbacks

Salary. The annual salary for project leaders varies with the individual's responsibilities, his or her experience, and the location and size of his or her organization. Generally, salaries range from $22,000 to $42,000.

Opportunity to Advance. Project leaders have a good opportunity to advance to higher DP management positions.

Travel. Up to one-fifth of a project leader's time is spent travelling to seminars and meetings.

Other Considerations. Overtime for which there is no direct compensation is often required of project leaders. The fast pace and daily deadlines that go with the position are difficult for some individuals to take. The position allows for a substantial amount of involvement with the company, however, which many project leaders enjoy. The position is a fairly powerful one, and it also allows for a great deal of interaction with other people.

Personality Required

The project leader must, of course, have management ability and leadership skills. The ability to communicate with others, poise, and self-control are essential to this position. Some aggressiveness is helpful, because the project leader is responsible for keeping the work moving along at a certain pace.

Technical skills are also necessary for this position, because sometimes the project leader becomes directly involved with the programming in an effort to solve a particular problem.

Outlook for the Future

The demand for project leaders is strong in large organizations and is expected to remain so in the near future.

Where to Find Openings

Most project leaders work in large companies or organizations, which have large computer systems or are developing their own applications to run on the systems. Openings may be found in hardware and software manufacturers and computer service organizations.

RETAIL STORE SALESPERSON

Retail store salespeople sell computers and computer equipment to people who come into the store, whether they are small businesspeople, homeowners, or college students. Many computer stores are connected to one or more major computer equipment manufacturers, and most stores limit their inventory—partly to avoid customer confusion—to about five computer lines. The products sold by retail computer stores include minicomputers, microcomputers, disk units, printers, software packages, and the literature that is associated with the equipment and software.

The average sale in a retail computer store amounts to approximately $5,000. A majority of the customers spending this amount of money are individuals in small businesses.

The retail salesperson needs to understand and be able to explain most of the technical aspects of the products sold in the store. Often, the characteristics of the products of various manufacturers vary from month to month and even week to week. One person working as a salesperson is often the store's manager and owner.

Job Environment

The retail store salesperson spends his or her time in the computer store, which can be quite small and cramped or roomy and very large.

Alternate Titles

There are no alternate titles for this position. For information on another position in computer sales, see the section of this chapter on sales representative.

Training and Background (or Experience) Required

The training expected for the position of retail store salesperson varies a great deal. A bachelor's degree, especially one which includes a few technical courses on computers, is preferred. Some knowledge of electronics is helpful. Generally, the more sophisticated the hardware or equipment the store sells, the higher the training requirements for the job.

Continuous on-the-job training is expected. Most of this consists in reading the literature regarding the most recent changes in the products carried by the store.

To some store managers and owners, a "sales personality" may be more important than an individual's particular level of training or background.

The position of retail store salesperson is entry level, although it is helpful for a person to have some previous sales experience. Salespeople often have some hands-on experience with the computer equipment sold by the store.

Benefits and Drawbacks

Salary. The salary of a retail store salesperson varies a great deal, but usually starts between $15,000 and $20,000 annually.

Opportunity to Advance. There is opportunity to advance to the position of a retail store manager, once an individual is knowledgeable enough about the products carried by the store to answer the most difficult technical questions raised by customers. Some salespeople eventually open their own retail store.

Travel. Any travel that is required of a retail store salesperson is limited to the local area.

Other Considerations. Retail store salespeople will be required to work some evenings and most Saturdays, which are usually busy days for retail stores.

Personality Required

A retail store salesperson must be able to translate technical information into nontechnical language. Patience is an asset in this position, because most customers will visit the store several times before making a purchase. A salesperson should be comfortable with strangers and like meeting and talking with people. Analytical ability is important, because a salesperson must thoroughly understand the products the store sells and needs to continually learn about updates in the product and/or product line. Having a "sales personality" is a prerequisite of the sales job. Individuals with this type of personality are dynamic, outgoing, easy to get along with, persuasive, and pleasant.

Outlook for the Future

Larger retail store chains are intense competition for small computer retailers, partly because the big stores usually get contracts with the better-known computer manufacturers. Openings are more likely to occur in stores affiliated with larger chains, but a very large staff is never required even by the most successful and largest retail stores. Demand for retail store salespeople, then, is only moderate and is not expected to increase greatly in the future.

Where to Find Openings

As mentioned above, more openings will be available in large retail stores and in stores affiliated with major chains.

SALES REPRESENTATIVE

A *computer sales representative* is responsible for selling a variety of equipment and/or services to distributors, retail outlets, or large businesses and service companies such as schools and colleges, factories, libraries, hospitals, banks, financial organizations, and department store chains. Each sales representative may work with customers within one particular industry, or he or she may sell to a variety of customers. The products sold by sales reps include computer mainframes and sometimes minicomputers and/or microcomputers, peripherals, and software; the services sold are often consulting, programming, or support services.

The actual activities of a computer sales representative are quite varied. Some of the time, he or she researches and draws up a list of sales prospects and studies and reviews the literature regarding the capabilities, limits, and strengths of the product or service he or she is selling. The sales rep then contacts the companies to set up an appointment for product demonstration and a presentation. The demonstration may involve testing the product with certain programs or comparing the product with a competitor's product. After the presentation, through a series of additional meetings at the customer's location, the sales rep helps analyze the company's needs, and then he or she will prepare a written proposal explaining what combination of products will best meet these needs. Finally, when the customer indicates a definite interest, the sales rep takes the order. He or she explains the different financing arrangements, such as leasing or purchasing, and handles the sale according to the customer's wishes. Most sales efforts require many months, but the size of the sale can be in the millions of dollars.

Job Environment

Computer sales representatives spend some preparation time at their home office, but most of their time is spent on the road and in their customers' offices.

Alternate Titles

Computer sales representatives are also referred to as *computing industry sales reps, customer reps, marketing reps,* or *manufacturers' sales workers.* They are also sometimes called *sales engineers* or *customer support representatives,* although these last two job titles sometimes imply additional support responsibilities after the sale is complete.

Training and Background (or Experience) Required

The training required for computer sales representatives is a bachelor's degree, preferably in computer science or in business or marketing, with courses in computer science. A master's degree in business administration (M.B.A.) is helpful for individuals who want to progress to management positions.

To some companies, a "sales personality" is more important than a person's particular training or background. Many of these employers have extensive sales training programs, which can last up to two years and involve apprenticeship with experienced sales reps, classes away from the home office, and personal study courses at the home office. Rotating among a variety of jobs is sometimes a part of sales training. Through the job rotation, the trainee has a chance to learn firsthand about the production, installation, and distribution of the product. Sales representatives commonly spend up to two weeks annually in classes designed to inform them of the most current modifications in the product or service that they sell.

The position of computer sales representative is an entry level position, but employers desire candidates with a proven track record in sales. Sometimes analysts, managers, engineers, and other persons are hired as computer sales representatives.

Benefits and Drawbacks

Salary. Computer sales representatives are compensated in a variety of ways. Some companies pay their sales reps a fixed salary (which often involves a quota system), and other organizations pay their reps a salary plus commission. Most sales representatives are paid extremely well, with their annual income varying from $50,000 to over $100,000 annually, depending in part on experience. Job perquisites (or perks) often include a car, an expense account, and special trips to resort areas.

Opportunity to Advance. Computer sales representatives can move into sales management positions within their own company in new area start-up situations. From there, they can progress to higher level management positions. Sales reps also have ample opportunity to advance to management, advertising, or market research positions in the companies to whom they have been selling computer equipment or services.

Travel. Extensive and constant travel is required for computer sales representatives. Many sales representatives, however, are responsible for a limited geographical area.

Other Considerations. One drawback of a career as a computer sales representative is the pressure of needing constantly to come up with a certain level of sales in order to justify a certain salary level. The job is also not appropriate, clearly, for a person who minds constant travel.

Computer sales reps enjoy interacting with a variety of people. They can experience a great deal of satisfaction when the equipment they have recommended has been installed, operational, and meeting the company's needs.

Personality Required

A computer sales representative must be able to assume a considerable amount of responsibility, because he or she is usually the primary contact with each customer. Initiative, energy, and self-confidence are required for this position. A sales rep should be comfortable with strangers and like meeting and talking with people. Analytical ability is important, because a rep needs to thoroughly understand the computer product or service that he or she is selling. Having a "sales personality" is a prerequisite of the sales job. Persons with this type of personality are dynamic, outgoing, persuasive, easy to get along with, and pleasant.

Outlook for the Future

There are presently excellent job opportunities in this area. The demand for computer sales representatives marketing software packages, communications interfaces, and mini- or microcomputer systems is expected to remain particularly high in the near future.

Where to Find Openings

Openings for computer sales representatives occur in large computer manufacturers and computer service firms. Many of the companies are located in or near major cities.

SYSTEMS ANALYSIS

Systems analysts plan and develop methods for computerizing business and scientific tasks or improving computer systems already in use. They are problem solvers and efficiency experts who must be well in tune with a variety of computer equipment and programming techniques as well as the specific needs of a particular department within their company. They function as the main link between the user department and the company's computer resources, so they often are expected to explain computer functions to users in everyday language and sometimes become involved in training end-users regarding the newly developed system.

Systems analysts usually perform five different steps for each project with which they are involved. The process begins with the gathering of information regarding exactly what the needs of the user department are and exactly how the job is performed manually. For example, if a retail chain wanted to computerize its inventory system, systems analysts would determine what information must be collected and what reports would need to be produced from it. The analysts may run feasibility studies at this stage and will study how the information is collected and processed manually: the speed with which the data is collected, the frequency of the produced reports, the sources of input that are processed, and many other variables.

The second stage is the planning or designing of a system that will incorporate computer equipment and procedures to increase the efficiency of the present operation. The problem must be stated clearly, based on all of the information that has been collected, and then several possible solutions devised. The solutions may involve the use of prewritten software packages, with some additional code, or programs that will be completely written by the company's programming staff. In many cases, the more cost-effective of these two approaches is the first of the two. One difficulty often experienced during this stage is the necessity of making the new or revised system compatible with the company's existing systems.

As part of the system design stage, *specifications* (or clear instructions to be used by programmers) are written by the systems analyst, who sometimes also completes system layout charts. Cost-benefit analyses are often prepared at this stage.

The third stage involves the presentation to management of one recommended system design. Discussions between the analyst and management usually continue until a design is approved.

Once the project has received formal approval, more detailed planning is done by the analyst. The system specifications, for example, will be made more complete.

The fifth and final stage includes the system implementation. This process sometimes involves the supervision by the analyst of a small group of programmers. The analyst usually decides exactly what hardware and software is needed for the project and works on acquiring them. Sometimes, the analyst actually does a little of the coding himself or herself.

Throughout the five steps for each project, the systems analyst is required to communicate both verbally and in writing with many different levels of employees within the company.

Job Environment

A systems analyst works in an office, which is usually in the computer department but may be located in the business department of the company. The normal work week for an analyst is 40 hours, although there are times just before deadline when substantial evening and/or weekend hours are required. A systems analyst does not receive paid overtime.

Alternate Titles

Systems analysts are also referred to as *information systems analysts, systems designers,* or *system engineers.* Senior or lead systems analysts have more experience than junior systems analysts.

Training and Background (or Experience) Required

There is no universally accepted way of preparing for a job as a systems analyst, because employers' preferences depend on the work being done. College graduates with a major in computer science or a related area are almost always sought for these jobs. Graduate degrees ranging from a Master of Business Administration (an M.B.A.) to a master's or doctoral degree in computer science are sometimes desired for the more complex jobs.

Technological advances occur so quickly in the computer field that continuous study is necessary to keep skills up to date. Training usually takes the form of one- and two-week courses offered by employers and software vendors. Additional training is sometimes acquired through professional development seminars offered by professional computing societies, listed in Appendix A.

Regardless of educational specialization, employers look for most people who are familiar with programming languages. Up to three years of work in programming is expected. In addition, several years of experience in the field in which the work is being performed, such as retailing, banking, or insurance, is considered a definite advantage. For information on certification, see Chapter 3.

Benefits and Drawbacks

Salary. The salary range of systems analysts, which varies with experience, is about $27,000 to $50,000. Some talented and experienced analysts are paid $100,000 annually. The highest salaries are paid by very large corporations located in urban areas.

Opportunity to Advance. The systems analysis position, partly because of its high visibility, is a good stepping stone to management positions. The analyst communicates with a variety of company employees of all different levels, and many of these people work in nontechnical positions. Because of his or her experience in working with users, a systems analyst can move into corporate management posts as well as positions in database administration or computing systems management. Experienced analysts sometimes work for or start their own consulting firms, which provide services to smaller companies that do not employ full-time systems analysts.

Travel. A small amount of travel, which revolves around training seminars or the visitation of the company's user departments, is required of systems analysts. The exact amount varies from organization to organization.

Other Considerations. A systems analyst is constantly working under deadline pressure and is often the one person held responsible by management for project completion or implementation by a specific target date.

The position can be very satisfying, however, especially when the analyst can see the improvement in operation that has resulted from his or her effort. The position carries with it intellectual status and high visibility within the company.

Personality Required

A systems analyst must be a poised individual who functions well under pressure and a good organizer and planner. He or she needs to have good interpersonal skills and the ability to communicate effectively, both orally and in writing, with technical personnel as well as end-users who have little or no computing background. Systems analysts need to be able to think logically and extract the real problem from a number of people's descriptions of it. They should be able to understand the functional specifics of the computer devices likely to be used in their projects, but they also should like working with people and ideas. Analysts often deal with a number of different projects simultaneously. The ability to concentrate and pay close attention to detail is essential for a systems analyst, who must also be able to research a problem or issue very thoroughly. Systems analysts often work independently, but on large projects, they also work in teams.

Outlook for the Future

Employment of systems analysts is expected to grow much faster than the average for all occupations through the mid-1990s. In fact, the Bureau of Labor Statistics has predicted a 69 percent increase in employment from 1984 to 1995. The exceptional increase in demand will be due partly to the proliferation of microcomputers in small businesses and also to the increase in the amount of problems regarding the compatibility of new and different kinds of computer equipment. The greatest need for systems analysts in the future is expected to be in database and data communications.

Where to Find Openings

Most system analyst jobs are located in urban areas, and many are found in large companies that are installing or putting up new databases or expanding in either the office automation or telecommunications area. Types of companies in which systems analysts work include computer consulting firms, insurance companies, banks, companies that deal in wholesale and retail trade, and large manufacturing companies.

SYSTEMS AND PROGRAMMING MANAGERS

The job of a *systems and programming manager* varies in at least two ways, depending upon the size of the company for which he or she is working. Company size determines the type of people who work for the systems and programming manager, as well as the type of projects for which he or she is responsible. Often, in a large company, a systems and programming manager has systems programmers and/or software engineers working for him or her, while a manager in a smaller company may direct the work of systems programmers and/or software engineers, applications programmers, and systems analysts. In large companies, a systems and programming manager is usually responsible for systems programming and development work done in one of the major areas of systems programming—telecommunications, for example (see section on systems programmer and section on telecommunications programmer). The manager's responsibilities in a sizeable company will include more administrative tasks than a smaller installation's systems and programming manager. A manager working for a smaller company will be responsible for a greater breadth of projects. For example, he or she may be in charge of all the modifications made to the operating system and the installation of all subsystems and products.

Despite the size of the company for which the systems and programming manager is working, he or she will be called upon to answer technical questions for the computing systems director or upper management, and he or she will be involved with planning the hardware and software needs of the area(s) for which he or she is responsible. For ex-ample, the systems and programming manager will need to understand what kind of hardware support future applications will need. His or her administrative functions will include seeing that products and subsystems and system upgrades are ordered at the proper time and arrive at the expected time. The systems and programming manager also usually oversees the training of his or her employees. He or she makes sure that the programmers responsible for installing and supporting a new product or subsystem will understand their responsibilities when or soon after the product or subsystem arrives.

Systems and programming managers' styles of working vary in the amount of programming they do (which varies from some to very little) and in the amount of technical discussions they have with their staff. Some systems and programming managers enjoy discussing the technical details of each project with programmers; others expect the programmers to work independently on their projects and to come to the manager with questions only if they cannot be answered any other way.

Job Environment

A systems and programming manager works in an office with a terminal, which is located in the data center.

Alternate Titles

Systems and programming managers who work with only systems programmers are sometimes called *systems programming managers*.

Training and Background (or Experience) Required

See the next section of this chapter for the training and experience required to become a systems programmer. To work as a systems and programming manager, a person must have an in-depth understanding of applications, user, and system problems. He or she must continually keep up with computer technology either by attending classes, seminars, or conferences, reading industry journals, or other means.

At least one year of experience as a *project manager* and four to five years of *systems programming* experience is typically required for a person to advance to the position of systems and programming manager.

Benefits and Drawbacks

Salary. The salary of a systems and programming manager varies with the size of the company for which he or she works and his or her experience level. Salaries usually range from about $35,000 to $55,000, depending on the size and location of the installation and the individual's experience.

Opportunity to Advance. A systems and programming manager can progress to the position of computing systems director if the opportunity arises. At that point, he or she may decide to focus on advancing into general management. In order to do this, he or she may need additional business education.

The position of systems and programming manager offers less opportunity to advance than other computer positions that are less technically oriented and more oriented to business, such as the position of an EDP auditor. Many companies, however, are now making an effort to structure two career paths for their technically oriented employees. One path leads to more and more challenging technical work, while the other focuses on the development of business and management skills. Systems and programming managers, as mentioned above, may hone their management skills in order to eventually progress into a nontechnical management position.

Travel. Usually the position of systems and programming manager involves only about 10 percent travel time.

Other Considerations. The job of a systems and programming manager can be very frustrating at times, as other computer careers can be. Deadlines must be met, and software development and modification must be synchronized with hardware upgrading. Also, it is sometimes difficult to switch from thinking about and working with bits and bytes to participating in long-term business planning meetings.

A systems and programming manager's position, however, can be very rewarding for a person who likes managing others and working in a highly technical area.

Personality Required

A systems and programming manager must be able to work well with both highly technical individuals and end-users or upper management. He or she must be flexible and capable of switching rapidly back and forth from the business world to the world of hi-tech, often on a minute-to-minute basis.

Outlook for the Future

The demand for systems and programming managers is expected to continue to be strong over the next decade, especially for managers experienced in the telecommunications and/or database/data communications fields.

Where to Find Openings

Systems and programming managers are employed by small and large companies that have computer installations. The number of people reporting to the manager varies by installation. Consulting firms, computer service firms, and computer manufacturers are among the types of companies in which systems and programming managers work.

SYSTEMS PROGRAMMER

Systems programmers maintain the instructions or programs that control the operation of the entire computer system. They are responsible for keeping the system running during normal operating hours, which are often around the clock. They also modify the sets of instructions that determine how the *central processing unit (CPU)* of the computer handles various jobs it's been given and communicates with peripheral equipment such as terminals, printers, or disk drives. Whatever tests a systems programmer runs must not interfere with normal production work, so in some companies (fewer as time goes on) testing must be done on weekends or in the early morning or evenings. Sometimes systems programmers serve as consultants to end-users, and usually, they are available to answer questions and assist applications programmers.

Systems programmers were generalists a decade ago, but over the past ten years they have become specialists. This happened partly because of the increasing complexity of operating systems and the ever-growing number of software products becoming available. The investment made by companies in systems personnel was more cost-effective if individuals specialized, and as more vendor-supplied software products replaced programs written by the company's programmers, it became important to have on-site specialists who could communicate with the vendor's staff when problems arose.

Today, systems programmers specialize to a varying degree depending on the size of the company or programming department in which they work. In small companies, systems programmers have broader and more general responsibilities than systems programmers employed by large companies.

An important part of every systems programmer's job is his or her continuing education. It is essential for him or her to keep up with the latest information related to his or her specialties. One way programmers keep up-to-date is by attending special classes or *symposiums* given by the company that makes the software with which he or she works. Usually, the employer pays for all expenses relating to outside classes that programmers need in order to do their job well. Sometimes companies have their own training departments, which make classes available to people in many different computer careers, although the past five years has seen the decline of corporate DP training programs. If enough people in the company need a certain kind of training, however, the company might invite the software producer to send an instructor to the company to give a class. For example, an Emdahl employee might give a class regarding how to use VM (*virtual machine*—one type of operating system) to do computing. End-users, as well as applications and systems programmers unfamiliar with the system, would probably attend the class. Reading manuals and other documentation is the second major way systems programmers keep their knowledge current. The reading material is usually very dry and very technical and often becomes better understood as the systems programmer gains hands-on experience in working with the system for which he or she is responsible.

There are a number of important differences between the position of an applications programmer and the position of a systems programmer. Although they both often spend part of their time coding or programming, and applications programmer modifies applications systems, which are programs or sets of instructions devised to perform a certain automated task. Common applications systems include the payroll system and the general ledger system, for example. Systems programmers, in contrast, code additions to or modifications for the operating system or related systems. These programs allow the applications programs to run and determine how the workload of the computer system is handled, among many other things. Systems and applications programming work also differs in the coding language that is used most of the time. COBOL is frequently used by applications programmers (see first section of this chapter), but systems programmers do almost all of their coding in BAL (*Basic Assembly Language*), a lower-level language that is closer to the machine language of 1s and 0s that the computer can immediately execute. Although both applications programmers and systems programmers have deadlines, systems programmers' deadlines are more critical to more people. For example, a company would stand to lose a lot more money if a new central processing unit (CPU) were delivered, and the software that ran the CPU was not in working order, than if a new general ledger system were completed a few days behind schedule. So although both applications and systems programmers have deadlines, the systems programmers' jobs usually carry more responsibility.

There are a wide variety of jobs or tasks that systems programmers perform. Described below are some examples of projects in which they specialize. The examples discussed are not always mutually exclusive; each company usually has its own unique subdivisions within the systems programming department. Subdivisions as a whole will normally include all of the following categories.

The first category involves software and hardware evaluation and planning or performance. These systems programmers run performance tests on new hardware and software and often provide management with reports that will help them make decisions regarding the hardware and software. They also perform tests and make recommendations regarding the efficiency of the data center. For example, if a new CPU is added to the present hardware configuration, but the channel to which it is attached is too busy, the result could be a bottleneck of activity and a decrease in *throughput*. Users could start to complain if they notice a difference in the amount of time the computer is taking to process their work. To avoid this problem and to ensure efficiency, performance systems programmers will run tests, analyze the performance of the new CPU, and make suggestions regarding changes needed to ensure the best use of the new hardware. Performance is an ongoing task, because the hardware and software in use and its configuration are constantly changing.

The second category of systems programming work is the modification of systems software to add new functions. Systems programmers working in this area either modify existing systems or create new software. For example, there are many exit points in large systems that are made available so installations can tailor the systems to their own needs. Systems programmers can then write exit programs to perform particular functions, such as implementing standards regarding the amount of temporary space each program is allowed to use concurrently.

A third category of work closely related to the second is the maintenance and upgrading of operating systems or subsystems. The software producers make available corrections to and improvements in their software, and the systems maintenance programmer does whatever is necessary to implement the changes. Sometimes documentation available for the upgrade procedure

is specific and sometimes it is not. The systems programmer working in this area is responsible for resolving any problems that arise from the application of maintenance to the system.

In the last five years, a change has occurred in the industry perception of systems or software maintenance programmers. Instead of being responsible only for finding coding errors, systems programmers who work with software maintenance become involved with major program enhancements. The role of software maintenance programmers has become more important as bigger and more complex products have become available; studies have shown that 40 percent of the costs expended throughout the life of a product pay for its development, while 60 percent pay for its maintenance. Despite the increase in respect that the DP industry has for software maintenance programmers, systems programmers often prefer to work on new projects rather than with those which have already been developed.

A fourth category of systems programming work entails the monitoring and maintenance of software vendor packages. These programs are smaller in scope than full operating systems or subsystems and may include, for example, PL1 or COBOL *compilers* (a compiler is a program that converts a higher level language into machine code of 1s and 0s), report writers, and accounting or billing packages. The systems programmers working in this area install the packages, help test them, and are responsible for solving any problems that arise with the products. Because many vendors do not make their products' source code available to their clients so they can make their own changes, often the programmers spend a substantial amount of times on the phone with a member of the vendor's staff. The vendor's software writers or developers usually write new code to fix problems reported by the programmer, and then send the changes to the programmer with installation instructions.

The fifth systems programming work category is security. This is sometimes only part of a systems programmer's responsibilities, although in a large company, all of one person's time can be devoted to working with software products that ensure the integrity of the computer system.

Data maintenance is a sixth type of systems programming work. It involves running and/or checking the backups that are made of the company's data. Usually, disk data is backed up to tape at periodical intervals so a copy of the data is available in case of a hardware failure or some other problem. Programmers working with data maintenance also work with software products dealing with data—for example, packages that perform backups and restores of disks.

The six categories described above do not include all types of systems programming tasks, but they reflect the primary activities of systems programmers. Be sure to see also the section on telecommunications programmers.

Job Environment

Systems programmers' offices are located in the data center, and their time is split between the computer room and their office. Each systems programmer has his or her own terminal and spends a substantial portion of the workday doing work on the terminal.

Alternate Titles

Systems programmers are usually referred to as systems programmer trainees; assistant, associate or junior systems programmers; senior systems programmers; and lead systems programmers. The highest echelon of systems programming work is sometimes referred to as *software engineering*. Newer systems programmers often start by performing the more routine tasks of the department under the supervision of a more experienced systems programmer.

Training and Background (or Experience) Required

A four-year degree, preferably a B.S. in computer science, is the training desired for systems programmers. The college degree should include courses in practical subjects such as assembly language and operating systems.

Usually, at least one year of assembly language

programming experience as an applications programmer is expected before an individual can become a systems programmer. It is possible, although more difficult, to move into systems programming from other jobs. Systems programming positions are not entry level positions; to progress as a systems programmer, in-depth experience with a new type of computer or with one part of the computer system is helpful.

Benefits and Drawbacks

Salary. Systems programmers are paid from $28,000 to $45,000 annually, depending on their experience. The top salaries are paid for specialists with more than seven years of time spent in the field.

Opportunity to Advance. The opportunity to advance from a systems programming area is somewhat limited and usually amounts to moves into other categories of systems programming work. It is possible to move from this area into a number of less technical areas, however. Sometimes people switch to less technical positions in order to have more interaction with people.

There are two other career moves that a seasoned systems programmer can make. He or she can become a *consultant* (see a previous section of this chapter). Or he or she can try to move into management. To become a manager, though, a systems programmer needs some broader education that will augment his or her technical expertise. (See a previous section of this chapter).

Travel. A systems programmer's travel is usually limited to the attendance of consortiums and vendor training classes.

Other Considerations. The work week of a systems programmer is usually very long—a minimum of 50 hours—and sometimes, the programmer is expected to work on evenings or weekends in order to run tests. In most installations, the experienced systems programmers are on call 24 hours a day in case of emergency. It is common for programmers to receive occasional late-night or early-morning phone calls when problems occur with the system. Sometimes the systems programmer will be able to give instructions to operations personnel over the phone that will correct the problem; sometimes he or she can fix it by logging on to his or her home terminal or computer. Once in a while, he or she may need to go in to work in order to solve the problem.

Some companies reward systems programmers for overtime with compensatory pay or time or a dinner out on the company for a job well done. The policy varies from company to company.

A systems programmer's day is usually fast-paced, and he or she has to contend with deadlines, just as many other people in computer careers do.

Systems programmers can get locked into working on a particular system, such as a billing system. When the programmer is ready to advance to higher levels of systems programming work, sometimes his or her employer will balk, because the job he or she is doing has become so important to the company, and because training a new person for the job would take so much time. In some cases, this is resolved by the programmer going to work for another company; sometimes it's resolved by a provision by the programmer's manager for a transition period. During this period, the programmer's work on the billing system could be automated, or he or she could teach the necessary skills to a more junior programmer. Meanwhile, the systems programmer can begin work and training on a more challenging project.

High frustration tolerance is essential for a systems programmer because higher-level projects are often very long.

One of the satisfactions of systems programming work is the intellectual involvement that the work requires. Pride can be taken in completing projects that are difficult or long; seeing the difference a finished project makes can be very rewarding. And there is always plenty of work to do. Many systems programmers enjoy the fast pace of their work and find the variety of tasks on which they work very challenging. They also enjoy keeping up with the latest changes in technology.

Personality Required

A systems programmer usually works alone, although he or she may consult or be consulted by other systems and applications programmers. Part of the personality required to be a successful systems programmer, then, is the ability to work alone and enjoy it. Individuals who work in systems programming are very technically oriented and love to find out how things work. They also must be patient and persistent and, as mentioned above, have a high frustration tolerance.

Outlook for the Future

The outlook for the future of systems programming is very good; the strong demand for programmers of this type is expected to continue. The areas which are becoming more important now include microcomputers and distributed DP, graphics, and database and data communications software.

Where to Find Openings

A large systems programming staff is usually retained by a company with a large computer system. The types of companies employing system programmers include computer service firms, computer manufacturers, and consulting firms.

TEACHERS

Computer science programs are offered in more than 1,000 colleges and universities in the United States. Many college professors teach courses in *computer science, information science,* or *software engineering.* Some of these courses are purely theoretical, and some are very practical. A college professor's responsibilities include developing courses; giving lectures; making reading assignments; supervising laboratory work; administering tests; and grading, evaluating, and advising students. Most college professors are also engaged in research activities; they submit articles regarding their findings to technical journals for publication. They are also expected to spend some time on academic committees whose concerns range from computing to more general administrative issues like university research policy. Some individuals teach part-time as instructors and adjunct professors; assistant, associate, and full professors are full-time faculty members. Many of the evening courses offered by colleges and universities are taught by part-time teachers who work as full-time systems analysts, technical writers, or programmers.

Computer science programs are now appearing in high schools and even elementary schools. Some secondary school students are instructed by teachers who specialize in computer science, while others learn computer science from their math teachers. Elementary school students are taught computer science by teachers with some special on-the-job training in computer science.

Job Environment

The college professor usually has his or her own office at the junior college or college where he or she works. He spends some time in classrooms on campus and some time in a computer laboratory. A high school computer science instructor works in a high school classroom.

Alternate Titles

There are no alternate titles for teachers besides those mentioned above.

Training and Background (or Experience) Required

Beginning college teachers or part-time college instructors are required to have at least a master's degree in computer science or a related field like math. Assistant, associate, and full professors all have their doctoral degrees, usually in computer science.

As mentioned above, large secondary schools sometimes have an instructor who teaches nothing but computer science, but in small high schools, computer science is often taught by a math teacher. Computer science in elementary schools is usually taught by elementary school teachers with some special training in computer science.

No experience is required to become a college professor or a computer science teacher in secondary schools. Experience in teaching during graduate school is viewed as a plus, however. Research and the ability to publish are the usual criteria that college and university faculty members use as a

measure of the college teacher's worth.

Benefits and Drawbacks

Salary. The annual salary of a college professor depends on the particular college. Four-year universities pay professors more than two-year junior or community colleges. The typical salary range is $20,000 to $43,000. Part-time instructors are usually paid a certain amount per course, and the exact amount varies with the school.

High school computer science instructors with a B.S. are normally paid from $15,000 to $24,000 annually.

Opportunity to Advance. As mentioned above, a computer science professor's research and publications, rather than his or her teaching ability, are the criteria usually used to determine whether he or she should be granted tenure. According to the American Association of University Professors, most colleges have a maximum probationary period of seven years, with a decision on whether or not to grant tenure made on year prior to the end of the period. A few colleges have a policy of waiting eight or ten years before the tenure decision is made. During this period, an individual has the rank of assistant professor. At the majority of colleges, assistant professors are given contracts that are renewed annually, but in the more prestigious schools, assistant professors are given either a one-year contract and then two three-year contracts, or just two three-year contracts. If a person is not granted tenure, he or she is given one year to find employment at another university. A professor who is granted tenure becomes an associate professor and is eligible to become a full professor at a later date. There is substantial opportunity for advancement in this career, then, although it usually involves employment at more than one college or university.

For high school computer science instructors there is a limited opportunity to advance.

Travel. Some travel to symposiums and association meetings is typically part of a college professor's job. There is usually no travel involved in a high school instructor's position.

Other Considerations. The major drawback

of being a computer science professor is the annual salary. Many professors leave academia to work in industry, because they are paid much more for doing a similar type of research.

For some individuals, the breadth of responsibility is irritating, but others enjoy it. There are professors who enjoy their research much more than their teaching and administrative duties, and some professors greatly prefer their teaching and their research to their committee work. Many individuals prefer the combination of all three, because it allows for a change in the type of work they do from day to day. The greatest benefit of the position for many professors is the personal fulfillment they find in their work.

The major disadvantages of being a high school computer science instructor are the pay and the limited opportunity to advance. As with computer science professors, however, many high school instructors really enjoy their work.

Personality Required

Computer science professors and high school instructors need to be technically oriented as well as people-oriented. They should enjoy explaining computer science concepts and answering students' questions. Also important is the priority of pursuing a career they enjoy over pursuing a career that pays very well.

Outlook for the Future

In recent years, a number of computer science professors have left their academic posts for more highly paid positions in industry. As a result, there is now a greater demand for computer science professors than for professors in other areas. The demand is expected to stay fairly constant until the middle of the 1990s, when many tenured university faculty are expected to retire. Demand for computer science professors, then, will increase in the future.

The demand for high school computer science instructors is fairly limited due to the fact that only large high schools can afford to hire them.

Where to Find Openings

More openings for computer science professors exist in urban than in rural areas, although they are employed by junior colleges, colleges, and universities across the country. Openings for high school computer science instructors can be found in sizable, progressive high schools.

TECHNICAL WRITERS

Technical writers research, write, edit, and proofread many different kinds of materials. They write the advertising copy or press releases used to promote a new system, software, or hardware product, and they write the sales or informational brochures that accompany the product. They also write user's manuals, which describe how to use certain programs or products, and reference manuals, which describe how to install new systems. Training manuals and instructional or educational materials for computer products and systems, reports, and technical proposals are also written by technical writers.

The quality of technical writing accompanying a computer product when it is first introduced on the market can have a big effect on the reception of the new product. For example, if a person with no computer background can use a microcomputer productively after reading the user's manual for only a half hour, then the microcomputer will probably sell much better than a micro with a highly technical user's manual—given that the other characteristics of the product are roughly the same. Programmers are more willing to work with complex products and systems with well-organized and easy-to-read reference manuals with good cross-indexing.

Some of the materials prepared by technical writers, like sales brochures and user's manuals, are written for individuals such as managers and end-users who have little or no technical background or expertise. Other materials, like technical reference manuals, are read by programmers or other computer specialists who are working with a computer product or system that is new to them. These readers are comfortable with technical language but need to have a clear description of the details of how the system works. So the technical writer prepares materials both in plain English and in technical computer language.

Regardless of whether or not he or she is writing for a technical or nontechnical audience, the technical writer's work usually involves several steps. First, the writer must thoroughly research the product, system, or process he or she will be describing, through library research, hands-on experience with the product, and/or detailed discussions with the systems and programming staff, users, or customers. After becoming very familiar with his or her topic, the technical writer often outlines and then writes the material. As the last step, he or she may revise the material several times based on the input of both technical and nontechnical individuals.

Depending on the particular task, a technical writer may work mostly as part of a team of computer professionals or mostly alone. The work is usually done at a fairly steady pace.

Job Environment

The technical writer works at a desk in an office, but the office's exact location in the company varies with the employer. It could be in the programming department, the advertising department or, in large companies, in the training division or an administrative department.

Alternate Titles

Technical writers occasionally used to be known as *documentation specialists*. Today, there really is no commonly used alternate title for the position of technical writer. A closely related occupation is that of a *journalist* (see a previous section of this chapter).

Training and Background
(or Experience) Required

A college degree is usually required of a technical writer. Some employers look for individuals with computer science degrees with a minor in journalism or English, while others stress experience and writing ability over a computer science major. A liberal arts degree with some credits in computer science is acceptable to the second type of employer.

Once a person is employed as a technical writer, his or her training will probably continue through his or her attendance of seminars and workshops on technical writing. The seminars are often sponsored by colleges and universities.

One or two years of experience as a programmer is highly desirable for a person interested in working as a technical writer, because he or she will need to have a good general knowledge of the computer industry. Employers also view actual writing experience very favorably. A person who is interested in entering this field may want to start by free-lancing as a technical writer while keeping a programming job, for example. Some individuals get their first writing experience by working without pay for a local newspaper or student journal.

Benefits and Drawbacks

Salary. The annual salary of a technical writer ranges from about $20,000 to about $36,000.

Opportunity for Advancement. A technical writer has a somewhat limited opportunity to advance. Usually, a writer needs some business or management experience in order to progress, and some technical writers get the necessary experience by combining their writing work with other special assignments. A technical writer can become a *training administrator* or a *publications manager* (a person who is responsible for producing all of the firm's technical material). Many technical writers take on free-lance assignments; some eventually form their own writing firms. Sometimes technical writers teach at a college or university, give writing seminars for companies, or write newspaper articles or computer books in addition to holding their full-time positions.

Travel. There is usually little or no travel in a technical writing job.

Other Considerations. The most trying part of a technical writer's job is the frustration of trying to find just the right words to describe or explain a product or procedure, but a great deal of personal satisfaction is often gained from expressing complex technical procedures or products in simple terms. Although a technical writer does have some deadline pressures, usually the pace of his or her work is fairly steady.

Personality Required

Sometimes a technical writer works as part of a team, and sometimes he or she works alone, so technical writers need to get along well with others but, at the same time, they should enjoy working alone. Writers must, of course, have good writing ability and like to write. They need to be very well-organized individuals, because they are often expected to organize a great deal of detailed information. Intellectual curiosity and patience are also important to being a successful technical writer, because the writer has to understand a product or process thoroughly before describing it in simple terms.

Outlook for the Future

The demand for technical writers is at present fairly strong, and it is expected to increase somewhat in the near future. Although computer scientists, software engineers, hardware designers, and other computer professionals may be very skilled in developing and designing new hardware and software, they are usually not as talented in providing clear, easy-to-understand documentation and instructions for the product or procedure they have developed. Therefore, technical writers will be in demand as long as new computer products continue to be developed.

In the future, however, it is predicted that technical writers will need a deeper understanding of technology than is required at present. They will be expected to be aware of and familiar with a broader range of documentation techniques.

Where to Find Openings

Openings for technical writers are likely to be found in computer manufacturing companies that develop software for their hardware and equipment, large firms that develop their own software, and software developers. Most technical writers work for large companies located in or near urban areas, although some technical writers are presently employed as journalists.

TELECOMMUNICATIONS PROGRAMMERS

Telecommunications programmers work with the software involved in the interconnecting of computers via communications lines. Some communications networks connect many individual remote workstations to one central computer, while others connect a number of large computers with many terminals or microcomputers. An example of the first type of telecommunications network is 24-hour-a-day electronic banking, which is now available from many commercial banks. A central computer controls the processing of a number of remote automated tellers. An example of the second kind of network is a company's internal communications network, which may link some 2,000 workstations around the country to several minicomputers and a mainframe located at the corporate data center. Since the divestiture of AT&T on January 1, 1984, more and more companies have been designing their internal communications network to function for voice as well as data transmission, so that one network can both provide phone service for employees and allow individuals to send data to other network users.

Telecommunications programmers are responsible for a variety of tasks related to the functioning of networks. Sometimes they are involved in the design stage of the network or an addition to an existing network; in this case, they work with systems analysts and other technical individuals to evaluate and then select the equipment or hardware to be used in the network. The telecommunications programmers may need to decide, for example, how many new ports will be needed for a new department's terminals to be connected to the mainframe. Or they may need to determine if the communications lines in part of the network need to allow for a very high speed of transfer for data files, while most of the lines need to allow for a moderately high speed of transfer.

Often, telecommunications programmers either

write and test the company's data communications software, or they are responsible for modifying vendor software so that it will interface properly with the software already in the network and thereby meet the company's communications needs. For example, telecommunications programmers may become involved in writing the programs required to allow different types of microcomputers to access the mainframe or central computer. Sometimes the microcomputer vendors market their own software which connects their micros to a certain type of mainframe. In these cases, the telecommunications programmer may need to modify the vendor's software in order to tailor it to the specific needs of the company purchasing the software.

Another responsibility of telecommunications programmers is the day-to-day monitoring of network operations and the solving of both the software and hardware problems experienced by network users. The maintenance or upgrading of communications software to keep it current is part of the telecommunications programmer's job, as is the task of advising applications programmers with questions about the network.

As you can see by comparing the above job description with the job description for systems programmers in an earlier section of this chapter, telecommunications programmers are systems programmers who specialize in communications. Sometimes this area is discussed separately, as it is here, because of the increasing importance of the telecommunications field in the computer job market.

Job Environment

Telecommunications programmers work in an office equipped with a terminal in the data center as well as in the computer room or telecommunications area.

Alternate Titles

The title of telecommunications programmer can be preceded by "junior" or "senior," as is the case with many other computer careers. Alternate titles for the job are: *data communications programmer, communications programmer,* and *data communica-*

tions specialist. Sometimes, if analysis as well as programming is involved in the position, the job title is *data communications analyst.*

Training and Background (or Experience) Required

The education expected for the position of telecommunications programmer is a four-year degree in a highly technical area, such as electrical engineering, computer science, or telecommunications. If the degree is not actually in communications, then it should include credits in communications and network theory. Sometimes engineers with graduate training take telecommunications programming positions if they are interested in working with software.

Two or more years of experience is usually required before a person can begin to work as a telecommunications programmer. The experience that is desired for this position includes in-depth use of BAL (Basic Assembly Language) as an applications programmer and as a systems programmer. Most individuals enter this position from a systems programming job.

Benefits and Drawbacks

Salary. As with other computer careers, a telecommunications programmer's salary varies with experience level and with the size and location of the company for which he or she works. Salaries range from $30,000 to $45,000.

Opportunity to Advance. Individuals working in this area often have a limited opportunity to advance unless they get additional and broader training.

Travel. Travel in this position is normally minimal (about 10 percent), because software modifications which affect the entire network are commonly made on the mainframe or the network's central computer, or on another computer that is accessible from the company's main data center.

Other Considerations. Odd hours are to be expected for telecommunications programmers, because sometimes changes must be made when the network is not busy. And telecommunications programmers work alone quite a bit of the time. Programmers working in this area find the work exciting, however, because it involves the latest advances in technology, and because the resulting network is used by hundreds and sometimes thousands of individuals.

Personality Required

A telecommunications programmer must be very logical and very thorough, and he or she should enjoy working alone. In recent years, communication skills have become more and more important to the position because it involves working with others who are less technical—for example, upper management or end-users.

Outlook for the Future

Telecommunications is one of the hottest areas in computers today. Demand for people experienced in this area is expected to continue to increase in the future; telecommunications has been and will continue to be one of the computer industry's largest growth areas. Of special interest in the future will be electronic mail and the integration of computers into networks.

Where to Find Openings

Telecommunications programmers work for large companies which have a communications network servicing internal and/or external users. These companies include banks and insurance companies as well as companies that manufacture computer and communications hardware and consulting firms that provide computer services to companies without their own computer. Most job opportunities for telecommunications programmers are located in or near large cities.

TRAINING SPECIALIST

A person who handles the training and education for a company is usually referred to as a *training specialist*. In large companies, one person is sometimes hired with this function as his or her sole responsibility. In smaller companies, the responsi-

bilities are usually divided among the respective managers. The training specialist needs to continually be aware of the educational needs of his or her company. Usually, the specialist administers or oversees the training programs of the company's employees and makes sure that they are kept up-to-date on the latest technological advances in their fields. Occasionally, the specialist is also in charge of classes which will be made available to the end-users of the firm's products, whether they are software or hardware products. The quality of this training can make a big difference in the company's sales.

One of a training specialist's activities is the careful development of a training schedule for individual employees. In planning the classes the person needs to take, the specialist keeps in mind both the productivity of the employee in his or her current position as well as the advancement of his or her career. Individualized training programs are sometimes utilized by companies in an effort to draw quality personnel who will feel they have a future at the company. Some companies with a history of employees moving to other firms as soon as their training is complete ask the employees to guarantee them a certain amount of service in return for the financial investment the company is about to make in them.

The training specialist designs and coordinates the educational programs of both new employees as well as more experienced computer personnel such as programmers or systems analysts. To this end, the training specialist sometimes teaches in-house classes and sometimes arranges for personnel to attend an outside course given by another company, a training institute, or a junior college. The specialist also organizes in-house classes to be given by a consultant or to be taught through the use of an audiovisual program or computer-aided instruction. The audiovisual program usually includes a videotape and written material. Computer-aided instruction involves the use of a program on either a microcomputer or a terminal (a VDT) connected to the mainframe. The advantage of either audiovisual instruction or computer-aided instruction is the employee's ability to progress at his or her own speed. Also, although time is usually set aside specifically for training, day-to-day business and responsibilities sometimes interfere; with this type of training it is fairly easy for an individual to pick up where he or she left off. It is up to the training specialist to decide which of the training options available will be the most effective for each individual or group.

Job Environment

The training specialist works in an office and usually spends a great deal of time in meetings and on the telephone.

Alternate Titles

The training specialist is also called an *education and training administrator* or a *DP training specialist*. In some companies, the functions of this individual are performed by a person who works in the information center (see an earlier section of this chapter).

Training and Background (or Experience) Required

A four-year college degree is required for this position, and some employers prefer a degree in computer science or a related field with business courses. Having a Master of Business Administration degree (an M.B.A.) opens the door to more opportunities.

The experience of people working as training specialists is varied. Some have experience in personnel training or high school or college teaching, while others have spent time as programmers, systems analysts, or technical writers. A move in training is common for computer professionals who are interested in getting out of very technical positions in which they are always on call.

Employers disagree as to which kind of background is more appropriate for a training specialist. Some companies are glad to hire former teachers or people who have worked in personnel training and then train them in the basics of computing. Other companies feel strongly that on-the-job computer experience is a prerequisite of being a good training specialist.

Benefits and Drawbacks

Salary. The annual salary of a training specialist depends on the size and location of his or her employer and on his or her level of experience. The typical salary range is from about $22,000 to about $37,000.

Opportunity to Advance. Training specialists have quite a visible corporate position and develop a number of contacts in many of the company's departments. For these reasons, the specialist has a good opportunity to advance to other management positions in the company.

Travel. Usually, the travel required of a training specialist is limited. The exception to this might be when the specialist teaches as well as coordinates training for users of the company's products; sometimes classes for these users are given in large cities across the country or at the users' installations.

Other Considerations. A training specialist has to contend with day-to-day deadline pressures, but many specialists find a great deal of personal satisfaction in their work.

Personality Required

A training specialist should have good organizational skills. He or she also needs to be creative enough to develop effective individualized training programs. Training specialists are generally more outgoing than people in more technical computer professions. The specialists need to be good at working with people and juggling their relationships with many different individuals. If the specialist does some teaching, he or she must be poised, able to handle large groups, and very good at giving oral presentations.

Outlook for the Future

Training specialists are not in as much demand as they once were, because some companies have discontinued their in-house DP training programs. A number of large companies, however, still have a separate computer training department and manufacturers of hardware and software will always need to provide some form of training for their customers; they are among the best prospects for openings in this field.

Where to Find Openings

The companies which presently employ training specialists are generally very large and located near big cities. The types of firms include hardware and software manufacturers and sizable users of computers—banks, government agencies, insurance companies, and wholesale and retail trade establishments. For more information, see the section on corporate training programs in Chapter 12, Training and Education.

WORD PROCESSING OPERATORS

A *word processor,* of course, is an electronic typewriter or a typewriter with an electronic memory. Some personal computers function as word processors when the computer is accessing word processing software. The introduction of word processors into the office has resulted in a substantial increase in the productivity of word processing operators or secretaries who sometimes use word processors. Word processors eliminate a great deal of the repetitive functions that secretaries used to be required to do, increase the speed and accuracy with which written material can be handled, and provide some new, previously unavailable functions such as the electronic storage of information.

Word processing operators (Fig. 5-9) perform a variety of tasks. First, they often need to type or enter text or documents into a computer. (The section on data entry, in this chapter, includes a description of jobs in which this is the major function of the position.) In entering the information, the word processing operator makes use of the many editing options or techniques available, for example, indentation, tabulation, underlining, and the centering of copy. Word processing operators work with many different kinds of text, including tables, lists, manuscripts, reports, contracts, and proposals. After typing in the information, often the word processing operator will store it. This is generally a precaution at this stage and avoids loss of the work if the operator needs to leave the machine and somehow an erase button is accidentally pushed. The third stage involves the reviewing and editing of the stored data. At this point, the document is checked for accuracy, spelling errors, and typos. Also, last-minute editing changes may be made now or at a later time. The fourth step involves the storing of the edited or corrected version of the document, which can then be accessed at any time in the future for additional changes. Finally, the document is printed, usually by pressing a few specific keys that tell the machine to send the text to a particular printer.

Besides increasing productivity, there are a number of other reasons that the use of word processing equipment in both small and large offices is rapidly expanding. Updating is much easier than it ever was when typewriters were used exclusively. A word processing operator can call up text from the floppy disk on which it has been stored and insert or delete only the material that is to be changed. The rearrangement of the text is all handled automatically. Word processing equipment also allows for the quick processing of repetitive tasks. A common example is the need to generate identical original letters to be sent to many different addresses. Specific aids are sometimes available with word processors that did not exist before. For instance, sometimes spelling-check programs are available, which can be used to automatically check a document for any misspellings. The possible misspellings are then displayed on the screen to be checked by the word processing operator. Another advantage that word processing equipment offers over typewriters is the quick and relatively easy printing of error-free documents.

Different approaches are used by different companies to integrate word processing equipment into the office. In some organizations, word processors simply replace typewriters, and the secretaries who had used typewriters are given word processing training. In these cases, word processing is usually only one of the responsibilities of the individual worker. Other organizations set up a centralized word processing department whose personnel re-

Fig. 5-9. The outlook for the future of word processing operator positions is excellent. Photograph courtesy of Sperry Corp.

ceive specific training for and specialize in the use of word processing equipment. A third approach that is quite common is a split in the responsibilities of different individuals once word processing equipment arrives in an office. Some secretaries work exclusively with typewriters and handle other secretarial tasks; other secretaries become word processing operators who deal only with word processing tasks.

Word processing involves business contact with individuals in an office setting, but most of the day the word processing operator is dealing with equipment. The work also usually involves following a set routine from day to day, although the content of the work often varies each day.

Job Environment

As mentioned previously, word processing operators usually work in an office setting.

Alternate Titles

The actual work of integrating word processing equipment into an office and the training of personnel on the new equipment is sometimes the responsibility of a person referred to as an *office automation specialist*. Another related career is that of *data entry*.

Training and Background (or Experience) Required

The minimum education required for word processing operators is a high school education; a college degree is important for any kind of more general advancement. Some employers provide on-the-job training for their secretarial personnel when word processing equipment is introduced in the company. Occasionally, though, it is up to individuals to get their own training, for which they will sometimes be reimbursed by the company. Courses are offered by the manufacturers of word processing equipment and also by some community colleges. Continuing education programs at four-year schools and vocational schools also sometimes have instruction in word processing.

A list of over 120 institutions in the United States that offer word processing training is available from the Association of Information Systems Professionals, 1015 North York Road, Willow Grove, PA 19090, (215) 657-6300. Besides listing individual schools, the pamphlet, which is entitled "Directory to Information/Word Processing Education," includes information about degree and job placement services.

In order to become a word processing operator, a person must have some typing and/or keypunching experience. The amount of experience an individual word processing operator has will help determine his or her salary level. When gaining experience, it is important to try to focus on the specific types of word processors that are widely used in your geographical area. The types of equipment that are most common will appear frequently in the want ads in local papers. Although it is true that a person trained and experienced on one type of word processing system can then more quickly learn another than a person with no word process-

ing experience, some employers prefer to hire individuals with prior experience using machines from a particular manufacturer.

Benefits and Drawbacks

Salary. The salary of a word processing operator varies with the workload, the exact responsibilities of the position, and the demand in the local area for word processing operators of that level. Generally, annual salaries range from about $15,000 to about $26,000.

Opportunity to Advance. There is little opportunity to advance from a word processing operator's position. Of course, it is possible to move into a supervisory position that involves overseeing a number of word processing operators, but in many companies, it is difficult to move into other computer careers. Common problems concerning advancement include overcoming the stereotype of being a secretary and moving up if your advancement is tied to your boss's advancement, and he or she has been promoted to the top of his or her career ladder. Problems can also arise when word processing operators are given additional responsibilities but no additional monetary recompense.

Overall, advancement from the position of a word processing operator is difficult. Sometimes personnel staffers or human resource managers can best advise a person in this position about making a career move in the same company.

Travel. Rarely, word processing operators travel for some additional training. Most word processing positions involve little or no travel.

Other Considerations. The work of a word processing operator is steady, and the hours are usually regular: a 40-hour work week. The job does involve the pressure that is associated with typing for the major part of the workday, however.

Personality Required

If word processing is only part of the responsibilities of a position which also involves secretarial duties, the individual must be able to handle many types of tasks at once. If the position involves word processing exclusively, accuracy and the ability to proofread or perceive details in documents is essential. Good spelling and grammar, good eye-hand coordination, and good organizational skills are also important to success as a word processing operator. The individual needs to be able to learn new information, such as how to use new word processing software, quickly. Finally, patience is a major asset in this position.

Outlook for the Future

The outlook for the future of word processing operator positions is excellent. The huge growth that has already occurred in this area is expected to continue over an inestimable period of time.

Where to Find Openings

In any large or small company where secretaries and other office help are employed, word processing operator positions are often available. As discussed earlier, some of these jobs involve only word processing work, while others include secretarial duties as well. The greatest need for word processing operators tends to exist in the largest organizations, simply because they generate more paperwork of various types.

Chapter 6

Computer Careers of the Future

The two most promising areas for future employment in computers are *CAD/CAM (computer-aided design/computer-aided manufacturing)* and *robotics*. These two quickly expanding areas are described below.

CAD/CAM

Computer-aided design/computer-aided manufacturing has to do with the use of computers in factories, product development laboratories, and other industrial environments. In most companies, the two areas go hand-in-hand, enabling products to be developed from five to 20 times as quickly as in the past (Fig. 6-1).

Computer-aided design systems (Fig. 6-2) are used by individuals trained as draftspersons, architects, designers, or engineers. The systems are used to design products, tools, and processes, such as new buildings, tables, or even computers. Computer graphics, including drawings, graphs, charts, and three dimensional forms, are produced on a CRT. The graphics are used by the engineer or designer to design every part of the product. The engineer can easily change the scale of the product, rotate a part of it on the screen, or punch in all the specifications for each piece of the product to make sure the pieces will not interfere with each other. The computer system allows the engineer to look for design flows at a very early stage, and then to modify the product accordingly. It can also be used to prepare the documentation for the product. A physical *prototype* (Fig. 6-3) which used to be built in every case, is now constructed only rarely, and then at the end of the engineering analysis and only for particularly critical projects. When the design is completed, the specifications are stored in the computer so that future modifications can be made with ease, and a copy of the specs are transferred electronically to another computer used in the manufacturing process, or to hardcopy via a *graphics printer* or *plotter* that can produce drawings or blueprints.

All of the design data are then used to set up the manufacturing process of the product. Master computers are used to control an assembly line of

Fig. 6-1. In computer-aided manufacturing, computers are used to control an assembly line of machines. (Photograph courtesy of Sperry Corp.)

Fig. 6-2. Computer-aided design systems are used by individuals trained as draftspersons, architects, designers, or engineers. (Photograph courtesy of Sperry Corp.)

machines, which may include robots, lathes, power saws, machine presses, and other equipment. The automated process that results is sometimes called *CIM (computer-integrated manufacturing)* instead of CAM.

For some CAD/CAM systems, which prompt their users at each step of the design process, not much special training is required. The use of other systems, however, can require up to six months of training. Most individuals who work with CAD/CAM systems have training in drafting, architecture, engineering, or product design, as well as computer science. Many persons gain previous experience working as mechanical or electrical engineers, architects, or draftspersons.

Although the use of CAD/CAM in industry has greatly increased productivity, it has been criticized for making jobs more routine and less challenging. As a result, some say, the employees involved experience much less job satisfaction. Another criti-

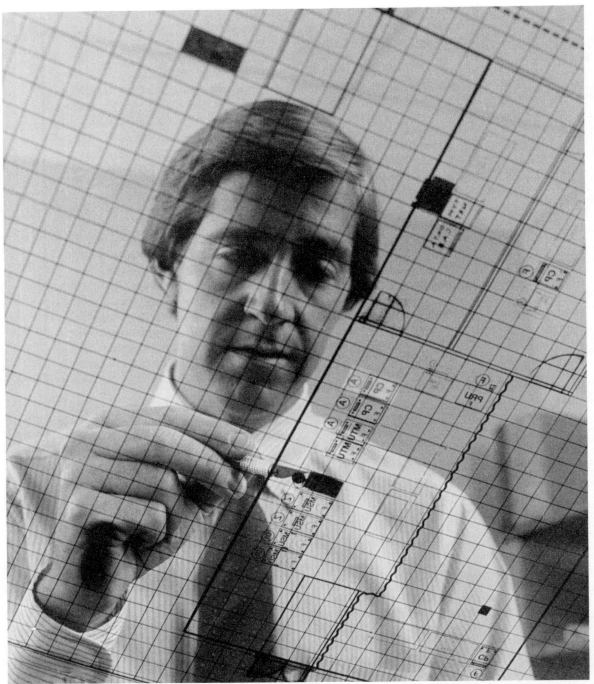

Fig. 6-3. Sometimes prototypes or designs are created manually in addition to being created and checked by computer. (Photograph courtesy of Honeywell, Inc.)

cism of the use of CAD/CAM is the resulting simplification of jobs, which means that workers become interchangeable and derive less of a sense of contribution.

Computer-aided design and computer-aided manufacturing, which sometimes include *computer-aided engineering*, has been used predominantly in the aircraft and automotive industries, although their use recently has been rapidly expanding to many industries. CAD/CAM, for example, has been used extensively in the development of smaller and lighter cars. Because of the decreasing price and increasing capabilities of the systems, they are now being used to design everything from skyscrapers to semiconductor circuits.

ROBOTICS

Robots are computer-controlled machines that can be integrated with other sophisticated machines to perform a number of different manufacturing operations. They can be reprogrammed to perform different tasks, many of which they can do with more accuracy and less cost than human manufacturing workers. In some cases, one robot can do the work of five humans. Robots of the future will probably look more like humans and be used in the home. Presently, most robots are used in factories. These large, one-armed machines can be used for welding, grinding, cutting, painting, drilling, handling, and assembling materials, and some have workable vision and sensor systems.

Training programs in robotics vary in the requirements and in the options offered. Usually, robot courses and/or programs are included as part of an engineering or technology program at colleges and universities. Many community colleges offer complete two-year programs or associate degrees in robotics for robot technicians.

An individual with an engineering degree has the option of working with the overall manufacturing process or climbing the corporate ladder into various management positions. As an engineer working in robotics, interaction with management will occur regarding cost proposals, efficiency studies, and quality control reports.

The job of *robotics technologist* or technician involves implementing the ideas of the engineer and improving them when applicable. The technologist or technician serves as a liaison between the engineer and the robot application or program(s).

Maintenance or service professionals, or robot repair specialists, may be involved with the initial setup of the robot as well as in-house repair and maintenance of the system. Sales and education or training in robotics are other career options in this area.

A list of robotics education and training institutions in colleges, universities, and technical institutes is provided at the end of this section. Included are institutions offering associate degree programs, institutions offering bachelor degree programs, master degree programs and doctorate degree programs.

Robots have been used mainly in the automotive industry, but they are being used more and more in aerospace, mining, computer, plastics, metal, textile, ski equipment, shoe, nuclear, cosmetics, oil, television and radio manufacturing, and candy production.

Presently, there is a very high demand for engineers capable of designing robots and programmers able to program them. This demand is expected to continue to increase at least through the middle of the 1990s.

It is unclear whether or not the demand for robot repairpersons will rise. Some predict that demand will increase greatly over the next decade, while other experts feel that the demand will never be high because robots have generally been designed with parts that are easily replaceable.

Robotics education and training institutions in colleges, universities, and technical institutes are shown below. For the most current information available on a particular program, write to the Education Department, Society of Manufacturing Engineers, One S.M.E. Drive, P.O. Box 930, Dearborn, MI 48121. Their new directory, entitled "Directory of Manufacturing Education," will be available as of November 1986. A complimentary copy will be provided upon request.

INSTITUTIONS OFFERING ASSOCIATE DEGREE PROGRAMS[2]

ALABAMA

Bessemer State Technical College
P.O. Box 308
Bessemer, AL 35021
(205) 428-6391
Contact: Rich Raymond
Robotics Laboratory: No

Jefferson State Junior College
Division of Technology
2601 Carson Road
Birmingham, AL 35215
(205) 853-1200, Ext. 271
Contact: Howard King
Robotics Laboratory: No

J.F. Drake State Technical College
Electronics Department
3421 Meridian Street
North Huntsville, AL 35811
(205) 539-8161
Contact: L. B. Kitchen
Robotics Laboratory: Yes

Wallace State Community College
Electronics Technology Department
P.O. Drawer 1049
Selma, AL 36701
(205) 875-2634
Contact: Jim Myers
Robotics Laboratory: Yes

Hobson State Technical College
Industrial Electronics Department
P.O. Box 489
Thomasville, AL 36784
(205) 636-9278
Contact: William A. Scott, Jr.
Robotics Laboratory: Yes

ALASKA

Islands Community College
1101 S.M.C. Boulevard
Sitka, AK 99835
(907) 747-6653
Contact: R.M. Griffin
Robotics Laboratory: No

ARIZONA

Scottsdale Community College
Electronics/Microprocessor Department
9000 East Chaparral Road
Scottsdale, AZ 85253
(602) 941-0999, Ext. 322
Contact: David Weaver
Robotics Laboratory: Yes

ARKANSAS

Westark Community College
Electronics Department
P.O. Box 3649
Fort Smith, AR 72913
(501) 785-4241, Ext. 481
Contact: Larry Fox
Robotics Laboratory: Yes

Twin Lakes Vo-Tech
Electronics Technololgy Department
Box 1496
Harrison, AR 72601
(501) 741-6175
Contact: Joe Johnson
Robotics Laboratory: Yes

Northwest Vo-Tech
Industrial Electronics Department
P.O. Drawer A
Highway 265 and Ford Avenue
Springdale, AR 72764
(501) 751-8824
Contact: Harold N. Harris
Robotics Laboratory: Yes

[2]Directory of Robotics Education and Training Institutions in Colleges, Universities, and Technical Institutes. Permission to reproduce granted by Education Department, Society of Manufacturing Engineers, P.O. Box 930, Dearborn, MI 48121.

CALIFORNIA

Glendale Community College
1500 North Verdugo Road
Glendale, CA 91208
(818) 240-1000, Ext. 311
Contact: Donald O. Ney
Robotics Laboratory: Yes

Long Beach City College
Electronics Department
4901 East Carson
Long Beach, CA 90808
(213) 420-4301
Contact: Dr. C.P. Bud Johnson
Robotics Laboratory: Yes

Cerritos College
Electronics Department
11110 East Alondra Boulevard
Norwalk, CA 90650
(213) 860-2451, Ext. 306
Contact: Anthony Austin
Robotics Laboratory: Yes

Laney College
Applied Technology Division
900 Fallon Street
Oakland, CA 94607
(415) 834-5574
Contact: Marcos R. Contreras
Robotics Laboratory: Yes

Riverside City College
Electronics Department
4800 Magnolia Avenue
Riverside, CA 92506
(714) 684-3240, Ext. 282
Contact: R. Vogel
Robotics Laboratory: No

Los Angeles Valley College
Engineering Department
5800 Fulton Avenue
Van Nuys, CA 91401
(213) 980-0431
Contact: William Lavoie
Robotics Laboratory: No

Tidewater Community College
Engineering Technologies Department
1700 College Crescent
Virginia Beach Campus
Virginia Beach, CA 23456
(804) 427-3070
Contact: Dr. Jag Mathur
Robotics Laboratory: Yes

Los Angeles Harbor College
Engineering Technology Department
1111 Figueroa Place
Wilmington, CA 90744
(213) 518-1000, Ext. 213
Contact: James Harter
Robotics Laboratory: No

COLORADO

Red Rocks Community College
Science & Technology Department
12600 West Sixth Avenue
Golden, CO 80401
(303) 988-6160, Ext. 388
Contact: P. Everett Perkins
Robotics Laboratory: N/A

Front Range Community College
3645 West 112th Avenue
Westminster, CO 80030
(303) 466-8811, Ext. 349
Contact: Ralph Duncan
Robotics Laboratory: N/A

CONNECTICUT

Thames Valley State Technical College
Engineering Technologies Department
574 New London Turnpike
Norwich, CT 06360
(203) 886-0177
Contact: Fred Gould
Robotics Laboratory: No

Waterbury State Technical College
Technologies Department
1460 West Main Street
Waterbury, CT 06708
(203) 575-8089
Contact: Dr. Seretny
Robotics Laboratory: Yes

DELAWARE

Delaware Technical & Community College-Terry Campus
Electromechanical Engineering Tech Department
1832 North DuPont Highway
Dover, DE 19901
(302) 736-5441
Contact: Sam Guccione
Robotics Laboratory: No

Delaware Technical & Community College-Newark
Electronics Department
400 Stanton-Christiana Road
Newark, DE 19701
(302) 454-3965, Ext. 3792
Contact: Gary Haas
Robotics Laboratory: Yes

FLORIDA

Brevard Community College
Electronic Engineering Technology Dept.
1519 Clearlake Road
Cocoa, FL 32922
(305) 632-1111
Contact: Warren B. Thiers
Robotics Laboratory: Yes

Edison Community College
Electronics Engineering Tech Department
College Parkway
Fort Myers, FL 33901
(813) 489-9300
Contact: Raymond E. Crimmel
Robotics Laboratory: Yes

Palm Beach Junior College
Engineering Technology Department
4200 Congress Drive
Lake Worth, FL 33461
(305) 439-8123
Contact: Phil N. Millard
Robotics Laboratory: No

Polk Community College
Electronics Technology Department
999 Avenue H, Northeast
Winter Haven, FL 33880
(813) 294-7771
Contact: Dr. Pearsall
Robotics Laboratory: Yes

GEORGIA

Dekalb Area Tech
Electromechanical Department
495 North Indian Creek Drive
Clarkston, GA 30021
(404) 299-4359
Contact: Glenn Pfautz
Robotics Laboratory: Yes

Clayton Junior College
Div. of Vo-Tech Education
P.O. Box 285
Morrow, GA 30260
(404) 961-3571
Contact: Ralph Clark
Robotics Laboratory: Yes

ILLINOIS

Belleville Area College
2500 Carlyle Road
Belleville, IL 62221
(618) 235-2700, Ext. 432
Contact: Robert L. Arndt
Robotics Laboratory: No

Olive-Harvey College
Applied Science Department
10001 South Woodland Avenue
Chicago, IL 60628
(312) 568-3700, Ext. 572
Contact: William Thanholt
Robotics Laboratory: Yes

Illinois Central College
Mechanical & Industrial Technology Departments
TKS
East Peoria, IL 61635
(309) 694-5510
Contact: W. Richard Polanin
Robotics Laboratory: Yes

College of Dupage
Glenn Ellyn, IL 60137
(312) 858-2800, Ext. 2495
Contact: James B. McCoral, Ph.D.
Robotics Laboratory: Yes

Joliet Junior College
Technology Department
1216 Houbelt Avenue
Joliet, IL 60431
(815) 729-9020, Ext. 293
Contact: Peter Kiefert
Robotics Laboratory: Yes

Black Hawk College
Electrical Technology Department
6600 34th Avenue
Moline, IL 61265
(309) 796-1311, Ext. 342
Contact: J. R. Lambert
Robotics Laboratory: Yes

Wabash Valley College
2200 College Drive
Mt. Carmel, IL 62863
(618) 262-8641
Contact: Bob Effland
Robotics Laboratory: Yes

Illinois Valley Community College
Engineering Department
Route One
Oglesby, IL 61348
(815) 224-2720
Contact: Don Haas
Robotics Laboratory: Yes

Triton College
Manufacturing Engineering Department
2000 Fifth Avenue
River Grove, IL 60171
(312) 456-0300, Ext. 433
Contact: Patrick Rubino
Robotics Laboratory: Yes

Waubonsee Community College
Business & Technology Department
IL. Route 47 at Harter Road
Sugar Grove, IL 60554
(312) 466-4811, Ext. 321
Contact: Norman Paul
Robotics Laboratory: Yes

INDIANA

Tri-State University
Technology Division
Angola, IN 46703
(219) 665-3141
Contact: Edward J. Nagle
Robotics Laboratory: Yes

Ivy Tech
Electronics Technology Department
4475 Central Avenue
Columbus, IN 47202
(812) 372-9925, Ext. 50
Contact: Gene Adair
Robotics Laboratory: Yes

Indiana Vocational Technical College
Industrial Maintenance Department
3501 1st Avenue
Evansville, IN 47710
(812) 426-2865
Contact: Curtis Palmer
Robotics Laboratory: Yes

Indiana Vocational Technical College
Electronics Department
3800 North Anthony Boulevard
Fort Wayne, IN 46805
(219) 482-9171
Contact: David W. Brown
Robotics Laboratory: Yes

Ball State University
Industry & Technology Dept.
Muncie, IN 47306
(317) 285-5656
Contact: Dr. Le Tang
Robotics Laboratory: Yes

Indiana Vocational Technical College
Instruction Department
8204 Highway 311
Sellersburg, IN 47172
(812) 246-3301
Contact: Jonathon W. Thomas
Robotics Laboratory: Yes

Indiana Vocational Technical College
1534 West Sample Street
South Bend, IN 46619
(219) 289-7001
Contact: D.W. Howard
Robotics Laboratory: Yes

Indiana Vocational Technical College
Electronics Department
7377 South Dixie Bee Road
Terre Haute, IN 47802
(812) 299-1121
Contact: Don Arney
Robotics Laboratory: Yes

Vincennes University
Robotics Technology Department
1002 North 2nd Street
Technology Building (TB-10)
Vincennes, IN 47591
(812) 885-4569
Contact: R. Dean Eavey
Robotics Laboratory: Yes

IOWA

Des Moines Area Community College
2006 S. Ankeny Boulevard
Ankeny, IA 50021
(515) 964-6277
Contact: Thomas Dunsmore
Robotics Laboratory: Yes

Marshalltown Community College
Industrial Technology Department
3700 South Center
Marshalltown, IA 50158
(515) 752-7106, Ext. 203
Contact: Jeff Dodge
Robotics Laboratory: Yes

Indian Hills Community College
High Technology Department
Grandview and Elm
Ottumwa, IA 52501
(515) 683-5201
Contact: Curt D. Bloomquist
Robotics Laboratory: Yes

Northwest Iowa Technical College
Industrial Manufacturing Department
Highway 18 West
Sheldon, IA 51201
(712) 324-2587
Contact: Dennis Davis
Robotics Laboratory: Yes

Southeastern Community College
Mechanical Technology Department
P.O. Drawer F
West Burlington, IA 52655
(319) 752-2731
Contact: John W. Smith
Robotics Laboratory: No

KANSAS

Hutchinson Community College
Technical Education Department
1300 North Plum
Hutchinson, KS 67501
(316) 665-3549
Contact: Bruce R. Balman
Robotics Laboratory: Yes

Kansas City Kansas Community College
Academic Computing Department
7250 State Avenue
Kansas City, KS 66112
(913) 334-1100
Contact: Bill Chennault
Robotics Laboratory: Yes

Johnson County Community College
Manufacturing Technology Department
12345 College at Quivira
Overland Park, KS 66210-1299
(913) 888-8500
Contact: Al Shopper
Robotics Laboratory: Yes

KENTUCKY

Louisville, University of
Industrial Engineering Department
Louisville, KY 49292
(502) 588-6342
Contact: Herman R. Leep
Robotics Laboratory: Yes

Maysville Community College of University of Kentucky
Industrial Technology Department
Route 2
Maysville, KY 41056
(606) 759-7141
Contact: James McMillan
Robotics Laboratory: Yes

LOUSIANA

Louisiana State University
Applied Sciences & Technology Division
P.O. Box 1129
Eunice, LA 70535
(318) 457-7311
Contact: Dr. Paul P. Pai
Robotics Laboratory: No

MARYLAND

Anne Arundel Community College
Mech. Engineering Technology Dept.
101 College Parkway
Arnold, MD 21017
(301) 269-7433
Contact: Ken Stibolt
Robotics Laboratory: Yes

Allegany Community College
Electro Mechanical Technology Dept.
Willow Brook Road
Cumberland, MD 21502
(301) 724-7700, Ext. 310
Contact: Larry Bloom
Robotics Laboratory: Yes

Prince Georges Community College
Engineering Technology Department
301 Largo Road
Largo, MD 20772
(301) 322-0174
Contact: William Lauffer
Robotics Laboratory: Yes

MASSACHUSETTS

Massasoit Community College
Engineering Technology Department
Brockton, MA 02402
(617) 588-9100, Ext. 242
Contact: Prof. Paul Hardy
Robotics Laboratory: Yes

Bristol Community College
Business & Engineering Dept.
777 Elsbree
Fall River, MA 02720
(617) 678-2811
Contact: Normand Lavigne
Robotics Laboratory: Yes

Mesabi Community College
Virginia, MA 55710
(218) 741-9200
Contact: Kenneth Pontimen
Robotics Laboratory: No

Mass Bay Community College
Science & Engineering Technology Department
50 Oakland Street
Wellesley, MA 02181
(617) 237-1100
Contact: Dr. Paul D. Anderson
Robotics Laboratory: No

MICHIGAN

Alpena Community College
Industrial Department
Alpena, MI 49707
(517) 356-9021, Ext. 233
Contact: A.E. Reed
Robotics Laboratory: No

Washtenaw Community College
Robotics Technology Department
P.O. Box D1
4800 East Huron River Drive
Ann Arbor, MI 48106
(313) 973-3300
Contact: George Agin
Robotics Laboratory: Yes

Oakland Community College
2900 Featherstone Road
Auburn Hills, MI 48057
(313) 853-4200
Contact: Dr. Bill J. Rose
Robotics Laboratory: Yes

Kellogg Community College
Business & Technology Department
450 North Avenue
Battle Creek, MI 49016
(616) 965-3931
Contact: Marut Patel
Robotics Laboratory: Yes

Henry Ford Community College
Industrial Technology Department
5101 Evergreen
Dearborn, MI 48128
(313) 271-2750, Ext. 360
Contact: John Nagohosian
Robotics Laboratory: Yes

Wayne County Community College
Electrical/Electronics/Robotics Technology
Department
1001 West Fort Street
Detroit, MI 48226
(313) 496-2691
Contact: John H. Spurlin
Robotics Laboratory: No

Mott Community College
Division of Applied Technology
1401 East Court Street
Flint, MI 48502
(313) 762-0516
Contact: John Ortiz
Robotics Laboratory: Yes

Grand Rapids Junior College
Technology Department
143 Bostwick
Grand Rapids, MI 49503
(616) 456-4860
Contact: Granville Brown
Robotics Laboratory: Yes

Mid Michigan College
Machine Tool Department
1375 South Clare Avenue
Harrison, MI 48625
(517) 386-7792
Contact: Tom Groner
Robotics Laboratory: No

Jackson Community College
Electro/Mechanical Technology Department
2111 Emmons Road
Jackson, MI 49201
(517) 787-0800
Contact: Ralph L. Burdick
Robotics Laboratory: Yes

Lansing Community College
Engineering Technology Department
P.O. Box 40010
Lansing, MI 48901
(517) 483-1380
Contact: Ronald Garthe
Robotics Laboratory: Yes

Schoolcraft College
Robotics Department
18600 Haggerty Road
Livonia, MI 48152
(313) 591-6400, Ext. 581
Contact: Jerry Wale
Robotics Laboratory: Yes

Delta College
Academic Department
University Center, MI 48710
(517) 686-9442
Contact: Donald Holzhei
Robotics Laboratory: Yes

Macomb Community College
Mechanical Technology Department
14500 Twelve Mile Road
Warren, MI 48093
(313) 445-7411
Contact: Laurence Ford
Robotics Laboratory: Yes

MISSISSIPPI

Itawamba Junior College
653 Eason Boulevard
Tupelo, MS 38801
(601) 842-5621
Contact: Harry Presley
Robotics Laboratory: Yes

Hinds Junior College—Utica Campus
Electronics Department
P.O. Box 280 UJC
Utica, MS 39175
(601) 885-6062
Contact: William J. Parks
Robotics Laboratory: Yes

MISSOURI

Jefferson College
Vocational-Tech Education
Box 1000
Hillsboro, MO 63050
(314) 789-3951
Contact: Paul Paulson
Robotics Laboratory: Yes

Penn Valley Community College
Electromechanical Technology Department
3201 Southwest Trafficway
Kansas City, MO 64111
(816) 932-7649
Contact: Robert L. Crockett
Robotics Laboratory: No

St. Louis Community College at Forest Park
Technology Department
5600 Oakland
St. Louis, MO 63110
(314) 644-9303
Contact: William D. Mason
Robotics Laboratory: Yes

NEBRASKA

Central Community College Platte Campus
Science Department
P.O. Box 1027
Columbus, NE 68601
(402) 564-7132
Contact: Bill Kucera
Robotics Laboratory: Yes

Southeast Community College
Electronics Department
AR2 Box 153
Milford, NE 68405
(402) 761-2131
Contact: Earl Fosler
Robotics Laboratory: Yes

NEW JERSEY

Camden County College
Engineering Technology Dept.
Box 200
Blackwood, NJ 08012
(609) 227-7200, Ext. 320
Contact: Prof. Weston Beale
Robotics Laboratory: Yes

Somerset County Technical Institute
P.O. Box 6350
North Bridge Street and Vogt Drive
Bridgewater, NJ 08807
(201) 526-8900
Contact: John A. Kuklis
Robotics Laboratory: Yes

Union County College
Electromechanical Technology Department
1033 Springfield Avenue
Cranford, NJ 07016
(201) 889-4100, Ext. 663
Contact: James Newman
Robotics Laboratory: Yes

Middlesex County College
Electrical Engineering Technology Department
Edison, NJ 08818
(201) 548-6000, Ext. 474
Contact: Jack I. Waintraub
Robotics Laboratory: Yes

Burlington County College
Div. of Science, Mathematics & Technology
Pemberton-Browns Mills Road
Pemberton, NJ 08068
(609) 894-9311
Contact: Jack Braun
Robotics Laboratory: No

Gloucester County College
Math/Science Department
Tanyard Road
Sewell, NJ 08080
(609) 468-5000, Ext. 254
Contact: John M. Cassady
Robotics Laboratory: No

NEW YORK

State University of New York—Alfred
Mechanical Engineering Technology Department
Alfred, NY 14802
(607) 871-6350
Contact: David F. Conde
Robotics Laboratory: No

Queensborough Community College
Mechanical Engineering Technology
56th Avenue and Springfield Boulevard
Bayside, NY 11364
(212) 631-6294
Contact: B.G. Schieber, Jr.
Robotics Laboratory: No

Erie Community College
Manufacturing Technology Department
121 Ellicott Street
Buffalo, NY 14203
(716) 675-5444
Contact: Thomas A. Lembke
Robotics Laboratory: Yes

State University of New York
Agricultural & Technology College
Delhi, NY 13753
(607) 746-4228
Contact: Charles D. Nichols
Robotics Laboratory: Yes

Herkimer County Community College
Mathematics & Science Division
Herkimer, NY 13352
(315) 866-0300
Contact: Frank J. Menapace
Robotics Laboratory: Yes

Columbia Greene Community College
Computer Science Dept.
P.O. 1000
Hudson, NY 12534
(518) 820-4111
Contact: William Thompson
Robotics Laboratory: Yes

Jamestown Community College
Engineering Department
525 Falconer Street
Jamestown, NY 14701
(716) 665-5220
Contact: Charles Rondeau
Robotics Laboratory: Yes

Orange County Community College
Technologies Department
115 South Street
Middletown, NY 10940
(914) 343-1121, Ext. 288
Contact: Arlin Bartlett
Robotics Laboratory: No

Niagara County Community College
Mechanical Technology Department
3111 Saunders Settlement
Sanborn, NY 14132
(716) 731-3271
Contact: Pascal Zanzano
Robotics Laboratory: Yes

Rockland Community College
Electronic Technology Department
145 College Road
Suffern, NY 10901
(914) 356-4650, Ext. 249
Contact: Ignacio R. Stanley
Robotics Laboratory: Yes

NORTH CAROLINA

Asheville-Buncombe Tech. College
340 Victoria Road
Asheville, NC 28801
(704) 254-1921
Contact: Olin R. Wood
Robotics Laboratory: No

Central Piedmont Community College
Electrical Engineering Technology Dept.
P.O. Box 35009
Charlotte, NC 28235
(704) 373-6786
Contact: T.A. Allison
Robotics Laboratory: Yes

Technical College of Alamance
Electronics Technology Department
P.O. Box 023
Haw River, NC 27258
(919) 578-2002
Contact: R.R. Stockard
Robotics Laboratory: Yes

Davidson County Community College
Engineering Department
P.O. Box 1287
Lexington, NC 27292
(704) 249-8186
Contact: Charles Su
Robotics Laboratory: Yes

Tri-County Community College
P.O. Box 46
Murphy, NC 28906
(704) 837-6810
Contact: Walter L. Tatha
Robotics Laboratory: No

Nash Technical College
Engineering Department
Old Carriage Road
Rocky Mount, NC 27809
(919) 443-4011
Contact: Jerome Hodges
Robotics Laboratory: Yes

Piedmont Technical College
P.O. Box 1197
Roxboro, NC 27573
(919) 599-1181, Ext. 204
Contact: Dr. William D. Rentz
Robotics Laboratory: Yes

Rowan Technical College
Manufacturing Engineering Technology
Department
P.O. Box 1595
Salisbury, NC 28144
(704) 637-0760
Contact: John K. Burns
Robotics Laboratory: Yes

Isothermal Community College
Mechanical Engineering/Drafting & Design
Departments
P.O. Box 804
Spindale, NC 28160
(704) 286-3636
Contact: N/A
Robotics Laboratory: Yes

Maryland Tech
Electronics Institute Department
P.O. Box 547
Spruce Pine, NC 28777
(704) 765-7351
Contact: Jerry Cox
Robotics Laboratory: No

Wilkes Community College
TV Program
Wilkesboro, NC 28697
(919) 667-7136
Contact: Josephine Hendrix
Robotics Laboratory: Yes

Forsyth Technical Institute
Manufacturing Engineering Technology Dept.
2100 Silas Creek Parkway
Winston-Salem, NC 27103
(919) 723-0371
Contact: John E. Beeson
Robotics Laboratory: Yes

NORTH DAKOTA

North Dakota State School of Science
Welding Department
Wahpeton, ND 58075
(701) 671-2434
Contact: John Cox
Robotics Laboratory: Yes

OHIO

Northwest Technical College
Engineering Technology Department
Route 1 Box 246A
Archbold, OH 43502
(419) 267-5511
Contact: Sanford A. Lane
Robotics Laboratory: No

Kent State University
Geauga Campus
14111 Claridon-Troy Road
Burton, OH 44021
(216) 834-4187
Contact: Gregory M. Shreve
Robotics Laboratory: Yes

Wright State University
Western Ohio Branch
Engineering Technology Department
7600 Street Route 703
Celina, OH 45822
(419) 586-2365
Contact: Art Burd
Robotics Laboratory: No

Cincinnati Technical College
Engineering Technology Dept.
3520 Central Parkway
Cincinnati, OH 45223
(513) 559-1520
Contact: Rob Speckert
Robotics Laboratory: Yes

Southern Ohio College
Robotics Department
4781 Hamilton Avenue
Cincinnati, OH 45223
(513) 681-0580
Contact: Robert L. Hoekstra
Robotics Laboratory: Yes

Terra Technical College
Engineering Technologies Department
1220 Cedar Street
Fremont, OH 43420
(419) 334-3886
Contact: Tom Kissell
Robotics Laboratory: Yes

Ohio University
Industrial Technology
1570 Granville Pike
Lancaster, OH 43130
(614) 654-6711
Contact: Zale Maxwell
Robotics Laboratory: Yes

Lima Technical College
Division of Engineering Technology
4300 Campus Drive
Lima, OH 45804
(419) 227-5131
Contact: Norman J. Rex
Robotics Laboratory: Yes

North Central Technical College
Mechanical Engineering Department
P.O. Box 698
Mansfield, OH 44901
(419) 747-4999
Contact: E.C. Boso
Robotics Laboratory: Yes

Shawnee State College
Engineering Technology Department
940 2nd Street
Portsmouth, OH 45662
(614) 354-3205
Contact: C.R. Irwin
Robotics Laboratory: Yes

Clark Technical College
Engineering Department
570 East Leffels Lane
Springfield, OH 45505
(513) 325-0691, Ext. 255
Contact: Dr. Monm Coffin
Robotics Laboratory: Yes

Owens Technical College
Engineering Technologies Department
Caller No. 10,000
Toledo, OH 43699
(419) 666-0580, Ext. 354
Contact: Dave Winters
Robotics Laboratory: Yes

Muskingam Area Technical College
Mechanical & Industrial Engineering Departments
1555 Newark Road
Zanesville, OH 43701
(614) 454-2501
Contact: Arthur N. Maupin
Robotics Laboratory: No

OKLAHOMA

El Reno Junior College
Electronics Technology Department
Box 370
1300 South Country Club Road
El Reno, OK 73036
(405) 262-2552
Contact: Miller Tiger
Robotics Laboratory: No

Rose State College
Engineering/Science Division
6420 Southeast 15th Street
Midwest City, OK 73110
(405) 733-7450
Contact: John H. Hansen
Robotics Laboratory: Yes

Oklahoma City Community College
7777 South May Avenue
Oklahoma City, OK 73159
(405) 682-1611
Contact: Curt Lezanic
Robotics Laboratory: No

Oklahoma State University Tech. Institute
Electrical Engineering Technology Department
900 North Portland
Oklahoma City, OK 73107
(405) 947-4421
Contact: Dr. Dewey Yeager
Robotics Laboratory: N/A

Oklahoma State Tech
Electronics Department
Okmulgee, OK 74447
(918) 756-6211
Contact: Bill J. Lyons
Robotics Laboratory: Yes

Tulsa Junior College
Science & Engineering Department
3727 East Apache
Tulsa, OK 74115
(918) 834-5071, Ext. 318
Contact: Ron Paquette
Robotics Laboratory: Yes

OREGON

Clatsop Community College
Electronics Department
16th and Jerome Street
Astoria, OR 97103
(503) 325-0910
Contact: Gilbert Doty
Robotics Laboratory: Yes

Mt. Hood Community College
Technology Department
26000 Southeast Stark Street
Gresham, OR 97030
(503) 667-7364
Contact: John Greenaway
Robotics Laboratory: No

Clackamas Community College
Industrial Department
19600 South Mollala Avenue
Oregon City, OR 97045
(503) 657-8400
Contact: G. Warren
Robotics Laboratory: No

PENNSYLVANIA

Delaware County Community College
Applied Sciences Department
Media, PA 19063
(215) 359-5288
Contact: Dr. Paul McQuay
Robotics Laboratory: Yes

Pennsylvania Institute of Technology
800 Manchester Avenue
Media, PA 19063
(215) 565-7900
Contact: William Koffke
Robotics Laboratory: Yes

Lehigh County Community College
Mechanical Technology Department
2370 Main Street
Schnecksville, PA 18078
(215) 799-1506
Contact: Cliff Miller
Robotics Laboratory: No

Alleghany County, Community College of
Engineering Technology Department
South Campus, 1750 Clairton Road
West Mifflin, PA 15122
(412) 469-1100, Ext. 226
Contact: Pearley Cunningham
Robotics Laboratory: No

Williamsport Community College
Division of High Technology
Williamsport, PA 17706
(717) 326-3761, Ext. 205
Contact: George Baker
Robotics Laboratory: Yes

Westmoreland County Community College
Technologies Department
Youngwood, PA 15697
(412) 925-4008
Contact: David Bruce
Robotics Laboratory: Yes

SOUTH CAROLINA

Aiken Technical College
Electro Mechanical Technology Department
P.O. Drawer 696
Aiken, SC 29801
(803) 593-9231
Contact: James B. Wertz
Robotics Laboratory: No

Piedmont Technical College
Robotics Resource Center
P.O. Drawer 1467
Greenwood, SC 29646
(803) 223-8357
Contact: James Rehg
Robotics Laboratory: Yes

Spartanburg Technical College
Engineering Technology Department
P.O. Drawer 4386
Spartanburg, SC 29305
(803) 576-5770
Contact: Jim Petroski
Robotics Laboratory: No

SOUTH DAKOTA

Northern State College
Industrial Technology Department
Aberdeen, SD 57401
(605) 622-2571
Contact: Terry Richardson, Ph.D.
Robotics Laboratory: Yes

TENNESSEE

Tri-Cities State Technical Institute
Mechanical Engineering Technology Department
P.O. Box 246
Blountville, TN 37617
(615) 323-3191
Contact: Jim Chandler
Robotics Laboratory: No

**Chattanooga State
Technical Community College**
Productivity Center
4501 Amnicola Highway
Chattanooga, TN 37406
(615) 697-4411
Contact: Oliver Benton
Robotics Laboratory: Yes

Columbia State Community College
Electronics Department
Hampshire Park
Columbia, TN 38401
(615) 388-0120, Ext. 329
Contact: Clyde M. Denton
Robotics Laboratory: Yes

Dyersburg State Community College
P.O. Box 648
Dyersburg, TN 38024
(901) 285-6910
Contact: John Moore
Robotics Laboratory: No

State Technical Institute at Knoxville
Electrical Engineering Technology Department
Division Street
Knoxville, TN 37919
(615) 584-6103, Ext. 221
Contact: Frank S. Darwin
Robotics Laboratory: N/A

Walters State Community College
Industrial Engineering Department
Morristown, TN 37814
(615) 581-2121, Ext. 369
Contact: Reza Safabakhsh
Robotics Laboratory: Yes

Nashville State Technical Institute
120 White Bridge Road
Nashville, TN 37209
(615) 741-1235
Contact: Joel Lavalley
Robotics Laboratory: No

Motlow State Community College
Engineering Technology Department
Tullahoma, TN 37388
(615) 455-8511
Contact: William J. Templeton, Jr.
Robotics Laboratory: No

TEXAS

Lee College
Technology Department
P.O. Box 818
Baytown, TX 77520
(713) 427-5666, Ext. 366
Contact: J.C. Lockett
Robotics Laboratory: Yes

Mt. View College
SS-Tech Div., Electronics Department
4849 West Illinois Avenue
Dallas, TX 75211
(214) 333-8722
Contact: Stan Fulton
Robotics Laboratory: Yes

Richland College
Engineering Technology Department
12800 Abrams Road
Dallas, TX 75243
(214) 238-6330
Contact: Harold Albertson
Robotics Laboratory: Yes

Grayson County College
Technical Occupation Department
6101 Grayson Drive
Denison, TX 75020
(405) 465-6030, Ext. 271
Contact: Joe Shults
Robotics Laboratory: Yes

**Tarrant County Junior
College—South Campus**
Engineering Technology Department
5301 Campus Drive
Fort Worth, TX 76119
(817) 531-0430
Contact: Jim Moore
Robotics Laboratory: Yes

Hill Junior College

Microelectronics Department
P.O. Box 619
Hillsboro, TX 76645
(817) 582-2555, Ext. 43
Contact: Jim Poole
Robotics Laboratory: N/A

Houston Community College

Technical Education Division
4310 Dunlavy
Houston, TX 77006
(713) 868-0787
Contact: Reddy Talusani
Robotics Laboratory: No

San Jacinto College

Electronics Department
5800 Uvalde
Houston, TX 77049
(713) 458-4050
Contact: Leo C. Wilson
Robotics Laboratory: No

UTAH

Utah Technical College at Salt Lake

Engineering Technology Department
P.O. Box 31808
Salt Lake City, UT 84131
(801) 967-9235
Contact: Joe Baker
Robotics Laboratory: Yes

VIRGINIA

J. Sargeant Reynolds Community College

Division of Engineering and Applied Science
Parham Road Campus
P.O. Box 12084
Richmond, VA 23241
(804) 264-3000
Contact: Dr. Thomas D. Diamond
Robotics Laboratory: No

Wytheville Community College

Business, Engineering Technology & Math
Department
1000 East Main Street
Wytheville, VA 24382
(703) 228-5541
Contact: Dr. Y.P. Hwu
Robotics Laboratory: No

WASHINGTON

Olympic College

Engineering Department
16th Chester
Bremerton, WA 98310
(206) 478-4777
Contact: Darrell A. Estep
Robotics Laboratory: No

Spokane Community College

Industrial Electricity/Robotics Department
N1810 Greene Street
Spokane, WA 99207
(509) 536-7158
Contact: Richard Cox
Robotics Laboratory: Yes

WISCONSIN

Fox Valley Technical Institute

Trade & Industry Department
P.O. Box 2277
Appleton, WI 54913
(414) 735-5783
Contact: Virgil Noordyk
Robotics Laboratory: Yes

Lakeshore Technical Institute

Electrical Service Department
1290 North Avenue
Cleveland, WI 53015
(414) 684-4408, Ext. 257
Contact: Mel DeSwarte
Robotics Laboratory: Yes

Black Hawk Tech. Institute
Trade & Industry Department
P.O. Box 5009
6004 Prairie Road
Janesville, WI 53547
(608) 756-4121, Ext. 273
Contact: Gene A. Hilst
Robotics Laboratory: Yes

Gateway Technical Institute
Trade & Industry Department
3520 30th Avenue
Kenosha, WI 53141
(414) 656-6940
Contact: Stuart Vorpagel
Robotics Laboratory: Yes

Western Wisconsin Technical Institute
Industrial Department
6th and Vine Streets
La Crosse, WI 54602
(608) 785-9178
Contact: William G. Welch, Jr.
Robotics Laboratory: Yes

Milwaukee Area Technical College
Welding Technology Department
1015 North 6th Street
Milwaukee, WI 53203
(414) 278-6247
Contact: Richard Tupta
Robotics Laboratory: Yes

Wisconsin Indianhead Technical Institute
Trades and Industrial Department
505 Pine Ridge Drive, Box B
Shell Lake, WI 54871
(715) 468-2815
Contact: Howard Sonnenberg
Robotics Laboratory: No

Wisconsin Indianhead Technical Institute
600 North 21st
Superior, WI 53403
(715) 394-6677
Contact: Raymond Johnson
Robotics Laboratory: N/A

North Central Technical Institute
1000 Campus Drive
Wausau, WI 54401
(715) 675-3331
Contact: Marvin D. Bausman
Robotics Laboratory: Yes

WYOMING

Casper College
Electronics Department
125 College Drive
Casper, WY 82601
(307) 268-2600
Contact: H.M. Dinges
Robotics Laboratory: Yes

INSTITUTIONS OFFERING BACHELOR DEGREE PROGRAMS

ARKANSAS

Arkansas, University of
Industrial Engineering Department
Room 309
Fayetteville, AR 72701
(501) 575-3156
Contact: William H. Rader
Robotics Laboratory: Yes

CALIFORNIA

California—Los Angeles, University of
Manufacturing Engineering Department
405 Hilgard Avenue
Los Angeles, CA 90024
(213) 206-8525
Contact: Dr. Watteau
Robotics Laboratory: Yes

California Polytechnic State University
Industrial Engineering Department
San Luis Obispo, CA 93407
(805) 546-2341
Contact: Dr. Donald E. Morgan
Robotics Laboratory: N/A

California State University, Los Angeles
Engineering Department
5151 State University Drive
Los Angeles, CA 90032
(213) 224-3541
Contact: Dr. Ram Manvi
Robotics Laboratory: Yes

Cogswell Polytechnical College
Mechanical Engineering Department
600 Stockton Street
San Francisco, CA 94108
(415) 433-5550, Ext. 221
Contact: Edwin J. Merrick
Robotics Laboratory: Yes

San Francisco State University
Division of Engineering
1600 Holloway Avenue
San Francisco, CA 94132
(415) 469-7386
Contact: Dr. W. Stadler
Robotics Laboratory: No

COLORADO
Colorado State University
Engineering Department
Fort Collins, CO 80523
(303) 491-8655
Contact: F.W. Smith
Robotics Laboratory: Yes

CONNECTICUT
Hartford, University of
College of Engineering
West Hartford, CT 06117
(203) 243-4786
Contact: Prof. C. Hemond
Robotics Laboratory: No

DELAWARE
Delaware, University of
Mechanical & Aerospace Engineering Depts.
Newark, DE 19711
(302) 451-2889
Contact: Dr. A. Kumar
Robotics Laboratory: N/A

FLORIDA
Florida Atlantic University
Electrical & Computer Engineering Departments
Boca Raton, FL 33431
(305) 393-3412
Contact: Yacov Shamash
Robotics Laboratory: Yes

Miami, University of
Industrial Engineering Department
Coral Gables, FL 33124
(305) 284-2344
Contact: Dr. David J. Sumanth
Robotics Laboratory: N/A

Florida, University of
Electrical Engineering Department
Dept. of Electrical Engineering
Gainesville, FL 32611
(904) 392-0814
Contact: Dr. Del Tesar
Robotics Laboratory: Yes

Florida International University
Mechanical Engineering Department
Tamiami Trail
Miami, FL 33199
(305) 554-2569
Contact: Dr. Ian Radin
Robotics Laboratory: No

Florida A & M University
Division of Engineer Tech and Computer Systems
307 Tech Unit 'A'
Tallahassee, FL 32307
(904) 599-3022
Contact: Barry A. McConnell
Robotics Laboratory: Yes

ILLINOIS
Southern Illinois University
Industrial Technology Department
Technology Building D
Carbondale, IL 62901
(618) 536-3396
Contact: Dr. John McLuckie
Robotics Laboratory: Yes

Millikin University
School of Business & Engineering
1184 West Main Street
Decatur, IL 62522
(217) 424-6338
Contact: James R. Gross
Robotics Laboratory: Yes

Illinois, University of
Mechanical & Industrial Engineering Departments
1513 University Avenue
Urbana, IL 61801
(217) 333-3432
Contact: Shiv Kapoor
Robotics Laboratory: Yes

INDIANA

I.T.T. Technical Institute
Automated Manufacturing Technology
Department
1415 Profit Drive
Fort Wayne, IN 46808
(219) 484-4107, Ext. 44
Contact: Dr. Edward A. Kimble
Robotics Laboratory: Yes

Indiana University—Purdue University at Ft. Wayne
Manufacturing Technology Department
2101 Coliseum Boulevard East
Fort Wayne, IN 46805
(219) 482-5761
Contact: Prof. Donald J. McAleece, CMfgE
Robotics Laboratory: Yes

Purdue University
Mechanical Engineering Technology Department
MGL 1209
Lafayette, IN 47907
(317) 494-7514
Contact: H. L. Banton
Robotics Laboratory: Yes

I.T.T. Technical Institute
9511 Angola Court
Indianapolis, IN 46268
(317) 875-8640
Contact: Milton J. Kalapach
Robotics Laboratory: Yes

Indiana State University
Electronics & Computer Technology Department
Terre Haute, IN 47809
(812) 232-6311
Contact: Dr. Larry Heath
Robotics Laboratory: Yes

IOWA

Iowa State University
Industrial Engineering Department
Ames, IA 50011
(515) 294-1682
Contact: Eric Malstrom
Robotics Laboratory: Yes

KANSAS

Cowley County Community College
Electronics Department
125 South 2nd
Arkansas City, KS 67005
(316) 422-0430, Ext. 273
Contact: William D. Hughes
Robotics Laboratory: No

KENTUCKY

Morehead State University
Industrial Education & Technology Department
UPO 774
Morehead, KY 40351
(606) 783-2419
Contact: Robert E. Newton
Robotics Laboratory: Yes

Eastern Kentucky University
Department of Industrial Education & Technology
Richmond, KY
(606) 622-3232
Contact: James Maslitsen
Robotics Laboratory: Yes

LOUISIANA

Louisiana State University
Industrial Engineering Department
3128 CEBA
Baton Rouge, LA 70803
(504) 388-5112
Contact: Dr. William E. Biles
Robotics Laboratory: Yes

Louisiana Tech
Mechanical Engineering Department
Ruston, LA 71272
(318) 257-2357
Contact: Robert O. Warrington Jr.
Robotics Laboratory: Yes

MARYLAND

U.S. Naval Academy
Weapons and Systems Engineering Department
Annapolis, MD 21402
(301) 267-3468
Contact: Dr. Kenneth A. Knowles
Robotics Laboratory: Yes

Maryland, University of
Electrical Engineering Department
College Park, MD 20742
(301) 454-6869
Contact: Robert W. Newcomb
Robotics Laboratory: Yes

MASSACHUSETTS

Massachusetts, University of
Mechanical Engineering Department
Amherst, MA 01003
(413) 545-2253
Contact: Dr. L.E. Murch
Robotics Laboratory: Yes

Southeastern Massachusetts University
Electrical Computer Engineering Department
North Dartmouth, MA 02747
(617) 999-8476
Contact: Gilbert Fain
Robotics Laboratory: Yes

MICHIGAN

Michigan—Dearborn, University of
School of Engineering
Dearborn, MI 48128
(313) 593-5080
Contact: Dr. Adnan Aswad
Robotics Laboratory: Yes

Michigan State University
College of Engineering
East Lansing, MI 48824
(517) 355-5066
Contact: R.L. Tummala
Robotics Laboratory: Yes

GMI Engineering & Management Center
Mechanical Engineering Department
1700 West Third Avenue
Flint, MI 48502
(313) 762-7877
Contact: Jack D. Lane
Robotics Laboratory: Yes

Michigan Technological University
Mechanical Engineering Department
Houghton, MI 49931
(906) 487-2551
Contact: Michael P. Deisenroth
Robotics Laboratory: Yes

Western Michigan University
Engineering Technology Department
Kohrman Hall
Kalamazoo, MI 49008
(616) 383-4992
Contact: Fred Z. Sitkins
Robotics Laboratory: Yes

Lake Superior State College
Engineering Technology Department
Sault Saint Marie, MI 49783
(906) 635-2597
Contact: James E. DeVault
Robotics Laboratory: Yes

Eastern Michigan University
Industrial Technology Department
104 Sill Hall
Ypsilanti, MI 48197
(313) 487-2040
Contact: Robert G. Parent
Robotics Laboratory: Yes

MISSISSIPPI

Southern Mississippi, University of
Industrial Technology
Box 5172, Southern Station
Hattiesburg, MS 39406-5172
(601) 266-4902
Contact: J.W. Lipscomb
Robotics Laboratory: Yes

Mississippi, University of
Electrical Engineering Department
University, MS 38677
(601) 232-7231
Contact: Dr. C.E. Smith
Robotics Laboratory: No

MISSOURI

Missouri, University of
Mechanical Engineering Department
Truman Engineering Labs
Independence, MO 64050
(816) 254-3663
Contact: Dr. J.K. Blundell
Robotics Laboratory: Yes

Missouri—Rolla, University of
Mechanical Engineering
Rolla, MO 65401
(314) 341-4614
Contact: R.T. Johnson
Robotics Laboratory: Yes

NEW JERSEY

Fairleigh Dickinson University
Mechanical Engineering Department
1000 River Road
Teaneck, NJ 07666
(201) 692-2725, Ext. 2316
Contact: Dr. B.D. Rivin
Robotics Laboratory: No

NEW YORK

Clarkson University
Engineering Department
Potsdam, NY 13676
(315) 268-6555
Contact: Dean Edward T. Misiaszek
Robotics Laboratory: Yes

Rensselaer Polytechnic Institute
Mechanical Engineering Department
Troy, NY 12181
(518) 266-6991
Contact: Dr. Stephen Derby
Robotics Laboratory: Yes

State University of New York
College of Technology
811 Count Street
Utica, NY 13502
(315) 792-3542
Contact: Prof. Atlas Hsie
Robotics Laboratory: Yes

NORTH CAROLINA

Duke University
Electrical Engineering Department
Durham, NC 27706
(919) 684-3123
Contact: Paul P. Wang
Robotics Laboratory: Yes

North Carolina State University
Electrical & Computer Engineering Departments
Box 7911
Raleigh, NC 27695-7911
(919) 737-2336
Contact: W.E. Snyder
Robotics Laboratory: Yes

OKLAHOMA

Ohio University
Department of Industrial Technology
19 West Union Street
Athens, OH 45701
(614) 594-5300
Contact: William H. Creighton
Robotics Laboratory: Yes

Cincinnati, University of
Mechanical and Industrial Engineering Depts.
ML #72
Cincinnati, OH 45242
(513) 475-5067
Contact: Ernest L. Hall
Robotics Laboratory: Yes

Oklahoma, University of
Industrial Engineering Department
202 West Boyd, Suite 124
Norman, OK 73019
(405) 325-3721
Contact: Yoichi Matsumoto
Robotics Laboratory: Yes

Toledo, The University of
Industrial Engineering Department
2801 West Bancroft Street
Toledo, OH 43606
(419) 537-2412
Contact: Dr. R.J. McNichols
Robotics Laboratory: Yes

PENNSYLVANIA

Swarthmore College
Engineering Department
Swarthmore, PA 19081
(215) 447-7080
Contact: Frederick L. Orthlieb
Robotics Laboratory: Yes

SOUTH CAROLINA

South Carolina, University of
Electrical and Computer Engineering Department
Columbia, SC 29208
(803) 777-4311
Contact: Ronald D. Bonnell
Robotics Laboratory: Yes

South Carolina State College
Industrial and Electrical Engineering Departments
Technology Department
Orangeburg, SC 29117
(803) 536-7117
Robotics Laboratory: No

SOUTH DAKOTA

Northern State College
Industrial Technology Department
Aberdeen, SD 57401
(605) 622-2571
Contact: Dr. Terry Richardson
Robotics Laboratory: Yes

**South Dakota School
of Mines & Technology**
Mechanical Engineering Department
Rapid City, SD 57701
(605) 394-2409
Contact: Dan Dolan
Robotics Laboratory: Yes

TEXAS

Texas, University of
Department of Mechanical Engineering
Austin, TX 78712
(512) 471-3059
Contact: A.E. Traver
Robotics Laboratory: Yes

Texas A & M University
Engineering Technology Department
College Station, TX 77843
(409) 845-4951
Contact: G.P. Peterson
Robotics Laboratory: Yes

Houston, University of
Mechanical Technology Department
4800 Calhoun
Houston, TX 77004
(713) 749-4652
Contact: Bill Drake
Robotics Laboratory: Yes

UTAH

Weber State College
Manufacturing Engineering Technology
Department
M.S. 1802
Ogden, UT 84408
(801) 626-6140
Contact: Roy D. Thornock
Robotics Laboratory: Yes

VERMONT

Vermont, University of
Mechanical Engineering Department
Votey Building
Burlington, VT 05405
(802) 656-3320
Contact: Prof. B. von Turkovich
Robotics Laboratory: Yes

VIRGINIA

Old Dominion University
MET Department
Norfolk, VA 23508
(804) 440-4644
Contact: Alok Verma
Robotics Laboratory: Yes

WISCONSIN

Wisconsin—Stout, University of
Material & Processes Department
FH 215
Menomonie, WI 54751
(715) 235-6323
Contact: Larry A. Schneider
Robotics Laboratory: Yes

WEST VIRGINIA

West Virginia Institute of Technology
Electrical & Industrial Technology Departments
312 Davis Hall, WVIT
Montgomery, WV 25136
(304) 442-3189
Contact: William C. Burns, Jr.
Robotics Laboratory: Yes

West Virginia University
Mechanical & Aerospace Engineering Departments
Morgantown, WV 26506
(304) 293-3111
Contact: John E. Sneckenberger
Robotics Laboratory: Yes

INSTITUTIONS OFFERING MASTER DEGREE PROGRAMS

ARKANSAS

Arkansas, University of
Industrial Engineering Department
Room 309
Fayetteville, AR 72701
(501) 575-3156
Contact: William H. Rader
Robotics Laboratory: Yes

CALIFORNIA

California—Davis, University of
Electrical & Computer Engineering Departments
Davis, CA 95616
(916) 752-1443
Contact: Dr. T.C. Hsia
Robotics Laboratory: Yes

California—Los Angeles, University of
Manufacturing Engineering Department
405 Hilgard Avenue
Los Angeles, CA 90024
(213) 206-8525
Contact: Dr. Watteau
Robotics Laboratory: Yes

California State University
School of Engineering
6000 J Street
Sacramento, CA 95825
(916) 454-7336
Contact: Dr. Mohammad H. Zand
Robotics Laboratory: Yes

COLORADO

Colorado State University
Engineering Department
Fort Collins, CO 80523
(303) 491-8655
Contact: F.W. Smith
Robotics Laboratory: Yes

DELAWARE

Delaware, University of
Mechanical and Aerospace
Engineering Departments
Newark, DE 19716
(302) 451-2889
Contact: Dr. Alok Kumar
Robotics Laboratory: N/A

FLORIDA

Florida Atlantic University
Electrical & Computer
Engineering Departments
Boca Raton, FL 33431
(305) 393-3412
Contact: Yocov Shamash
Robotics Laboratory: Yes

Miami, University of
Industrial Engineering Department
Coral Gables, FL 33124
(305) 284-2344
Contact: Dr. David J. Sumanth
Robotics Laboratory: N/A

Florida, University of
Electrical Engineering Department
Gainesville, FL 32611
(904) 392-0814
Contact: Dr. Del Tesar
Robotics Laboratory: Yes

Central Florida, University of
Industrial Engineering Department
P.O. Box 25000
Orlando, FL 32816
(305) 275-2615
Contact: John E. Biegel
Robotics Laboratory: Yes

South Florida, University of
College of Engineering
4202 Fowler Avenue
Tampa, FL 33620
(813) 974-2269
Contact: D.L. Kimbler
Robotics Laboratory: Yes

GEORGIA

Georgia Institute of Technology
School of Mechanical Engineering
Atlanta, GA 30332
(404) 894-3247
Contact: Wayne J. Book, Ph.D.
Robotics Laboratory: Yes

ILLINOIS

Northwestern University
Industrial Engineering Department
Evanston, IL 60201
(312) 492-5066
Contact: Prof. C.H. Wu
Robotics Laboratory: Yes

Illinois, University of
Mechanical and Industrial
Engineering Departments
1513 University Avenue
Urbana, IL 61801
(217) 333-3432
Contact: Shiv Kapoor
Robotics Laboratory: Yes

IOWA

Iowa State University
Industrial Engineering Department
Ames, IA 50011
(515) 294-1682
Contact: Eric Malstrom
Robotics Laboratory: Yes

LOUISIANA

Louisiana State University
Industrial Engineering Department
3128 CEBA
Baton Rouge, LA 70803
(504) 388-5112
Contact: Dr. William E. Biles
Robotics Laboratory: Yes

Louisiana Tech
Mechanical Engineering Department
Ruston, LA 71272
(318) 257-2357
Contact: Dr. Robert O. Warrington
Robotics Laboratory: Yes

MARYLAND

Maryland, University of
Mechanical Engineering Department
College Park, MD 20742
(301) 454-7373
Contact: Jackson C.S. Yang
Robotics Laboratory: Yes

MASSACHUSETTS

Massachusetts, University of
Mechanical Engineering Department
Amherst, MA 01003
(413) 545-2253
Contact: Dr. L.E. Murch
Robotics Laboratory: Yes

Southeastern Massachusetts University
Electrical Computer Engineering Department
North Dartmouth, MA 02747
(617) 999-8476
Contact: Gilbert Fain
Robotics Laboratory: Yes

MICHIGAN

Michigan—Dearborn, University of
School of Engineering
Dearborn, MI 48128
(313) 593-5080
Contact: Dr. Adnan Aswad
Robotics Laboratory: Yes

Michigan State University
College of Engineering
East Lansing, MI 48824
(517) 355-5066
Contact: R.L. Tummala
Robotics Laboratory: Yes

Michigan Technological University
Mechanical Engineering Department
Houghton, MI 49931
(906) 487-2551
Contact: Michael P. Deisenroth
Robotics Laboratory: Yes

MISSOURI

Missouri, University of
Mechanical Engineering Department
Truman Engineering Labs
Independence, MO 64050
(816) 254-3663
Contact: Dr. J.K. Blundell
Robotics Laboratory: Yes

NEW YORK

Columbia University
Mechanical Engineering Department
234 Southwest Mudd
New York, NY 10027
(212) 280-2955
Contact: G. Klein
Robotics Laboratory: Yes

Rensselaer Polytechnic Institute
Electrical Computer Systems
Engineering Department
Troy, NY 12181
(518) 266-6440
Contact: F. DiCesare
Robotics Laboratory: Yes

NORTH CAROLINA

Duke University
Electrical Engineering Department
Durham, NC 27706
(919) 684-3123
Contact: Paul P. Wang
Robotics Laboratory: Yes

North Carolina State University
Electrical & Computer
Engineering Departments
Box 7911
Raleigh, NC 27695-7911
(919) 737-2336
Contact: W. E. Snyder
Robotics Laboratory: Yes

OHIO

Ohio University
Mechanical Engineering
Athens, OH
(614) 594-5862
Contact: Roy A. Lawrence
Robotics Laboratory: Yes

Cincinnati, University of
Mechanical & Industrial Engineering Departments
ML #72
Cincinnati, OH 45242
(513) 475-5067
Contact: Ernest L. Hall
Robotics Laboratory: Yes

Toledo, University of
Mechanical & Electrical Engineering Departments
2801 West Bancroft
Toledo, OH 43606
(419) 537-2140
Contact: S. Kramer
Robotics Laboratory: Yes

OKLAHOMA

Oklahoma, University of
Industrial Engineering Department
202 West Boyd, Suite 124
Norman, OK 73019
(405) 325-3721
Contact: Yoichi Matsumoto
Robotics Laboratory: Yes

PENNSYLVANIA

Drexel University
Electrical & Computer Engineering Department
32nd and Chestnut
Philadelphia, PA 19104
(215) 895-2220
Contact: Dr. Richard Klatter
Robotics Laboratory: Yes

Carnegie—Mellon University
Mechanical Engineering Department
Pittsburgh, PA 15213
(412) 578-3529
Contact: Paul K. Wright
Robotics Laboratory: Yes

RHODE ISLAND

Rhode Island, University of
Robotics Research Center
College of Engineering
Kingston, RI 02881
(401) 792-2186
Contact: Dean of Engineering
Robotics Laboratory: Yes

SOUTH CAROLINA

Clemson University
Mechanical Engineering Department
Clemson, SC 29631
(803) 656-3291
Contact: F.W. Paul
Robotics Laboratory: Yes

South Carolina, University of
Electrical and Computer
Engineering Departments
Columbia, SC 29208
(803) 777-4311
Contact: Ronald D. Bonnell
Robotics Laboratory: Yes

SOUTH DAKOTA

**South Dakota School
of Mines & Technology**
Mechanical Engineering Department
Rapid City, SD 57701
(605) 394-2409
Contact: Dan Dolan
Robotics Laboratory: Yes

TEXAS

Texas, University of
Mechanical Engineering Department
Austin, TX 78712
(512) 471-3059
Contact: A.E. Traver
Robotics Laboratory: Yes

UTAH

Brigham Young University
Mechanical Engineering
242 P Clyde Building
Provo, UT 84601
(801) 378-5539
Contact: W. Edward Red
Robotics Laboratory: Yes

WEST VIRGINIA

West Virginia University
Mechanical & Aerospace Engineering Departments
Morgantown, WV 26506
(304) 293-3111
Contact: John E. Sneckenbergen
Robotics Laboratory: Yes

WISCONSIN

Wisconsin—Madison, University of
Manufacturing Systems Engineering Department
1513 University Avenue
Madison, WI 53706
(608) 262-0921
Contact: M.E. DeVries
Robotics Laboratory: Yes

INSTITUTIONS OFFERING DOCTORATE DEGREE PROGRAMS

CALIFORNIA

California—Los Angeles, University of
Manufacturing Engineering Department
405 Hilgard Avenue
Los Angeles, CA 90024
(213) 206-8525
Contact: Dr. Watteau
Robotics Laboratory: Yes

COLORADO
Colorado State University
Engineering Department
Fort Collins, CO 80523
(303) 491-8655
Contact: F.W. Smith
Robotics Laboratory: Yes

FLORIDA

Florida, University of
Electrical Engineering Department
Gainesville, FL 32611
(904) 392-0814
Contact: Dr. Del Tesar
Robotics Laboratory: Yes

MARYLAND

Maryland, University of
Mechanical Engineering Department
College Park, MD 20742
(301) 454-7373
Contact: Jackson C.S. Yang
Robotics Laboratory: Yes

NORTH CAROLINA

Duke University
Electrical Engineering
Durham, NC 27706
(919) 684-3123
Contact: Paul P. Wang
Robotics Laboratory: Yes

North Carolina State University
Electrical & Computer Engineering Departments
Box 7911
Raleigh, NC 27695-7911
(919) 737-2336
Contact: W. E. Snyder
Robotics Laboratory: Yes

RHODE ISLAND

Rhode Island, University of
College of Engineering
Kingston, RI 02881
(401) 792-2186
Contact: Dean of Engineering
Robotics Laboratory: N/A

Chapter 7

Computer Employment Agencies

A *computer employment agency* or *personnel agency* can be useful in locating a new position that is better fitted to your personal needs, offers the opportunity for more growth, or offers greater financial reward than your present position.

Sometimes personnel agencies can be helpful in job-hunting when you are switching from your present career into a computer career or when you have just finished school and want to start working in a computer job. Some companies have a policy of not handling people new to the field, while others do. You should call or visit at least three or four agencies in your area to see which handle newcomers to the field. If you're unsure of which agencies to contact first, you may want to choose one or two mentioned below. Or you could call the personnel department of two or three large companies to which you are applying and ask the person who answers the phone which personnel agency the company uses most often when hiring computer personnel. You may be able to find an agency who handles individuals who are new to the field, but even if you do, it is important to do some job-hunting on your own (see Chapter 8 on "How to Get Your First Job In Computers"). If you do become interested in a job you learned about through a recruiter, be sure to ask the recruiter whether the client company will pay the agency's fee or whether you will be asked to pay the agency's fee once the company makes you an offer.

Once you are an experienced computer professional, you will begin to get calls from recruiters or "headhunters" with job openings related to your background and experience. You may at the time be interested in moving to another position, or you may want to interview for the position just to find out more about it. Once you have some experience working in a computer field, you will be in great demand. You will find that even if you are not interested in changing jobs at a certain time, the recruiter will be happy to call you back in six months to discuss new openings with you then.

If you are interested in changing jobs, get in touch with one or two personnel agencies. Start with those mentioned below. No matter which agency you work with, remember to find out up front who is expected to pay the agency fee.

Source EDP is the largest recruiting firm in the United States that devotes itself to handling computer professionals. All of its charges are paid for by its client companies. Information on its regional branches can be obtained from the central office at Source EDP, Department DT, P.O. Box 7100, Mountain View, CA 94039. The central office or a branch office can provide you with a free booklet called "Digest of Computer Opportunities" with the opportunities listed according to the region of the U.S. in which they are located.

The *National Association of Personnel Consultants* is an organization whose 1500 members are required to practice business according to the NAPC Standards of Ethical Practice, shown below.

All of its members perform most of their work on a *contingency search* basis, although many also work for client companies on a retainer basis. Occasionally, the office has a temporary placement service.

When a firm is working on a contingency basis, its service charge is paid only when a person is hired by a company as a full-time employee. Specifically, the person must be hired, begin work, and often complete a certain period of time on the job in which his or her job performance is acceptable. Sometimes the person seeking employment through the personnel agency is asked to pay a registration fee, and, depending upon the circumstances, a contingency placement firm may charge the employer, the job applicant, or both.

If you are asked by a personnel consultant to sign a contract, read it very carefully first. Usually, contracts are used only if the individual may be asked to pay part of the service charge. It is important to understand all of your obligations before you sign the contract—what is your liability, for example, if you start work at a company and then change your mind or leave the job before the stipulated amount of time? If you have questions about any specifics, discuss them with the personnel recruiter or consultant. According to the *NAPC*, more and more often the employer is paying the service charge. And, of course, contingency placement agencies are not paid a fee by either the ap-

plicant or the employer for unsuccessful job searches.

When a personnel agency works for a client company on a *retained search* basis, the applicant does not pay the service charge. The company pays the agency fee, and fee payment is not contingent on the actual hiring of an employee.

The members of the National Association of Personnel Consultants who specialize in data processing are shown below, after an explanation of the NAPC ethical standards.

NAPC STANDARDS OF ETHICAL PRACTICE[3]

Personnel consulting firms are an important part of the nation's free enterprise system. In seeking to bring qualified applicants and potential employers together, they perform a valuable service for both business and the public.

The National Association of Personnel Consultants operates for the mutual benefit of its members, employers, and the employment-seeking public.

The following areas of responsibility present general principles recognized by *association members,* who shall to the best of their ability:

Responsibility to the Community

. . . Be a contributing part of the community through participation in community activities.

. . . Serve as a reliable source of information on matters pertaining to the employment field.

Responsibility to the Applicant

. . . Strive for the right of all individuals who want the dignity of work to choose their field of endeavor and utilize their abilities and talents for personal fulfillment and the good of our country.

. . . Extend professional service to all qualified employed and unemployed applicants regardless of race, color, creed, religion, national origin, sex, age, income level, or physical handicap.

---

[3]Copyright © 1984 by the National Association of Personnel Consultants. Reprinted with permission.

Responsibility to the Employer

. . . Represent the best interest of the employer by acting as an effective extension of the employer's recruitment effort and respect every confidence entrusted by client companies.

Responsibility to the Nation

. . . Engage actively in preserving the free enterprise system as essential to a continuation of the nation's growth and strength.

. . . Cooperate in local and national efforts to maintain a high-level economy through reduction of national levels of unemployment.

To this end, the Association, through its Ethics Committee, has developed and promulgated the Standards of Ethical Practices to which all members have agreed in writing.

Relations with Applicants

☐ Applicants shall be referred to employers for interviews only on job openings for which at least verbal authority has been given by the employer.

☐ Representations made to applicants about the duties, probable length of the employment, hours, and salary of prospective positions shall be in conformance with the best knowledge of the personnel consultant.

☐ Precaution shall be taken against referring any applicant to employers who are known to engage in illegal, immoral, or questionable business practices.

☐ Information about an applicant will be used only for the purpose of finding employment for that applicant. Confidential information shall be treated accordingly.

☐ An applicant shall be aware of changes, if any, before being permitted to incur any obligations for services rendered. Any fee obligations shall be fully disclosed in a written agreement, a copy of which shall be provided to the applicant, and it shall set forth any circumstances meriting adjustment.

☐ No applicant shall be referred to any employer where a strike or lockout exists or is impending (according to the best knowledge of the personnel consultant) without being notified of such condition.

Relations with Employers

☐ An applicant's employment record, qualifications, and salary requirements shall be stated to the employer as accurately and fully as possible, or as requested.

☐ An applicant shall be referred to the employer for interview only with prior authorization of the employer, which may be given verbally.

☐ Confidential information relating to the business policy of employer, which is imparted as an aid to the effective handling of their job requirements, shall be treated accordingly.

☐ Applicants shall not be solicited for other positions while they are still in the employ of the employer with whom they have been placed by the personnel consulting firm in question, unless the applicant initiates reactivation of his/her application.

☐ Direct mail, bulletins, and resumes of applicants that are presented to employers shall represent bonafide candidates.

Relations Between Personnel Consulting Firms

☐ An applicant or employer who has a complaint about another consulting firm should be directed to file the complaint with the Chairperson of the Ethics Committee in his/her state or in care of NAPC headquarters of Washington. The firm receiving the complaint should not become involved.

☐ The Association provides adequate means for assuring adherence by members to its standards of ethics. To further the effectiveness of these procedures, each member shall be responsible for bringing to the attention of the Association's Ethics Committee (or local counterpart) any violations of these standards. The Ethics Committee shall process any such complaint in accordance with its usual procedure, and, where the facts warrant it, the Ethics Committee shall bring the matter to the attention of the appropriate government authority for its action.

☐ A member shall not, in the course of advertising, public relations efforts, or any other activity, permit the demeaning or criticizing in any manner whatsoever of any other personnel consulting firm.

Advertising

☐ Positions listed in newspapers or other media shall be factual and refer to bonafide openings available at the time that copy is given to these publications.

☐ All advertising promotion or announcements regarding certification must conform to the standards and format of the NAPC Certification Program.

Service Charge

☐ No applicant shall be obligated for a contingency service charge until an offer and acceptance has been made between employer and applicant.

☐ Adjustments and refunds of service charges shall be made promptly, in accordance with the highest ethical standards.

General

The member shall cooperate with, and permit at any time, complete and thorough investigation of an alleged violation of ethics or standards that tends to reflect on the business practices of the individual service and the Association, by the elected officers of duly appointed committee of the National Association of Personnel Consultants and shall abide by decisions of the investigative committee.

Note: These standards of ethical practices are in no way to supersede or replace the requirements of local ordinances or state and Federal laws.

INQUIRIES RELATING TO ETHICAL CONDUCT

Members of the National Association of Personnel Consultants must subscribe to the Code of Ethics and Standards of Ethical Practices. Local, state, and national Ethics Committees ensure compliance with these standards. Guidelines for these committees establish a three-step program of education, persuasion, and enforcement in handling complaints brought by client employers, the public, and member and nonmember placement services. An NAPC Ethics Committee has no enforcement powers over the nonmember office, but the tools of education and persuasion are frequently effective in resolving complaints against nonmembers.

Inquiries or complaints relating to the ethical conduct of private personnel placement services may be directed to: Chairperson, NAPC Ethics Committee, National Association of Personnel Consultants, 1432 Duke Street, Alexandria, VA 22314, (703) 684-0180.

NAPC MEMBERS SPECIALIZING IN DATA PROCESSING[4]

ALABAMA

Cruit Executive Search
P.O. Box 59353
Birmingham, AL 35259
(205) 870-8170

Diversified Pers. Consultants
P.O. Box 19003
Birmingham, AL 35219
(205) 942-1115

Gary W. Little and Associates
One Riverchase Office Plaza
Suite 106
Birmingham, AL 35244
(205) 987-7989

Placement Experts
944 Central Bank Building
Huntsville, AL 35801
(205) 539-2467

Snelling & Snelling
1813 University Drive
Huntsville, AL 35801
(205) 533-1410

Clark Personnel Service
578 Azalea Road #108
Mobile, AL 36609
(205) 666-6892

Longs Personnel Services
P.O. Box 16704
Mobile, AL 36616
(205) 476-4080

Dunhill of Montgomery
500 East Boulevard, Suite 301
Montgomery, AL 36117
(205) 279-0494

ARIZONA

Far Western Placement Svc.
4744 North Central
Phoenix, AZ 85012
(602) 264-1025

General Employment Enterprises
3443 North Central Avenue #1104
Phoenix, AZ 85012
(602) 265-7800

Great Southwestern Pers. Co.
2747 East Camelback Road
Biltmore Fountains, #215
Phoenix, AZ 85016
(602) 242-3792

Staff One
7505 East Main Street, #600
Scottsdale, AZ 85251
(602) 941-1764

A. R. Hutton Agency
350 West 16th Street, #408
Yuma, AZ 85364
(602) 782-2549

ARKANSAS

Dunhill Personnel - Little Rock
2024 Arkansas Valley Drive, #704
Little Rock, AR 72212
(501) 225-8080

CALIFORNIA

Gary D. Nelson Associates
10050 North Wolfe Road
Suite 275
Cupertino, CA 95014
(408) 255-7400

General Employment Enterprises
39175 Liberty Street, #229
Fremont, CA 94538
(415) 797-5680

General Employment Enterprises
2130 Main Street, #150
Huntington Beach, CA 92648
(714) 960-2431

Input Search Agency
23161 Lake Center Drive, #203
Lake Forest, CA 92630
(714) 855-4999

Business & Professional Agency
3255 Wilshire Boulevard, 17th Floor
Los Angeles, CA 90010
(213) 380-8200

General Employment Enterprises
3699 Wilshire Boulevard, #850
Los Angeles, CA 90010
(213) 386-4630

Input Search Agency
5757 Wilshire Boulevard, #493
Los Angeles, CA 90036
(213) 938-9137

Robert Half Personnel-L.A.
3600 Wilshire Boulevard
Los Angeles, CA 90010
(213) 386-6805

XXCAL
2001 South Barrington Avenue, #114
Los Angeles, CA 90025
(213) 477-2902

JPM & Associates
4621 Teller Avenue, Suite 110
Newport Beach, CA 92660
(714) 553-0311

Midcom Agency
1940 North Tustin, #117
Orange, CA 92665
(714) 998-6041

General Employment Enterprises
2471 East Bayshore Road, #510
Palo Alto, CA 94303
(415) 494-3441

JPM & Associates, DBA
Sales Consultants-Mgt. Recr.
635 Camino De Los Mares, #210
San Clemente, CA 92672
(714) 496-2000

Allied Search
2001 Union Street, #300
San Francisco, CA 94123
(415) 921-1971

Gary D. Nelson Associates
311 California Street
San Francisco, CA 94104
(415) 398-3232

General Employment Enterprises
One Market Plaza, #2015
San Francisco, CA 94105
(415) 896-0511

Robert Half of No. Calif.
111 Pine Street
San Francisco, CA 94111
(415) 434-1900

General Employment Enterprises
1550 The Alameda, #320
San Jose, CA 95126
(408) 288-8700

Abraham & London Ltd.
Personnel Franchise System
13440 Ventura Boulevard, #205
Sherman Oaks, CA 91423
(800) 227-3800

General Employment Enterprises
5930 Vareil, Suite 1
Woodland Hills, CA 91367
(818) 703-6908

COLORADO

John Heckers & Associates
8795 Ralston Road
Aruada, CO 80002
(303) 422-8072

Kenex Consultants
3025 South Parker Road, Penthouse S
Aurora, CO 80014
(303) 696-8490

Scully & Associates
6285 Lehman Drive, Suite D-202
Colorado Springs, CO 80918
(303) 594-0106

Phillips Personnel Service
1675 Broadway, #2280
Denver, CO 80202
(303) 893-1850

Riley Recruiting Enterprises
1410 High Street, Suite 300
Denver, CO 80218
(302) 388-1467

Rocky Mountain Recruiters
1430 Larimer Square, #201
Denver, CO 80202
(303) 628-9400

Margaret Hook's Personnel
5650 South Syracuse Circle
Englewood, CO 80111
(303) 770-2100

CONNECTICUT

Professional Employment Registry
2 Stony Hill Road
Bethel, CT 06801
(203) 743-3050

Vannah / Rowe, Inc.
11 Mountain Avenue
P.O. Box 514
Bloomfield, CT 06002
(203) 243-0424

Bailey Employment Service
5 South Main Street
Branford, CT 06405
(203) 488-2504

AAA Personnel Associates
14 Hayestown Avenue
Danbury, CT 06810
(203) 744-1820

Employment Opportunities
213 Main Street
Danbury, CT 06810
(203) 792-9536

Executive Register
34 Mill Plain Road
Danbury, CT 06810
(203) 743-5542

Nemeth Associates
57 North Street
Danbury, CT 06810
(203) 797-0414

KGC Associates
100 Connecticut Boulevard
East Hartford, CT 06108
(203) 528-1728

Amity Consultants
2505 Black Rock Turnpike
Fairfield, CT 06430
(203) 372-4316

Corporate Resource Group
457 Castle Avenue
Fairfield, CT 06430
(203) 787-5791

Business Personnel Associates
61 A Wells Street
P.O. Box 923
Glastonbury, CT 06033
(203) 659-3511

Power Industry Personnel
1064 Poq Road
Groton, CT 06340
(203) 446-9930

Gilbert Lane Personnel
1952 Whitney Avenue
Hamden, CT 06517
(203) 281-3984

Management Recruiters-Hamden
2911 Dixwell Avenue
Hamden, CT 06518
(203) 248-0770

Arthur J. Langdon
750 Main Street
P.O. Box 31496
Hartford, CT 06103
(203) 724-3441

Availability of Hartford
179 Allyn Street
Hartford, CT 06103
(203) 247-5566

Corporate Resource Group
60 Washington Street
Hartford, CT 06106
(203) 547-0900

Hallmark Personnel
242 Trumbull Street
Suite 210
Hartford, CT 06103
(203) 527-5779

Human Resource Consultants Ltd.
15 Lewis Street Suite 503
Hartford, CT 06103
(203) 522-0400

Kinkead Associates
One Financial Plaza
Hartford, CT 06103
(203) 246-1901

Options Unlimited
18 Asylum Street Suite 208
Hartford, CT 06103
(203) 278-7872

Positions, Inc.
60 Washington Street
Hartford, CT 06106
(203) 547-0010

RJS Associates
241 Asylum Street
Hartford, CT 06103
(203) 278-5840

UNI / Search of Hartford
15 Lewis Street
Hartford, CT 06103
(203) 278-8040

A.R. Mazzotta Associates
50 Riverview Center
Middletown, CT 06457
(203) 347-7626

Auden Associates
505 Main Street
P.O. Box 1077
Middletown, CT 06457
(203) 344-9847

Diversified Employment Service
531 Whalley Avenue
New Haven, CT 06511
(203) 397-2500

Spectra Professional Search
419 Whalley Avenue
New Haven, CT 06511
(203) 288-2803

Executive Management Associates
50 Glover Avenue
Norwalk, CT 06850
(203) 846-7790

Conlon Associates
833 Summer Street
Stamford, CT 06901
(203) 359-0860

Data Management Resources
100 Prospect Street
Stamford, CT 06901
(203) 324-4358

Fortune Personnel Consultants
400 Main Street
Stamford, CT 06901
(203) 324-1313

Herz, Stewart & Company
1200 Summer Street
Stamford, CT 06905
(203) 324-5400

Hipp Waters Professional Recr.
707 Summer Street
Stamford, CT 06901
(203) 357-8400

Fairfield Whitney
88 Ryders Lane Suite 213
Stratford, CT 06497
(214) 377-8900

Quinn Associates, Ltd.
33 King Street
Stratford, CT 06497
(203) 386-1300

Bailey Employment Service
115 Main Street
Torrington, CT 06790
(203) 489-0494

Jaci Carroll Personnel Services
37 Leavenworth Street
P.O. Box 1525
Waterbury, CT 06721
(203) 574-4838

Professional Computer Personnel
111 West Main Street
Waterbury, CT 06702
(203) 575-1651

Executive Recruiters
630 Oakwood Avenue
West Hartford, CT 06110
(203) 521-7400

Executive Services
10 North Main Street, #212
West Hartford, CT 06107
(203) 236-1971

Hire Counseling & Personnel Svc.
115-H Hillcrest Avenue
West Hartford, CT 06110
(203) 522-0307

Richard Clark Associates
45 South Main Street
West Hartford, CT 06107
(203) 236-6886

Career Decisions Employment
393 Meloy Road
West Haven, CT 06516
(203) 932-1600

Nicastro Associates
246 Post Road East
Westport, CT 06880
(203) 226-6945

Dunhill of Greater Stamford
213 Danbury Road
Wilton, CT 06897
(203) 762-7722

DELAWARE

Ellie Mack Associates
3411 Silverside Road
S107 Weldin Building, Concord Plaza
Wilmington, DE 19810
(302) 478-6955

Placers, The
2000 Pennsylvania Avenue, #201
Wilmington, DE 19806
(302) 575-1414

Robert Half of Wilmington
Brandywood Plaza
Foulk and Grubb Roads
Wilmington, DE 19810
(302) 475-4500

DISTRICT OF COLUMBIA

Management Recruiters
2020 K Street, Northwest, Suite 350
Washington, DC 20006
(202) 466-5300

FLORIDA

Benson and Associates
Pers. & Management Cons.
800 West Cypress Creek Road, #208
Fort Lauderdale, FL 33309
(305) 491-5004

Retail Recruiters
Spectra Professional Search
2550 West Oakland Park Boulevard #109
Fort Lauderdale, FL 33311
(305) 731-2300

Snelling & Snelling
3500 North State Road 7
Suite 300
Fort Lauderdale, FL 33319
(305) 485-5700

Keegan & Keegan
24 West Hollywood Boulevard Suite 2
Fort Walton Beach, FL 32548
(904) 244-7694

Personnel Center
919 Northwest 13th Street
P.O. Box 1111
Gainesville, FL 32602
(904) 372-6377

BMR Associates
2500 Hollywood Boulevard, #310
Hollywood, FL 33020
(305) 921-4585

Advantage Personnel Agencies
7861 Bird Road
Miami, FL 33155
(305) 264-7060

Circare
6660 Biscayne Boulevard #101
Miami, FL 33138
(305) 757-6655

Corporate Advisors
250 Northeast 27th Street
Miami, FL 33137
(305) 573-7753

Hastings and Hastings
1201 Brickell Avenue
Miami, FL 33131
(305) 374-2255

Markett Personnel
P.O. Box 162-211
Miami, FL 33116
(305) 386-0005

Career Associates
640 Northeast 124 Street
North Miami, FL 33161
(305) 893-0810

ACI
3101 Maguire Boulevard, #200
Orlando, FL 32803
(305) 894-6551

Action Personnel
P.O. Box 20904
Orlando, FL 32814
(305) 896-4591

General Employment Enterprises
600 Courtland Street, #430
Orlando, FL 32804
(305) 629-9222

United Consulting Services
Suite 218, 5151 Adanson Street
Orlando, FL 32804
(305) 629-0075

Keegan & Keegan
5514 North Davis Highway, #102
Pensacola, FL 32503
(904) 474-0990

Landrum Personnel Associates
1207 West Garden Street
P.O. Box 1373
Pensacola, FL 32501
(904) 434-2321

Snelling and Snelling
428 Plaza Building
Pensacola, FL 32505
(904) 434-1311

R.L. Brown & Associates
1620 South Federal Highway, #800
Pompano Beach, FL 33062
(305) 946-4682

Personnel Inc.
1020 East Lafayette Street
Suite 108 C
Tallahassee, FL 32301
(904) 877-7055

Frank Leonard Personnel
1211 North Westshore Boulevard
Suite 100
Tampa, FL 33607
(813) 872-1853

Professional Pers. Cons.-Tampa
1211 North Westshore Boulevard
Suite 314
Tampa, FL 33607
(813) 877-7008

David Wood Personnel
1897 Palm Beach Lakes Boulevard
West Palm Beach, FL 33409
(305) 686-4571

Dalindy Personnel Consultants
2443 Lee Road
Winter Park, FL 32789
(305) 628-4065

GEORGIA

Albany Personnel Service
235 Roosevelt Boulevard
Suite 216 Albany Towers
Albany, GA 31701
(912) 439-2231

B.A.I. Limited
3475 Lenox Road, Northeast
Suite 490 Live Oak Center
Atlanta, GA 30303
(404) 231-4545

Bell Oaks Company
3390 Peachtree Road, #924
Atlanta, GA 30326
(404) 261-2170

Computer Network Resources
1835 Savoy Drive, #315
Atlanta, GA 30341
(404) 451-6100

EDP Research
4300 Paran Walk Northwest
Atlanta, GA 30327
(703) 821-2188

General Employment Enterprises
225 Peachtree Street, #414
Atlanta, GA 30303
(404) 681-3810

Management Search
1550 Harris Tower
233 Peachtree Street, Northeast
Atlanta, GA 30303
(404) 659-5050

Niermann Personnel Service
3390 Peachtree Road, Suite 110
Atlanta, GA 30326
(404) 262-2760

Noble & Anglin
3088 Mercer University Drive, #200
Atlanta, GA 30341
(404) 451-0030

Robert Half of Atlanta
3379 Peachtree Road Northeast, #810
Atlanta, GA 30326
(404) 266-2153

Went Mackenzie
4920 Winters Chapel Road (L-2)
Atlanta, GA 30360
(404) 396-1292

Whitlow and Associates
3390 Peachtree Road, Northeast
Suite 236
Atlanta, GA 30326
(404) 262-2566

Personnel Concepts
National Bank & Trust Building
1246 First Avenue
Columbus, GA 31902
(404) 324-1837

Mutual Personnel Service
415 First National Bank Building
Macon, GA 31201
(912) 743-3757

Niermann Personnel Services
1331 Citizens Parkway, #105
Morrow, GA 30260
(404) 996-6170

ILLINOIS

EJ Ashton & Associates, Ltd.
3223 North Frontage Road, #2313
Arlington Heights, IL 60004
(312) 577-7900

General Employment Enterprises
85 West Algonquin Road, #130
Arlington Heights, IL 60005
(312) 364-9450

Banner Personnel Service
7 West Madison, #1100
Chicago, IL 60602
(312) 641-6456

General Employment Enterprises
150 South Wacker Drive, #600
Chicago, IL 60606
(312) 346-7001

General Employment Enterprises
150 South Wacker Drive, #512
Chicago, IL 60606
(312) 782-1024

Protech Group, The
2 North Riverside Plaza, #2400
Chicago, IL 60606
(312) 559-1990

Wills and Company
333 North Michigan Avenue, #812
Chicago, IL 60601
(312) 236-5356

Warren & Associates
P.O. Box 173
Geneseo, IL 61254
(309) 441-5700

Career Link
1926 Waukegan
Glenview, IL 60025
(312) 562-5465

Prestige Personnel
2066 Ridge Road
Homewood, IL 60430
(312) 798-9010

Systems Network Assistance
523 'A' North Milwaukee Avenue
Libertyville, IL 60048
(312) 367-1286

General Employment Enterprises
350 West Shuman Boulevard
Naperville, IL 60540
(312) 357-8005

Professional Executive Cons.
3000 Dundee, Suite 418
Northbrook, IL 60062
(312) 564-3900

Murphy Employment Service
1301 West 22nd Street
Suite 911A
Oak Brook, IL 60521
(312) 655-2011

Johnson Personnel Co.
110 South Alpine Road
Rockford, IL 61108
(815) 229-0840

Ned E. Dickey and Associates
P.O. Box 1598
Rockford, IL 61110
(815) 968-1883

Cari
1501 Woodfield Road, #108 South
Schaumburg, IL 60105
(312) 490-7140

Career Sources Plus
201 Route 45, Suite A
Vernon Hills, IL 60061
(312) 367-9252

INDIANA

Hart Line, The
P.O. Box 2687
Bloomington, IN 47402
(812) 336-7600

Careers Unlimited
1238 South Main
Elkhart, IN 46516
(219) 293-0659

Career Consultants
107 North Pennsylvania
Indianapolis, IN 46204
(317) 639-5601

General Employment Enterprises
Circle Tower, 5 East Market, #32
Indianapolis, IN 46204
(317) 636-2261

Kordick & Associates
5610 Crawfordsville Road, #906
Indianapolis, IN 46224
(317) 244-1500

L. Deane Shepard
3737 North Meridian Street
Indianapolis, IN 46208
(317) 924-1216

Resource Group, The
6100 North Keystone Suite 651
Indianapolis, IN 46220
(317) 259-0107

Chevigny Personnel Agency
100 West 79th Avenue
Merrillville, IN 46410
(219) 769-4880

Roberts Placement Service
423 West McKinley
P.O. Box 531
Mishawaka, IN 46544
(219) 255-3139

Miriam Black Personnel Service
310 Merchants National Bank Building
P.O. Box 35
Terre Haute, IN 47808
(812) 232-1394

IOWA

Mgmt. Recruiters Quad Cities
Alpine Center North, #45
Suite 45
Bettendorf, IO 52722
(319) 359-3503

Dunhill of Cedar Rapids
119 3rd Street Northeast
121 Professional Park
Cedar Rapids, IO 52401
(319) 366-8273

Midtown Personnel Ltd.
P.O. Box 1547
Council Bluffs, IO 51502
(712) 328-3153

Executive Resources Ltd.
4515 Fleur Drive
Des Moines, IO 50321
(515) 287-6880

Key Employment Services
1001 Office Park Road
Suite 320
West Des Moines, IO 50265
(515) 224-0446

City & National Employment
504 Jefferson - P.O. Box 83
Waterloo, IO 50704
(319) 232-6641

KENTUCKY

General Employment Enterprises
Executive Park Suite 616
Louisville, KY 40207
(502) 897-5347

J C Malone Associates
1941 Bishop Lane
Suite 100
Louisville, KY 40218
(502) 456-2380

LOUISIANA

Professional Personnel Services
5629 Government Street
P.O. Box 66592
Baton Rouge, LA 70896
(504) 926-7350

National Employment Services
P.O. Box 53544
Lafayette, LA 70505
(318) 269-0112

Search Personnel
116 Fountain Bend Drive
P.O. Box 31808
Lafayette, LA 70503
(318) 988-4400

Edna Loposer Personnel Service
3929 Veterans Boulevard
Suite 200
Metairie, LA 70002
(504) 454-0333

Executive Locators of America
P.O. Box 1337
3124 49th Street
Metairie, LA 70004
(504) 838-8262

Professional Staffing
3500 North Causeway Boulevard
P.O. Box 8775
Metairie, LA 70011
(504) 837-8722

Corporate Consultants
806 Perdido, Suite 205
New Orleans, LA 70112
(504) 523-5442

Creative Career Corporation
200 Carondelet Street, #100
American Bank Building
New Orleans, LA 70130
(504) 522-7180

MAINE

Bartlett Agency, The
P.O. Box 1666
1115 Lisbon Street
Lewiston, ME 04240
(207) 786-0134

Kuebler Associates
Two Monument Square
Executive Office Center
Portland, ME 04101
(207) 774-9100

Romac & Associates
Three Canal Plaza
P.O. Box 7469 DTS
Portland, ME 04112
(207) 773-6387

MARYLAND

Futures Personnel Services
601 Oxford Building
8600 LaSalle Road
Baltimore, MD 21204
(301) 321-1984

Gabriel & Bowie Associates, Ltd.
Route 175 and Gambrills Road
P.O. Box 21160
Baltimore, MD 21228
(301) 987-6670

R.M. Hiebel Associates
101 West Read Street, #611
Baltimore, MD 21201
(301) 234-0800

Don Richard Associates
7315 Wisconsin Avenue #303 East
Bethesda, MD 20814
(301) 652-1182

Clark, Clark & Clark Associates
7338 Baltimore Boulevard
College Park, MD 20740
(301) 864-1117

Tellis & Dean Associates
5410 Indian Head Highway
Oxon Hill, MD 20745
(301) 839-5200

A.G. Fishkin & Associates
6121 Executive Boulevard
Rockville, MD 20852
(301) 770-4944

Perry Newton Associates
932 Hungerford Drive, #23
P.O. Box 1158
Rockville, MD 20850
(301) 340-3360

Target Search
932 Hungerford Drive Suite 7B
Rockville, MD 20850
(301) 340-7009

Tech Search
11428 Rockville Pike
Rockville, MD 20852
(301) 984-6282

Wallach Associates
6101 Executive Boulevard, #380
P.O. Box 6016
Rockville, MD 20850
(301) 231-9000

M.D. Mattes & Associates
P.O. Box 291
30 East Padonia Road, #203
Timonium, MD 21093
(301) 252-8071

MASSACHUSETTS

T.J. Hayes Associates
Two Geneva Avenue
Assonet, MA 02702
(617) 644-2350

Professional Recruiters
23 Midstate Drive
Auburn, MA 01501
(617) 832-5757

Barclay Personnel Systems
200 Clarendon Street
Boston, MA 02116
(617) 247-6800

CIS Personnel Services
711 Boylston Street
Boston, MA 02116
(617) 266-1000

General Employment Enterprises
545 Boylston Street, #501
Boston, MA 02116
(617) 267-9119

Hipp Waters Professional Recruit
50 Milk Street
Boston, MA 02109
(617) 267-8300

Positions, Inc.
One McKinley Square
Boston, MA 02109
(617) 367-9212

Robert Half Of Boston
100 Summer Street
Suite 2905
Boston, MA 02110
(617) 423-1200

Emerson Professionals
12 New England Executive Park
Burlington, MA 01803
(617) 861-0808

Retail Recruiters-Massachusetts
850 Providence Highway
Dedham, MA 02026
(617) 329-5850

The Software Alliance
Office at Mill Falls
385 Elliot Street
Newton, MA 02164
(617) 965-2808

BFH Associates
P.O. Box 358
Sharon, MA 02067
(617) 668-0960

Gilbert Lane Personnel Service
1500 Main Street
Springfield, MA 01115
(413) 733-2133

Nationwide Business Service
145 State Street
Springfield, MA 01103
(413) 732-4104

New Dimensions
Exec Search / Technical Plcmnts.
67 Pleasant Street
Swampscott, MA 01907
(617) 592-6420

Management Search
1111 Elm Street
West Springfield, MA 01089
(413) 732-2384

Positions, Inc.
117 Park Avenue
West Springfield, MA 01089
(413) 781-3412

Executive Selection
303 Wyman Street, Suite 300
Waltham, MA 02154
(617) 890-0402

Management Resource Associates
7 Wheeling Avenue
Woburn, MA 01801
(617) 933-1600

Lane Employment Service
370 Main Street Suite 820
Worcester, MA 01608
(617) 757-5678

New England Search
390 Main Street, #657-659
Worcester, MA 01608
(617) 792-0330

Positions, Inc.
446 Main Street
Worcester, MA 01608
(617) 765-8800

SCI
390 Main Street, #620
Worcester, MA 01608
(617) 754-8499

Sweidel & Associates
446 Main Street, 15th Floor
Worcester, MA 01608
(617) 755-3424

MICHIGAN

P.P.L.
842 East Columbia
P.O. Box 1127
Battle Creek, MI 49016
(616) 968-9391

Snelling and Snelling-Birmingham
30100 Telegraph, #474
Birmingham, MI 48010
(313) 644-4600

General Employment Enterprises
1200 South Street, #1120
Detroit, MI 48226
(313) 963-8470

Professional Personnel Cons.
18189 West 10 Mile Road
Southfield, MI 48075
(313) 357-4810

Dunhill of Troy
755 West Big Beaver Road, #423
Troy, MI 48084
(313) 362-3115

Littman Associates
2525 Crooks Road
Troy, MI 48084
(313) 649-1150

MINNESOTA

Roth Young Pers. of Minneapolis
4530 West 77th Street
Suit 250
Edina, MN 55435
(612) 831-6655

Rainbow Personnel
5730 Duluth Street
Golden Valley, MN 55422
(612) 757-7252

Accounting Personnel-Minnesota
5354 Cedar Lake Road,
#104
Minneapolis, MN 55416
(612) 544-1005

Andcor Companies
600 South County Road 18, #575
Minneapolis, MN 55426
(612) 546-0966

Computer People
5353 Wayzata Boulevard, #604
Park National Bank Building
Minneapolis, MN 55416
(612) 542-8520

Electronics Systems Pers. Agency
121 South 8th Street
858 TCF Tower
Minneapolis, MN 55402
(612) 338-6714

Employment Specialists
7200 France Avenue, South
Minneapolis, MN 55435
(612) 831-6444

MISSISSIPPI

Allied Personnel of Gulfport
Hardy Court Office Plaza
100 Courthouse Road #126
Gulfport, MS 39501
(601) 896-8131

Dunhill of Greater Jackson
Suite 'F'
5285 Galaxie
Jackson, MS 39206
(601) 981-3151

Resource Staffing Group
633 North State Street, #402
Jackson, MS 39201
(601) 354-4475

M.D. Treadway & Company
9369 Goodman Road
Olive Branch, MS 38654
(601) 895-4106

MISSOURI

Professional Career Development
7777 Bonhomme, #1326
Clayton, MO 63105
(314) 727-7670

Associated Ventures
1534 Saint Ives
Dellwood, MO 63136
(314) 867-7357

Executive Placement Consultants
12900 New Halls Ferry Road
Florissant, MO 63033
(314) 831-1996

Career Consultants
8550 Holmes, Suite 120
Kansas City, MO 64131
(816) 444-9600

General Employment Enterprises
1100 Main Street #1010
Kansas City, MO 64105
(816) 421-0011

Professional Career Development
1125 Grand Avenue
Suite 1500
Kansas City, MO 64106
(816) 471-4206

Sales Recruiters of Kansas City
1125 Grand Avenue Suite 2002
Kansas City, MO 64106
(816) 471-1010

Davis Company
408 Olive Street, #333
St. Louis, MO 63102
(314) 241-7100

Executive Career Consultants
111 North Taylor Avenue
St. Louis, MO 63122
(314) 965-3939

Executive Resource
1010 Collingwood Drive
St. Louis, MO 63132
(314) 993-3232

General Employment Enterprises
720 Olive Street, #602
St. Louis, MO 63101
(314) 231-740

HDB Incorporated
300 Ozark Trail Drive, #101
St. Louis, MO 63011
(314) 391-7799

L.P. Banning
610 Locust, Suite 1825
St. Louis, MO 63101
(314) 231-2474

SJ. Associates
5865 Hampton Avenue, Suite B
St. Louis, MO 63109
(314) 481-2715

NEBRASKA

Eggers Personnel & Consulting
Eggers Plaza
11272 Elm Street
Omaha, NE 68144
(402) 333-3480

Personnel Search
1126 South 72nd Street
Omaha, NE 68124
(402) 397-2980

Staff America
Suite 900 Commercial Federal
2120 South 72nd Street
Omaha, NE 68124
(402) 391-2065

NEW HAMPSHIRE

Craig's Criterion
P.O. Box 700
Contoocook, NH 03229
(603) 669-8810

Fortune Personnel Consultants
505 West Hollis Street, #208
Nashua, NH 03062
(603) 880-4900

Preferred Positions
157 Main Dunstable Road
Nashua, NH 03060
(603) 889-0112

NEW JERSEY

American Placement Services
1999 East Marlton Pike
Cherry Hill, NJ 08003
(609) 424-6542

National Contact Network
3100 West Chapel Avenue
Cherry Hill, NJ 08002
(609) 667-4080

RSVP Services
Suite 700
One Cherry Hill Mall
Cherry Hill, NJ 08002
(609) 667-4488

Careers First
305 U. S. Route 130
Cinnaminson, NJ 08077
(609) 786-0004

Applied Personnel
760 Route 18
East Brunswick, NJ 08816
(201) 238-2500

Brandon Associates
2175 Lemoine Avenue
Fort Lee, NJ 07024
(201) 461-5544

H. Neuman Associates
2500 Brunswick Avenue
Lawrenceville, NJ 08648
(609) 883-3700

Steeple Associates
25 Notch Road
Little Falls, NJ 07424
(201) 256-2444

Systems Search II
90 Milburn Avenue
Millburn, NJ 07041
(201) 761-4400

Associates Personnel Service
20 Church Street, Suite 10
Montclair, NJ 07042
(201) 783-5700

Paul James Associates
25 Airport Road
Morristown, NJ 07960
(201) 540-8900

Scientific Search
Plaza Office Center, Suite 200
Route 73 and Fellowship Road
Mt. Laurel, NJ 08054
(609) 866-0200

Normann Personnel Consultants
625 From Road
Paramus, NJ 07652
(201) 261-1576

Personnel Associates, Inc.
225 Old New Brunswick Road
Piscataway, NJ 08854
(201) 981-1466

Professional Plcmt.-Princeton
1150 Hillside Avenue
Plainfield, NJ 07060
(201) 753-1800

Bette I. Kantor Personnel
318 Wall Street Building J
Princeton, NJ 08540
(609) 921-8907

Career Path
1156 East Ridgewood Avenue
Ridgewood, NJ 07450
(201) 652-2500

Personnel Service
1172 East Ridgewood Avenue
Ridgewood, NJ 07450
(201) 444-6643

Gerotoga - A-1 In Personnel
219 Park Avenue
Scotch Plains, NJ 07076
(201) 322-8300

Lancaster Associates
94 Grove Street
Somerville, NJ 08876
(201) 526-5440

Newcrest
21 Hillcrest Road
West Caldwell, NJ 07006
(201) 226-2022

Purcell Employment Systems
900 Route 9
Woodbridge, NJ 07095
(201) 636-5100

NEW MEXICO

Dunhill of Albuquerque
1717 Louisiana, Northeast #218
Albuquerque, NM 87110
(505) 262-1871

Hallmark Personnel Consultants
4213 Montgomery Boulevard Northeast
Albuquerque, NM 87109
(505) 884-7101

New Mexico Employment Bureau
8500 Menaul Northeast #B-195
Albuquerque, NM 87112
(505) 265-6655

Snelling and Snelling
2601 Wyoming Northeast
Albuquerque, NM 87112
(505) 293-7800

NEW YORK

Anton Wood Associates
1692 Central Avenue
Albany, NY 12205
(518) 869-8477

London Scott Associates
1741 Route 9
P.O. Box 209
Clifton Park, NY 12065
(518) 383-2302

Career Placements
1975 Hempstead Turnpike
East Meadow, NY 11554
(516) 794-4850

Mar-El Employment Agency
2233 Broadhollow Road
Farmingdale, NY 11735
(516) 454-8100

Case Personnel Systems
550 Old Country Road
Hicksville, NY 11801
(516) 433-2133

Huntington Personnel Consultants
234 Main Street
Huntington, NY 11743
(516) 549-8888

Woodbury Personnel
375 North Broadway
Jericho, NY 11753
(516) 938-7910

Hank Ward Associates Ltd.
8 Stanley Circle, Guptill Park
Latham, NY 12110
(518) 783-5145

Mar-El Employment Agency
3000 Hempstead Turnpike
Levittown, NY 11756
(516) 579-7777

Trimbec
425 Electronics Parkway
Drawer 40
Liverpool, NY 13088
(315) 451-4220

Dunhill of Huntington
535 Broadhollow Road
Melville, NY 11747
(516) 293-0055

Global Search
One Huntington Quadrangle
Melville, NY 11747
(516) 293-3555

Snelling & Snelling
900 Walt Whitman Road
Melville, NY 11747
(516) 549-1313

Better Careers
213 Main Street
Mt. Kisco, NY 10549
(914) 666-2468

Botal Associates
7 Dey Street
New York, NY 10007
(212) 227-7370

Com-Tek Agency
295 Madison Avenue, #725
New York, NY 10017
(212) 682-8282

Cor Management SVCS. Ltd.
420 Lexington Avenue
New York, NY 10170
(212) 599-2640

Don Allan Associates
521 Fifth Avenue
New York, NY 10017
(212) 697-9775

E.J. Rhodes Personnel Consultants
580 Fifth Avenue
New York, NY 10036
(212) 575-5990

Kanon Personnel
8 West 40th Street
New York, NY 10018
(212) 391-2610

Leslie Kavanagh Associates
505 Fifth Avenue, #1300
New York, NY 10017
(212) 661-0670

Omni Recruiting
275 Madison Avenue
New York, NY 10016
(212) 683-7800

Preston Associates
11 East 44th Street
Suite 505
New York, NY 10017
(212) 661-1950

Robert Half of New York
522 Fifth Avenue, 19th Floor
New York, NY 10036
(212) 221-6500

Stead-Fast Permanent Agency
Stead-Fast Temporaries
160 Broadway
New York, NY 10038
(212) 374-1292

Tact Employment Agency
80 Wall Street
New York, NY 10005
(212) 668-0022

Ethan Allen Personnel Agency
59 Academy Street
Poughkeepsie, NY 12601
(914) 471-9700

Executive Placement Corporation
949-51 Sibley Tower Building
Rochester, NY 14604
(716) 454-1424

College & Professional Plcmt.
600 East Genesee Street
Syracuse, NY 13202
(315) 475-6179

Dapexs Consultants
One Park Place
Syracuse, NY 13202
(315) 474-2477

Personnel Associates
731 James Street, #206
Syracuse, NY 13203
(315) 422-0070

NORTH CAROLINA

Personnel Placement
537 D Huffman Mill Road
Burlington, NC 27215
(919) 584-5591

Keyop Corp
P.O. Box 3032
Chapel Hill, NC 27515
(919) 967-7522

Corporate Personnel Consultants
3705 Latrobe Drive, #310-320
Calcutta Office Condominums
Charlotte, NC 28211
(704)-366-1800

Dunhill of Charlotte
6401 Carmel Road
Charlotte, NC 28211
(704) 554-8771

Executive Search
P.O. Box 220689
Charlotte, NC 28222
(704) 364-8315

Positions, Inc.
4601 Park Road - IBM Building, #640
Charlotte, NC 28209
(704) 527-5310

SHS International-Charlotte
Schneider Hill & Spangler
310 Northwestern Bank Building
Charlotte, NC 28202
(704) 377-3414

VIP Personnel
3101 Guess Road, Suite C
Durham, NC 27705
(919) 471-6404

National Career Centers - USA
P.O. Box 447
1830 Owen Drive, Suite L
Fayetteville, NC 28302
(919) 483-0413

Dunhill of Gastonia
260 West Main Avenue
P.O. Box 87
Gastonia, NC 28053
(704) 861-1516

Dunhill of Greensboro
P.O. Box 9189
Greensboro, NC 27408
(919) 282-2400

Graham & Associates Empl. Cons.
2100-M West Cornwallis Drive
Greensboro, NC 27408
(919) 288-9330

Kosier Careers
3717A West Market Street
Greensboro, NC 27403
(919) 855-7600

Regency Personnel Consultants
Regency Building
823 North Elm Street
Greensboro, NC 27401
(919) 373-1991

Sto Fox Personnel Consultants
1834 Banking Street
P.O. Box 29269
Greensboro, NC 27429
(919) 378-9894

W.R. Atchison & Associates
612 Pasteur Drive Suite 301
Greensboro, NC 27403
(919) 855-5943

Dunhill of Greenville
223 West 10th Street, Suite 101
Greenville, NC 27834
(919) 758-2107

Dunhill of Hickory, N.C.
42 3rd Street, Northwest
Suite 1
Hickory, NC 28601
(704) 322-7420

Professional Recruiters
3948 Browing Place, #345
Raleigh, NC 27609
(919) 782-2350

Winston Placement
P.O. Box 15366
Winston-Salem, NC 27103
(919) 768-4040

OHIO

Sanford Rose Associates
265 South Main Street
Akron, OH 44308
(216) 762-6211

J.B. Brown & Associates
24100 Chagrin Boulevard, #340
Beachwood, OH 44122
(216) 464-5570

Snelling & Snelling-Canton
315 West Tuscarawas Street
Canton, OH 44702
(216) 456-4511

CBS Personnel Services
One East Fourth Street, #1300
Cincinnati, OH 45202
(513) 651-1111

Centennial Personnel
2211 Carew Tower
Cincinnati, OH 45202
(513) 381-4411

Opportunity Consultants
432 Walnut Street
Suite 208 Tri-State Building
Cincinnati, OH 45202
(513) 241-8675

Riethmiller & Associates
7265 Kenwood Road, #273
Cincinnati, OH 45236
(513) 793-7373

Robert Half of Cincinnati
1 East 4th Street
Cincinnati, OH 45202
(513) 621-7711

Black's Employment Service
7206 Melrose Avenue
Cleveland, OH 44103
(216) 881-3694

J.B. Brown & Associates
Terminal Tower Suite 1114
Cleveland, OH 44113
(216) 696-2525

Maerkle French Associates
804 Hanna Building
Cleveland, OH 44115
(216) 861-5865

Marvel Consultants
3690 Orange Place, #395
Cleveland, OH 44122
(216) 292-2855

Midland Consultants
4715 State Road
Cleveland, OH 44109
(216) 398-9330

Westgate Personnel
20325 Center Ridge Road
Suite 514
Cleveland, OH 44116
(216) 333-1344

Heagren, Burk Systems
1560 Fishinger Road
Columbus, OH 43221
(614) 457-2551

Thomas Group, The
5341 Acevedo Court
Columbus, OH 43220
(614) 457-2688

Your Employment Service
3400 North High Street
Columbus, OH 43202
(614) 261-0552

CBS Personnel Services
One First National Plaza, #1910
Dayton, OH 45402
(513) 222-2525

Deveny & Associates
3864 Kettering Boulevard
Dayton, OH 45439
(513) 298-4955

Executive Resources
3077 Kettering Boulevard, #215
Dayton, OH 45439
(513) 298-8168

Hahn and Associates
111 West First Street, #510
Dayton, OH 45402
(513) 223-8130

Robert Half of Dayton
One First National Plaza
Dayton, OH 45402
(513) 224-0600

Elyria Placement Service
1110 Garford Avenue
706 Elyria Savings & Trust Building
Elyria, OH 44035
(216) 322-0229

Ryan Personnel Services
417 West Sandusky Street, Building B
Findlay, OH 45840
(419) 422-3119

General Employment Enterprises
6100 Rockside Woods Boulevard, #130
Independence, OH 44131
(216) 524-4444

Flowers and Associates
420 Holland Road
Box 538
Maumee, OH 43537
(419) 893-4816

Longberry Employment Service
6 East Park Avenue, #303
P.O. Box 471
Niles, OH 44446
(216) 652-5871

Renhil Group, Inc.
P.O. Box 527
Perrysburg, OH 43551
(419) 874-2203

Corporate Research
3540 Secor Road, #300
Toledo, OH 43606
(419) 535-1941

Technical Employment Services
31601 Vine
Willowick, OH 44094
(216) 585-0200

KBK Management Associates
4800 Market Street
Youngstown, OH 44512
(216) 788-6508

Sanford Rose Associates
25 East Boardman Street
400 Ohio One Building
Youngstown, OH 44503
(216) 744-4361

OKLAHOMA

Career Employment Service
P.O. Box 2096
Bartlesville, OK 74005
(918) 336-4122

J. Edward Smith Associates
P.O. Box 983
Claremore, OK 74018
(918) 582-9863

Dunhill Personnel Tulsa
8221 East 63rd Place
Tulsa, OK 74133
(918) 252-9667

International Search Corp.
3303 South Yale Avenue, #210
Tulsa, OK 74135
(918) 494-7936

Lloyd Richards Personnel Svc.
Oil Capital Building
507 South Main, Suite 502
Tulsa, OK 74103
(918) 582-5251

OREGON

Dunhill of Portland
620 Southwest Fifth Avenue, #604
Portland, OR 97204
(503) 224-1850

Murphy Symonds and Stowell
1001 Southwest Fifth Avenue, #1110
Portland, OR 97204
(503) 242-2300

PENNSYLVANIA

Becker Personnel Services
1 Bala Cynwyd Plaza
Bala Cynwyd, PA 19004
(215) 667-3010

T.A.C. Professional Recruiters
Suite GK, 1 Bala Avenue
Bala Cynwyd, PA 19004
(215) 667-7351

JFC Personnel Agency
1520 Market Street
Camp Hill, PA 17011
(717) 761-8095

Meck Associates Prof. Pers. Agcy.
1517 Cedar Cliff Drive
Camp Hill, PA 17011
(717) 761-4777

Robert Harkins Associates
1433 West Main Street
Box 236
Ephrata, PA 17522
(717) 733-9664

Science Center
550 Pinetown Road
Ft. Washington, PA 19034
(215) 643-3700

Heberling Personnel
P.O. Box 2332
Harrisburg, PA 17105
(717) 763-8222

National Career Services
P.O. Box 2833
Harrisburg, PA 17105
(717) 652-1200

Phoenix Personnel Services
P.O. Box 1733
Harrisburg, PA 17105
(717) 763-7871

D. Jackson and Associates
20 Briarcrest Square
Hershey, PA 17033
(717) 533-3213

Kenneth James Associates
207 Buck Road
Holland, PA 18966
(215) 322-5080

Kogen Personnel
202 Fisher Building
Johnstown, PA 15901
(814) 536-7571

Kennett Group, The
143 Beverly Drive
Kennett Square, PA 19348
(215) 356-4070

Bryant Bureau
8 North Queen Street, #508
Lancaster, PA 17603
(717) 299-6647

Systems Personnel
Philadelphia / Wilmington Division
115 West State Street
Media, PA 19063
(215) 565-8880

CMA
P.O. Box 184
Narberth, PA 19072
(215) 664-1756

Atomic Personnel
1518 Walnut Street, #1504
Philadelphia, PA 19102
(215) 735-4908

General Employment Enterprises
8 Penn Center Plaza, #333
Philadelphia, PA 19103
(215) 564-3101

General Employment Enterprises
3 Penn Center Plaza, #2007
Philadelphia, PA 19103
(215) 569-3226

J. White & Company
1700 Walnut Street, #700
Philadelphia, PA 19103
(215) 545-8588

O'Shea System of Employment
12 South 12th Street
PSFS Building Suite 1113
Philadelphia, PA 19107
(215) 925-7272

Pratt Placement Service
1547 Pratt Street
Suite 300
Philadelphia, PA 19124
(215) 537-1212

Sanmar Staffing Consultants
1211 Chestnut Street, #200
Philadelphia, PA 19107
(215) 563-9399

International Business Assocs.
1301 Chamber of Commerce Building
Pittsburgh, PA 15219
(412) 281-6263

N. Dean Davic Associates
Suite 645
400 Penn Center Boulevard
Pittsburgh, PA 15235
(412) 824-8100

Provident Personnel Consultants
P.O. Box 72
Prospect Park, PA 19076
(215) 586-5888

Nancy Jackson, Inc.
4th Floor Bank Towers Building
Corner Wyoming Avenue and Spruce Street
Scranton, PA 18503
(717) 346-8711

Precision Search
850 Easton Road
Warrington, PA 18976
(215) 343-3900

Peter Depasquale Associates
454 Pine Street Suite A
Williamsport, PA 17701
(717) 326-1736

United Consultants
1508 East Market Street
York, PA 17403
(717) 846-2009

RHODE ISLAND

Career Systems
2224 Pawtucket Avenue
East Providence, RI 02914
(401) 431-0001

Becker Associates
Division of LILA
126 Congdon Avenue
North Kingstown, RI 02852
(401) 737-9054

ERA Placements
509 Armistice Boulevard
Pawtucket, RI 02861
(401) 724-3871

Bay Search Group
112 Union Street, #510
Providence, RI 02903
(401) 751-2870

Greene Personnel Consultants
809-811 Fleet National Bank Building
Providence, RI 02903
(401) 272-4472

Positions, Inc.
10 Orms Street
Providence, RI 02904
(401) 273-7600

Retail Recruiters - Rhode Island
245 Waterman Street
Suite 303 Doris Building
Providence, RI 02906
(401) 421-9200

New England Consultants
156 Centerville Road
P.O. Box 6756
Warwick, RI 02887
(401) 732-4650

Peterson Personnel Recruiters
500 Jefferson Boulevard
Warwick, RI 02886
(401) 732-3405

SOUTH CAROLINA

Southern Recruiters & Cons.
215 Park Avenue, Southeast
P.O. Box 2745
Aiken, SC 29802
(803) 648-7834

RH Unlimited
9440 Two Notch Road, Suite D
Columbia, SC 29223
(803) 788-8680

Excel Personnel
20 West Antrim Drive
Greenville, SC 29607
(803) 233-2546

Snelling & Snelling
600 Columbia Avenue
Lexington, SC 29072
(803) 359-7644

Management Recruiters-Spartanburg
10 Metro Drive, Suite A-1
Spartanburg, SC 29303
(803) 573-7427

Thomas Glover Associates
200 East Main Street
Spartanburg, SC 29301
(803) 585-9890

TENNESSEE

Shiloh Careers International Inc.
Two Maryland Farms, Suite 105
Brentwood, TN 37027
(615) 373-3090

H & H Personnel Consultants
P.O. Box 21371
Chattanooga, TN 37421
(615) 899-1235

Baker & Baker Employment Service
1191 West Main Street
Hendersonville, TN 37075
(615) 824-5253

Professional Placement Service
112 West Baltimore, #102
First Tennessee Bank Building
Jackson, TN 38301
(901) 422-6637

Galloway Employment Service
4646 Poplar Avenue, Suite 402
Memphis, TN 38117
(901) 683-6356

Jean's Personnel
5100 Poplar Avenue, Suite 514
Memphis, TN 38137
(901) 682-3700

Baker & Baker Employment Service
224 South Church Street
Murfreesboro, TN 37130
(615) 896-9580

Dealy-Rourke Personnel Service
3401 West End, #310
Nashville, TN 37203
(615) 292-0931

Fanning Personnel
Two International Plaza, #210
Nashville, TN 37217
(615) 361-8000

TEXAS

Vance Employment Service
Suite 917, Barfield Building
Amarillo, TX 79101
(806) 372-3456

Career Cons. Professional Search
3624 North Hills Drive, #B-205
Austin, TX 78731
(512) 346-6660

Dunhill of Austin
1106 Clayton Lane
Suite 280 West
Austin, TX 78723
(512) 458-5271

Snelling and Snelling
8200 MoPac Expressway
One Park North, #130
Austin, TX 78759
(512) 346-6920

Tarrant / Cavness Personnel Svc.
710 Brazos Street
Austin, TX 78701
(512) 477-5737

Dunhill Personnel-Corpus Christi
5155 Flynn Parkway
Conoco Tower, #204
Corpus Christi, TX 78411
(512) 854-1424

Babich & Associates
6060 North Central Expressway
Twin Sixties Towers #544
Dallas, TX 75206
(214) 361-5735

Datapro Personnel Consultants
12720 Hilcrest, Suite 520
Dallas, TX 75230
(214) 661-8600

General Employment Enterprises
5501 LBJ Freeway, #1022
Dallas, TX 75240
(214) 788-4462

General Employment Enterprises
8350 North Central Expressway, #518
Dallas, TX 75206
(214) 987-0762

General Employment Enterprises
Plaza of Americas, Suite 402, Bo
Dallas, TX 75201
(214) 742-1117

King Computer Search
9221 LBJ Street #208
Dallas, TX 75238
(214) 238-1021

Robert Half of Dallas
2 Northpark East, #750
Dallas, TX 75231
(214) 363-3300

Sumrall Personnel Consultants
4020 McEwen Suite 123
Dallas, TX 75234
(214) 387-4801

Babich & Associates
602 Mallick Tower
One Summit Avenue
Fort Worth, TX 76102
(817) 336-7261

Robert Shields & Associates
1550 West Bay Area Boulevard, #101
Friendswood, TX 77546
(713) 488-7961

Emjay Computer Careers
4615 Southwest Freeway
Suite 815 Executive Plaza
Houston, TX 77027
(713) 840-9114

General Employment Enterprises
1235 North Loop West, #713
Houston, TX 77008
(713) 861-6588

Richard, Wayne & Roberts Pers.
24 Greenway Plaza Suite 1304
Houston, TX 77046
(713) 629-6681

Scientific Placement
14925 Memorial Drive
P.O. Box 19949
Houston, TX 77224
(713) 496-6100

Stevenson & Goss
12012 Wickchester Lane, #5
Houston, TX 77079
(713) 556-0505

Agape Personnel Agency
2161 50th, Suite 105
Lubbock, TX 79412
(806) 747-3578

Snelling and Snelling
2222 Indiana Avenue
Lubbock, TX 79410
(806) 797-3281

Career Path
201 Oak Ridge Square
Midland, TX 79705
(915) 682-5166

Locke Employment Service
2446 Ceegee Street, #200
San Antonio, TX 78217
(512) 826-9671

Professional Recruiting Cons.
45 Northeast Loop 410, Suite 850
Suite 103
San Antonio, TX 78216
(512) 349-7801

Robert Half of San Antonio
#850 - 6243 IH 10 West
San Antonio, TX 78201
(512) 736-2467

Snelling & Snelling
96 Gill Road, Suite 250
San Antonio, TX 78201
(512) 732-2261
1610 Woodstead Court, #195
Executive Employment Service

The Woodlands, TX 77380
(713) 367-3700

UTAH

Professional Recruiters
220 East 3900 South Suite 9
Salt Lake City, UT 84107
(801) 268-9940

VIRGINIA

Dunhill of Alexandria
4810 Beauregard Street, Suite 203
Alexandria, VA 22312
(703) 354-7227

Old Dominion Personnel Service
1901 North Fort Myer Drive, #1010
Arlington, VA 22209
(703) 522-3100

McCormick Group, The
9000 B Crownwood Court
Burke, VA 20015
(703) 978-0200

Bill Young & Associates
7309 Arlington Boulevard, #202
Falls Church, VA 22042
(703) 573-0200

Nexus Associates
5881 Leesburg Pike, #101
Falls Church, VA 22041
(703) 998-6363

Personnel, Inc.
7297-C Lee Highway
Falls Church, VA 22042
(703) 532-6550

Houston Personnel
2015 Wards Road
Lynchburg, VA 24502
(804) 237-5984

Dan Buckley and Associates
6708 Whitier Avenue
McLean, VA 22101
(703) 448-0553

Mid-Atlantic Power Service
7808 Wildwood Drive
Norfolk, VA 23518
(804) 583-2301

Don Richards Assoc.-Richmond
519 East Main Street
Richmond, VA 23219
(804) 644-0651

Hunter Search
7011 Backlick Court
Springfield, VA 22151
(703) 354-6000

NRI Computer Resources
8133 Leesburg Pike, #220
Vienna, VA 22180
(703) 442-0320

Herb Gretz Associates
414 25th Street
Virginia Beach, VA 23451
(804) 422-4872

Lendman Associates Limited
P.O. Box 62682
5500 Greenwich Road
Virginia Beach, VA 23462
(804) 497-8971

WASHINGTON

Western Power Services
1201 Jadwin Avenue
Richland, WA 99352
(509) 943-6633

Pacific Power Services
P.O. Box 2178
Silverdale, WA 98383
(206) 692-7281

WISCONSIN

Harry Case Associates
828 Cherry Street
Green Bay, WI 54301
(414) 432-5188

Lee Franzen & Associates
6601 C Northway
Greendale, WI 53129
(414) 421-3380

Availability of Madison
aka / A+ Ability Consultants, NPC
202 North Midvale Boulevard
Madison, WI 53705
(608) 231-2421

Life Style Careers
415 West Main Street
Madison, WI 53703
(608) 257-0511

Qualified Personnel
302 East Washington Avenue
Madison, WI 53701
(608) 257-1057

Robert Half of Wisconsin
First Wisconsin Center
777 East Wisconsin Avenue
Milwaukee, WI 53202
(414) 271-4253

CANADA

P J. Ward Associates Ltd.
214 King Street West, #400
Toronto, Ontario M5H 1K4
(416) 593-1660

Chapter 8

Computer Professionals: What Are They Like?

Insight into what computer professionals are actually like may help you decide if you are the type of person who will enjoy working in a computer field. (See Chapter 5 for a discussion of the personality required for each position.) Included in this chapter is more general information pertaining to the personality of individuals employed in computer jobs (Fig. 8-1).

In general, people who work with computers are able to reason logically, are very responsible, and like to be challenged in their work. They also have good oral and written communications skills, because most computer jobs involve some interaction with other people. Communication skills include the ability to read and understand business information ranging from equipment requirements to directives from superiors. Very important to many computer jobs is the ability to work with a high degree of accuracy with persistence and patience. Computer professionals often need to draw on their own ingenuity and imagination to solve problems, which makes many computer jobs

challenging. People who work in computer fields are also willing to continue to learn something new; it has been estimated that in the computer industry, job skills are outdated every three years.

Gerald M. Weinberg, in his well-known book *The Psychology of Computer Programming*, pointed out a number of personality traits that are essential to computer programming. These traits would apply to systems and applications programmers, telecommunications and database programmers, and microcomputer programmers, as well as others. He mentioned that programmers must be able to tolerate stressful situations, because the work often involves rigid deadlines. Adaptability to change is important, as is neatness and orderliness in one's work. A programmer needs to have a certain type of humility which will lead him to look through the entire program for similar errors once he or she has found an error of a certain type, instead of only fixing the first error of that type and then assuming that the rest of the program will be correct. A programmer must also be assertive, however, and

Fig. 8-1. As a group, computer professionals work hard. (Photograph courtesy of Applied Data Research, Inc., Princeton, NJ 08540.)

self-confident enough to get things done. The final trait of importance to working as a programmer is a sense of humor.

The results of a study done by Columbia University for "Business Week" magazine, comparing managers to computer specialists (hardware designers, software designers, and management information systems computer employees), showed that in relation to managers, computer professionals rated responsibility, salary, and title as less important, but better hours and the opportunity to learn new skills as more important.

A number of studies have been done on the personality characteristics of the computer or data processing professional. Many of these studies point to traits like good problem solving ability, practicality, reliability, and shyness. The most comprehensive study of the computer professional done in recent years is the survey done by the Dewar's Center for Career Development in 1983, entitled *The Dewar's Profiles of Americans at Work: Dewar's*

Career Profile: Computer Professionals. It was designed to provide insight into "the human aspects of a computer profession, dealing with individual aspirations and attitudes, rewards, and satisfaction . . . how much time they devote to their work how they spend their leisure time, and how they view their own profession from the inside."[5] Excerpts from the study appear below.

The findings are based on telephone interviews with over 300 active members of six different computer professions, including educators, systems analysts, programmers, consultants, entrepreneurs, and computer sales or marketing personnel. The interviews cover a wide range of topics including career and job satisfaction, professional aspirations, motivations and rewards, views on where the field

---

[5] *The Dewar's Profiles of Americans at Work: Dewar's Career Profile: Computer Professionals.* Copyright © 1983 by Schenley Imports Co. & Dewar's White Label Scotch. Reprinted with permission.

143

is headed, and advice to those considering pursuing a computer career.

In addition, the report provides information on educational and salary levels, methods used to land first jobs, hours devoted to work, and how leisure time is spent. Together, this information shapes an accurate, up-to-date profile of the computer profession as a whole and provides insight into various distinct types of computer professionals.

The first report focuses on six different types of computer professionals:

☐ Educators
☐ Systems analysts
☐ Computer programmers
☐ Data-processing consultants
☐ Entrepreneurs
☐ Computer sales or marketing personnel.[6]

Together, they cover a wide spectrum of the computer field, ranging from those involved in teaching and research to those who sell hardware or software or run their own businesses.

As might be expected, certain differences regarding both habits and attitudes among these different fields emerge and are discussed in the report. On a number of key factors however, including job satisfaction and adherence to career paths, career motivation, and working rewards, this seemingly eclectic group demonstrates a true sense of coherence. The report begins, then, with a composite profile of the computer professional that cuts across all job categories.

COMPUTER PROFESSIONALS —A COMPOSITE PROFILE

Computer professionals are a highly satisfied and motivated group of hard working individuals, who achieve a large measure of fulfillment through their work. This composite profile emerges from their attitudes toward their jobs and career choices, both in terms of motivation and satisfaction, and holds

---

[6]A small number (7 percent) of the people interviewed did not place themselves in any of these categories.

true for the entire spectrum of computer professionals.

Work Satisfaction

Satisfaction with work is a very subjective attitude. Essentially, it is a product of two factors—work experience itself, and the expectations brought to the job, which are also highly subjective. Truly satisfied workers who enjoy their work tend to regard the tasks involved as pleasurable, even "fun," rather than drudgery.

Behavioral scientists have identified three psychological states relating to work experience that contribute to job satisfaction and distinguish motivated, satisfied workers from their tired and disaffected counterparts:

☐ Experiencing meaningfulness.
☐ Experiencing responsibility.
☐ Knowledge of results.

Computer professionals are overwhelmingly satisfied with their jobs. Most (70 percent) say they are "very satisfied" with their present position, while nearly all the rest say they are "somewhat satisfied." This enthusiasm is particularly strong among entrepreneurs and weakest among systems analysts (Table 8-1).

It can be assumed, then, that for most computer professionals, work experience involves a fair amount of meaningfulness, responsibility, and knowledge of results.

The second factor (besides work experience) that determines job satisfaction is expectations. The high level of job satisfaction among computer professionals apparently stems in part from their overall rate of professional advancement. Eight in ten (82 percent) say they are at least as far advanced in their careers as they thought they would be five years ago, and over a quarter (28 percent) say they are even further along. Not surprising, those exceeding their expectations are also happiest with their jobs (Table 8-2).

About three of four computer professionals (73 percent), however, identify some aspects of their work that they don't like. Among this group, four

Table 8-1. Job Satisfaction by Work Category.

	Educators	Systems analysts	Computer programmers	Consultants	Entrepreneurs/ run own business	Sales
	%	%	%	%	%	%
Percent saying they are *very satisfied* with their position	71	61	68	69	78	68
(Number of respondents)	(55)	(57)	(37)	(32)	(41)	(57)

of ten (42 percent) cite the burdens of excessive paperwork far outstripping any other specific complaint. Pressure is the bane of 12 percent while 9 percent complain about their salary (Table 8-3).

Personal Motivation: Career Goals and Rewards

Computer professionals find the personal goals that led them to seek a career in the computer field fulfilled through the rewards derived from their jobs.

What are the hoped for goals or incentives which lead people to choose a career in computer field? Strong personal interests in the field tops the list, receiving an average score of 8.25 on a 10-point scale, with personal growth close behind at 8.1. The practical consideration of employment opportunities also plays a major role, but status and relocation possibilities do not provide strong incentives.

What are the rewards actually gained from the work experience? Being creative is the most important aspect of their present positions. It receives the highest average ranking, 8.62 on a second 10-point scale among 10 such rewarding aspects of work. Learning new skills and helping people or businesses solve problems follow in close succession.

Financial considerations and job security rank somewhat lower, while status falls to the bottom of the list, even below physical working conditions and environment.

Computer professionals as a group, therefore, value the creative, learning and problem-solving rewards of their work above all else. Certain social considerations, such as the ability to work independently and enjoy the company of colleagues, also rank fairly high. But the most purely practical aspects—money, security, and status—appear to be the least important.

Table 8-2. Career Advancement by Job Satisfaction.

	Career Advancement			
	Even further along	As far as expected	Not quite as far as expected	Not nearly as far as expected
	%	%	%	%
Percent saying they are *very satisfied* with their present position	81	70	51	17
(Number of respondents)	(84)	(161)	(43)	(6)

Table 8-3. Work Complaints.

What aspects of your present work don't you like?	%
Paper work and bureaucracy	42
Pressure/ long hours	12
Financial rewards	9
Inadequate facilities	4
Location/physical conditions	5
Dealing with customers	4
Lack of advancement	3
Not able to use full capabilities	3
Teaching load	3
Travel	2
Other	13
(Number of respondents) (220)	

The linkage between creatively and job satisfaction can be seen from the fact that nearly half (46 percent) of those "very satisfied" with their jobs give creativity a top ranking of ten, compared to only 29 percent of those only somewhat satisfied (Table 8-4).

Combining the top-ranking (intrinsic) aspects of both scales produces a model of the dynamic interplay between career goals and rewards that helps produce such a high level of job satisfaction. Computer professionals are primarily motivated by genuine interest and the pursuit of personal growth, which in the daily routine find expression in the challenge of creativity and the ongoing desire to learn new skills. These rewards, in turn, achieve their full realization through applications that help people or businesses solve problems.

Computer professionals, then, achieve their high level of job satisfaction not only by expanding their own knowledge and skills, but also by channeling their creativity to the service of others.

TYPES OF COMPUTER PROFESSIONALS

The composite profile just presented fits most members of the computer professions. But within the group, certain distinct types emerge, distinguished by the degree of commitment they give to their jobs, both in terms of time and intensity.

At one extreme are the "computerholics," who devote at least 50 hours a week to their jobs, frequently work on weekends, and function in a work environment they themselves describe as "extremely hectic." About one in five (22 percent) computer professionals corresponds to this type.

At the opposite end of the spectrum are the "nine-to-fivers," who devote 40 hours or less to their jobs, hardly—if ever—work weekends, and describe the pace at their work environments as "generally steady or relaxed." About one-fifth of the group (21 percent) fall into this category. In be-

	Job satisfaction	
	Very satisfied	Somewhat satisfied
	%	%
Rating creativity 10 on a 10-point scale:	46	29
(Number of respondents)	(210)	(74)

Table 8-4. Rating of Creativity by Job Satisfaction.

Table 8-5. Computer Type by Job Category.

Computer worker type:	Educators	Systems analysts	Computer programmers	Consultants	Entrepreneurs/ run own business	Sales
	Work category					
Computerholics	% 22	% 20	% 8	% 12	% 43	% 31
Overtimers	63	54	59	64	50	52
Nine-to-fivers	15	27	33	24	7	17
(Number of respondents)	(54)	(56)	(36)	(33)	(42)	(58)

tween, lie the "overtimers," comprising 57 percent of the total number of professionals.[7]

It is important to note that computerholics, overtimers, and nine-to-fivers are equally satisfied with their jobs and, with few exceptions, do not differ in terms of the goals they seek or the rewards they find in their work. The exceptions are, however, quite telling:

Computerholics are nearly twice as likely as nine-to-fivers to seek personal growth in their careers; 55 percent ranked this nine or ten, compared to 41 percent of overtimers and 29 percent of nine-to-fivers. Computerholics are more likely to be motivated by strong personal interests in choosing their career paths; 58 percent ranked this nine or ten compared to 50 percent of overtimers and 43 percent of nine-to-fivers. In terms of work rewards, computerholics are far more likely to achieve satisfaction from helping people or businesses solve problems; 59 percent ranked this nine or ten, compared to 42 percent of overtimers and 36 percent of nine-to-fivers.

On the whole, computerholics bring an intensity to everything they do, including leisure activities. Specifically, they distinguish themselves in many facets of their work and lives: Computerholics are over twice as likely as nine-to-fivers to believe their careers are further advanced than they ex-

pected in school; 46 percent, compared to 26 percent of overtimers and 18 percent of nine-to-fivers.

Their work experiences are twice as likely as nine-to-fivers to correspond very closely to their expectations while in school; 31 percent versus 23 percent of overtimers and 13 percent of nine-to-fivers.

As a group, they are better educated; 86 percent have graduate or professional training, compared to 70 percent of overtimers and 46 percent of nine-to-fivers.

They tend to value nonmath and noncomputer science courses more than their less-driven colleagues: 59 percent say these courses were "valuable," compared to 42 percent of overtimers and 39 percent of nine-to-fivers. They are about as likely to have come to their present position from a related field as are overtimers (67 percent versus 70 percent), but more so than nine-to-fivers, half of whom (51 percent) came to their present position from outside the field.

Nine-to-fivers, on the other hand, are much more likely to work independently than computerholics. Half (49 percent) of them work on their own, compared to 30 percent of computerholics and 36 percent of overtimers. And nine-to-fivers, as might be expected, value their leisure activities more than others: 62 percent consider them "very important," compared to 55 percent of overtimers and 49 percent of computerholics.

But computerholics tend to take the rewards of leisure activities more seriously. They are far more likely than nine-to-fivers to consider challenge

---

[7]Respondents were assigned to each of the extreme types in the basis of fulfilling two of three conditions. The rest were assigned to the "overtimers" category.

and excitement "very important." For challenge, 46 percent to 32 percent of overtimers and 22 percent of nine-to-fivers; for excitement, 37 percent to 19 percent for the other two types. Computerholics are also more likely to value creativity, competition, and the ability to learn new things as leisure rewards.

Computerholics are most prevalent among entrepreneurs and computer marketing personnel (Table 8-5).

ASPIRATIONS AND EXPECTATIONS

The distance between school and work can seem light-years apart. For those still in college or graduate school, the route to a desirable position may appear tortuous or obscure. Once having found a comfortable position or career track, people may find their prior expectations uninformed or naive.

Expectations in Retrospect

How closely does the work experience of today's computer professionals correspond to their expectations when they were in college or graduate school? The sample is split into four roughly equal quarters. About half believe their work experience corresponds "very closely" (23 percent) or "somewhat closely" (29 percent) to their earlier expectations, while the other half believe it doesn't correspond "very closely" or "at all."

The experiences of computer professionals who teach correspond particularly closely to their expectations: nearly half (47 percent) claim they are "very close." This makes sense, because role models—their professors—were readily available and highly visible during their college years. Entrepreneurs are least likely to cite a strong correspondence: only 10 percent. But no more than 30 percent of those in any of the computer professions claim that their experiences have no relationship to their expectations (Table 8-6).

Landing that First Job

Finding the first full-time position in the desired field can be the hardest—and often the most discouraging—experience for recent graduates. They find themselves thrust into an employment system that does not simply rely on neutral measures of ability such as exams and grades, but operates under its own set of marketplace values. Learning how that system works can be an education in itself.

More computer professionals landed their first job through a third-party contact such as a relative or teacher than through any other means. A quarter (25 percent) of the sample landed their first job this way.

About one in six (17 percent) attained his/her first position through the campus recruitment process, while one in ten did so by answering a

Table 8-6. Expectations and Work Experience by Work Category.

Correspondence between expectation and work experience:	Educators	Systems analysts	Computer programmers	Consultants	Entrepreneurs/ run own business	Sales
	%	%	%	%	%	%
Very close	47	16	19	17	10	27
Not at all close	13	29	28	27	24	29
(Number of respondents)	(55)	(57)	(37)	(32)	(41)	(57)

specific advertisement (11 percent) or pounding the pavement or making *cold calls* (12 percent). A fifth of the sample (22 percent) depended on "other" means, which underscores the individuality of career experiences.

Consistent Loyalty, Evolving Ambition

Once launched on their career paths, an overwhelming majority of computer professionals demonstrate unswerving commitment to their chosen profession. Only one in five (19 percent) is even considering moving into another area of data processing, and only one in nineteen (6 percent) is considering leaving the data processing field altogether.

Even in terms of adhering to their original aspirations, many computer professionals display impressive consistency. Over half (56 percent) the sample say their ambitions and aspirations have not changed since they entered the field.

For those whose ambitions have undergone some type of change, the most frequent shift is an increased interest in pursuing a managerial role (33 percent). A number of other specific career roles attract far fewer computer people, including interest in the more technical aspects of the field and in sales. Some respondents, thinking in more general terms, simply say they have become more ambitious, or their horizons have expanded (14 percent), while a third as many (5 percent) say they have lowered their sights (Table 8-7).

INDIVIDUALISTS ON THE JOB

Computer professionals are, by and large, hard working, self-motivated types who value the opportunity to work independently. As indicated in Part One, the ability to work independently ranked fairly high, 7.94 on the 10-point reward scale.

Work Situation

Most computer professionals either work independently (37 percent) or as a member of a small group (32 percent). Most of the remainder primarily manage others (28 percent). As might be expected, consultants and educators are most likely to work independently; over half of each group do so. En-

Table 8-7. Changing Ambitions.

In what ways do you think your ambitions have changed since you entered the data-processing field?	%
More interested in management	33
More ambitious/ raised sights	14
More interested in technical end	9
More interested in sales/marketing	7
More interested in teaching	5
More interested in computer science	5
Less ambitious/ lowered sights	5
More interested in money	4
Other	18
(Number of respondents) (132)	

trepreneurs, on the other hand, most frequently manage others, while systems analysts are the most likely to operate in small groups (Table 8-8).

Time, Intensity, and Work Environment

Computer professionals as a group work hard. They prove this in both the time they devote to their jobs and the intensity with which they work. Three in four computer professionals (73 percent) operate in a hectic or intense work environment, and one in four describes it as "very hectic or intense." This intensity decreases somewhat, however, with the length of time spent in the field (Table 8-9). This suggests that "veterans" have learned to cope with the demands of their profession or have made choices about how to balance their work and leisure time.

But while the computer workplace may be anything but relaxed, the character or atmosphere of

Table 8-8. Present Work Situation by Work Category.

Present work situation:	Educators	Systems analysts	Computer programmers	Consultants	Entrepreneurs/ run own business	Sales
	%	%	%	%	%	%
Work mostly independently	55	12	38	59	17	47
Work closely in a small group	22	53	27	28	22	30
Primarily manage others	22	33	35	9	59	14
(Number of respondents)	(55)	(57)	(37)	(32)	(41)	(57)

the work environment tends to be informal. Eight of 10 (79 percent) computer professionals describe their workplaces as "moderately" or "very informal."

The second measure of job commitment is the amount of time actually devoted to work. Nearly three-quarters (74 percent) of computer professionals put in 41 hours or more in a typical workweek, and a third (31 percent) put in over 50 hours. Entrepreneurs clearly devote the most time to their jobs: six of 10 put in over 50 hours a week. Programmers spend the least hours on work: nine of 10 (89 percent) spend 50 hours or less (Table 8-10).

Female computer professionals appear to devote less time to their jobs than male: half of the women, but only a fifth of the men, work 40 hours or less a week. At the other extreme, a third of the men, but only a tenth of the women, spend 51 hours or more a week working for their jobs (Table 8-11).

Computer work is not restricted to the traditional business week. One in four computer professionals (25 percent) frequently spends time on the weekend doing work for his or her job, while fully 60 percent do this at least some of the time.

The amount of time devoted to a job is directly linked to satisfaction with that position. Those who work more than 50 hours a week are more likely to be "very satisfied" with their current positions than are others (Table 8-12).

Curiously, job satisfaction decreases somewhat with the frequency of weekend work (Table 8-13).

Table 8-9. Intensity at Work by Length of Experience.

Intensity of work environment:	1 year or less	2-4 years	5-7 years	8-10 years	10 or more years
	%	%	%	%	%
Very hectic or intense	38	31	24	17	23
(Number of respondents)	(6)	(22)	(12)	(9)	(26)

Table 8-10. Length of Workweek by Work Category.

Length of workweek:	Work category					
	Educators	Systems analysts	Computer programmers	Consultants	Entrepreneurs/ run own business	Sales
	%	%	%	%	%	%
Less than 35 hrs/week	0	0	3	9	2	4
35-40 hrs/week	19	31	38	25	7	19
41-50 hrs/week	46	48	48	47	29	37
51-60 hrs/week	24	16	8	10	37	23
More than 60 hrs/week	11	5	3	9	25	17
(Number of respondents)	(55)	(57)	(37)	(32)	(41)	(57)

Table 8-11. Length of Workweek by Gender.

Length of workweek:	Male		Female	
Less than 35 hours/week	2		7	
		22%		52%
35-40 hours/week	20		45	
41-50 hours/week	44		36	
51-60 hours/week	22		7	
		34%		12%
60 hours or more hours/week	12		5	
(Number of respondents)	(259)		(42)	

Table 8-12. Length of Workweek by Job Description.

	Length of workweek	
	Less than 50 hrs/wk	More than 50 hrs/wk
	%	%
Percent saying they are *very satisfied* with their present position	66	78
(Number of respondents)	(206)	(93)

Table 8-13. Working on Weekends by Job Satisfaction.

	Work on Weekends			
	Frequently	Sometimes	Rarely	Never
	%	%	%	%
Percent saying they are *very satisfied* with their present position	64	71	72	75
(Number of respondents)	(75)	(106)	(92)	(28)

The most likely explanation for this seeming contradiction is that no matter how much time is devoted to work during the workweek, bringing work home on the weekend interferes with another vital component of the computer professional's life: leisure activities—the subject of Part Four.

THE REWARDS OF LEISURE

Leisure activities are a vital component of the computer professional's life. Over half the sample (55 percent) consider leisure activities "very important," and 37 percent consider them "somewhat important."

What rewards do computer professionals seek in their leisure activities? Relaxation heads the list, with 55 percent citing this as a very important objective, followed by the chance to learn new things (44 percent), companionship (42 percent), and creativity (39 percent). Competition falls to the bottom of the list, called "very important" by only 14 percent.

The leisure activities of a third of computer professionals involve computers. This involvement increases among those whose offices are the most relaxed. Presumably, those operating in a more intense computer work environment have a greater need to "get away" from the machine altogether (Table 8-14).

Among social activities enjoyed with spouse, romantic partner, or friends, the most frequently engaged in (at least once or twice a week) are attending a religious service or sponsored event (38 percent), engaging in outdoor activities, such as hiking (36 percent), visiting friends or relatives (35 percent), and participating in sports (31 percent). For a complete list of leisure activities, see Table 8-15.

Most computer people spend the bulk of their free time with others, or divide it equally alone and with others. Only one in five says he/she spends more free time alone. In fact, despite the "loner" image of computer devotees, computer professionals are less likely than members of the general

Table 8-14. Computers as a Leisure Activity by Intensity of Work Environment.

	Intensity of Work Environment				
Do your leisure activities include computers:	Very hectic or intense	Moderately hectic or intense	Generally steady pace	Fairly relaxed	Very relaxed
	%	%	%	%	%
Yes	21	37	37	44	67
No	79	63	63	56	33
(Number of respondents)	(75)	(145)	(54)	(18)	(9)

Table 8-15. Leisure Activities.

How frequently do you enjoy doing the following *social* activities with spouse, romantic partner, or friends?

	At least once or twice a week	Less frequently	Never
	%	%	%
Attend religious service or sponsored event	38	36	26
Engage in outdoor activities (hike, hunt, etc.)	36	53	11
Visit friends or relatives	35	62	3
Participate in sports	31	46	23
Participate in community or political activities	16	56	28
Play cards or board games	13	58	29
Go to movies	11	90	9
Attend cultural performances: plays, opera, classical music, concerts, dance	10	84	6
Go to bars or nightclubs	10	47	43
Attend sports events	10	45	25
Host and attend informal (barbecue and beer) parties	8	86	6
Host and attend dinner and evening parties	8	85	7
Go dancing	5	61	34
Attend wine tastings	4	37	59
Go to museums or exhibitions	2	88	10
Attend rock, folk, jazz, or popular concerts	1	59	40

public to spend the bulk of their free time alone: 20 percent compared to 31 percent.

THE ROAD TO SUCCESS

As one would expect, professionals in the computer field tend to be highly educated. But the routes travelled—in terms of educational program or major—are not as limited as might be expected. While math, computer science, and electrical engineering are the most frequently utilized paths, many people have entered the field successfully from other directions. And computer professionals themselves emphasize the value of other areas of knowledge in their work.

Table 8-16. College Training by Gender.

	Male	Female
	%	%
Yes	91	76
No	9	24
(Number of respondents)	(259)	(42)

The Major Path

Most computer professionals (89 percent) have completed college, and two-thirds of these (69 percent) have graduate or other postgraduate education. Women in the field are somewhat less likely than men to have a college degree (Table 8-16).

Mathematics heads the list of college majors (pursued by 30 percent of computer professionals), followed by computer science and electrical en-

gineering (each pursued by 15 percent). One in ten (11 percent) followed a business/management program in college (see Table 8-17).

Together, these four subjects account for three-quarters of the sample. The remainder studied the other sciences, engineering, the social sciences, and the arts and humanities, from English literature to theater and music.

Advanced training again focuses on computer science and math (23 percent and 22 percent respectively), business and management (17 percent), and electrical engineering (12 percent). Other science and engineering specialties account for most of the remainder (Table 8-18).

The Broader Person

Computer professionals are nearly unanimous in recognizing that narrow training alone is not the only thing conducive to career achievement. Almost half (45 percent) consider their studies other than computer sciences and math "very valuable" to

Table 8-17. Major In College.

College Major	
Mathematics	30
Computer science	15
Electrical engineering	15
Other sciences	13
Business/ management	11
Arts and humanities	7
Other engineering	5
Social sciences	4
Other	1
(Number of respondents) (260)	

Table 8-18. Subject Area In Graduate School.

Main Area of Study in Graduate School	
	%
Computer science	23
Mathematics	22
Business/ management	17
Electrical engineering	12
Other sciences	10
Other engineering	8
Arts and humanities	4
Other	3
(Number of respondents) (181)	

their success in their present positions, and only 18 percent don't consider them at least "somewhat valuable."

In terms of general areas of knowledge, three-quarters (77 percent) believe traditional English language skills are "very important" to the successful pursuit of their careers, compared to 58 percent who believe statistics and math are "very important," and 44 percent who feel this way about the sciences. Philosophy and logic were the only other liberal arts subjects to be considered "very important" by more than a third (37 percent) of the sample (Table 8-19).

VIEWS ON THE FIELDS— PEOPLE AND OPPORTUNITIES

Computer professionals bring their own perspective and insights to the world of data processing. Opportunities, of course, are very much on everyone's mind, and computer people have definite ideas about where the field is headed.

For them, however, this field is not only one of opportunity, but a sphere of activity where they have found their place. Their views on their col-leagues explain to a large extent why they feel at home in the field.

Observations on People

Most computer people have positive attitudes about their colleagues as a group. When asked what distinguishes them from other professionals, however, no single descriptive characteristic predominates. Problem-solving abilities, along with dedication and professionalism and intelligence (including imagination and curiosity) were mentioned by a fifth of the sample.

Ambitious, aggressive, and independent characteristics stood out for some, while one in ten focused on the perceived "weird" or eccentric qualities of their peers (Table 8-20). (The difficulty in characterizing the field is indicated by the fact that 18 percent of the responses did not fall into the seven general categories established.)

But regardless of the term expressed (with the exception of "weird"), most computer people believe their description applies to themselves as well. This serves as strong proof that computer people identify with their colleagues. Thus, they not only

Table 8-19. Importance of Areas of Knowledge.

How important do you believe the following general areas of knowledge are the to the successful pursuit of your career?	Rated "very important"
	%
Traditional English skills (writing, grammar, etc.)	77
Statistics/math	58
Science (physics, chemistry, biology)	44
Philosophy/logic	37
Economics	27
Broad cultural background (literature, arts, etc.)	16
Social sciences	11
World history/geography/foreign affairs	7
(Number of respondents)	(269)

Table 8-20. Characterizing Their Peers.

In a word or phrase, what characteristics distinguish most of your colleagues from people in other professions?	
Problem solvers	20
Dedicated/ professional	20
Intelligent/imaginative/ inquisitive	19
Weird	10
Independent	5
Aggressive/ ambitious	5
Motivated	3
Other	18
(Number of respondents)	(301)

feel at home with what they do, but feel they belong to the field in terms of who they are.

Opportunities Observed

Programming and software development is far and away the data processing field offering the best job opportunities, according to people in the field. Two-thirds named this area in terms of its increasing employment needs in the foreseeable future. Computer applications (such as medical and industrial) was the second choice, attracting the endorsement of a third of the sample. Seven job opportunity choices each attracted between 20 and 29 percent of the sample, with systems development, computer graphics, and teaching at the high end, and sales and marketing at the low end. Only one in ten (12 percent) cited entrepreneurship (Table 8-21).

Computer people strongly believe (98 percent) the data processing field offers more opportunity to women and minorities than other fields. In fact,

Table 8-21. Future Job Opportunities.

Which area or areas of the data-processing field offer the best job opportunities, in terms of increasing needs in the foreseeable future?*	
	%
Programming/software development	65
Computer applications (medical, industrial, etc.)	34
Systems development	29
Computer graphics	28
Teaching computer sciences	26
Electronic communications	24
Hardware R&D	23
Artificial intelligence	22
Sales and marketing	20
Entrepreneurial	12
Other	4
(Number of respondents)	(301)
*Note: Respondents were allowed up to three choices.	

half (48 percent) believe it offers "much more opportunity."

Each computer professional, when asked to provide advice—or caution—to young people thinking of entering the data processing field, offers his or her own individual thoughts. These messages can be distilled into the following list of suggestions.

☐ Get a broad education.
☐ Be sure you're really interested and capable.
☐ Get practical experience during college.
☐ Be prepared to work hard.
☐ Don't specialize too soon.
☐ Stay current in the field.

Some respondents emphasize the necessity of having math and computer science credentials to succeed, while others point out the competitive and demanding nature of the business.

When asked to advise people over 30 who are considering switching into the computer field, today's professionals add a few caveats to their advice:

☐ Be prepared to compete with younger, skilled people.
☐ Think it through very carefully.
☐ Get the necessary training.

Others cite the value of a degree and the importance of the first job in the computer field.

Chapter 9

The Future

The following information is based on a December, 1985 report completed by the Office of Technology Assessment in December, 1985. The Office's job is to provide congressional committees with objective analyses of the emerging, difficult, and highly technical issues of the late 20th century. If you are interested in perusing the 348-page report, a free copy is available from the Office of Technology Assessment, Congress of the United States, Washington, DC 20510.

THE DOMINANT TRENDS
OF OFFICE AUTOMATION: 1985 to 2000

The Office of Technology Assessment discerned four dominant trends in office automation over the next 15 years. It also pointed out 12 possible consequences of the increasing use of technology to accomplish information-related tasks.

The first trend that the Office discussed in its recent report is an increase in distributed information processing and *networking*. The strong movement toward the use of microcomputers and distributed or *decentralized data access and handling*

is expected to continue, and the trend toward networking microcomputers, minicomputers, mainframes, and peripheral equipment into integrated systems is predicted to grow. Because of the increasing use of networking, there is expected to be a merging of two types of computing: centralized computing and decentralized or end-user computing. In *centralized computing*, most of the computer processing is done on large systems and by computer specialists. In *decentralized* or *end-user computing*, which is gaining in popularity today, much computer processing takes place on microcomputers used at various locations by individuals who are not computer specialists. As a result of the merging of the two approaches, an individual, for example, will be able to access the same information and perform about the same functions whether he or she is using a terminal or a microcomputer.

The second major trend in office automation over the next 15 years, according to the Office of Automation Technology, will be the continuing proliferation of technological options available for office automation. There will be a very broad choice

Fig. 9-1. A major trend in office automation over the next 15 years will be the continuing proliferation of technological options available for office automation. (Photograph courtesy of Sperry Corp.)

among vendors, systems, software packages, connecting devices, and communications technologies. As a result, users will find it difficult to formulate long-term automation plans. It will be possible, however, for the process of office automation to occur a few tasks at a time, if that is the approach preferred by the users. One effect of the broad choice of technological options that has already started to occur is the convergence of separate office technologies. For example, typewriters now have microelectronic components that enable them to do some of the tasks that can be done with word processors, and word processors are becoming almost indistinguishable from microcomputers. Users are able to put together devices and components to meet their specific needs.

The third dominant trend in office automation is expected to be an increase in the amount of data captured at the point of origin. More clients or consumers will enter data directly into the computer as they do now, for example, when they do their banking with an automated teller machine. Instead of the data being rekeyed when it is received from another organization, it will be received electronically—that is, it will be sent via telecommunications lines from one company's computer to another company's computer. This trend, and the changes which are presently occurring in computer input technology (such as the improvement of *optical scanners* and the development of computers with *speech recognition*), are expected to result in a decrease in the number of data entry jobs and in the costs of handling at least some types of data.

The fourth major trend covered by the Office of Technology Assessment is implied by the first and third trends discussed above; there will continue to be an increasing amount of communication, via computers and telecommunications lines, between organizations. For instance, a hospital's computer may send bills directly to a health insurer's computer, which may instruct a bank's computer to transfer funds. The bank's computer would make the payment and then notify both the hospital's and the insurer's computer that the funds have been transferred.

POSSIBLE CONSEQUENCES OF OFFICE AUTOMATION

In addition to discussing four major trends that are expected to dominate office automation over the next 15 years, the Office of Technology Assessment pointed out 12 possible consequences of office automation that will occur between 1985 and 2000.

First, office automation is predicted to lead to increased productivity. By the mid-1990s, according to the Office of Technology Assessment, almost every office in the U.S. will have at least one computer, just as almost every office now has a phone. There will probably be a terminal of some kind for, at the most, every two or three employees.

Second, the Office indicated that the number of office jobs is likely to decrease, due to office automation. There will be a substantial lessening of clerical and, in particular, data entry work to be done. There may also be a decrease in the number of lower level managers needed, because their tasks may be automated or taken over by clerical workers. Office automation may have the same type of effect, although to a lesser degree, on the tasks of paraprofessionals and technical employees.

To date, this expectation has not been borne out in real life. Many companies in the process of automating their offices have in fact hired more personnel. The Office of Technology Assessment suggests that the need for more workers is only temporary. It results from the short-term inefficiencies that occur when a new technology is introduced into a workplace that is not yet designed to use it to best advantage. Given time, office automation is expected to result in a significant savings of both time and labor, or a decrease in the number of office jobs.

The third possible consequence of office automation discussed by the Office of Technology Assessment is an increase in the number of employees who will be made part-time or temporary instead of full-time. Some individuals who now work full-time may work instead as independent contractors. This could result in a decrease in the number of full-time jobs available.

Training and education is expected to change in two ways, according to the Office. First, more of the training provided by vendors and employers is expected to be very narrow in scope. Much of it will be specifically related to a certain system or task. Employees with this kind of training are more likely to become trapped in dead-end jobs; they will have a limited opportunity to advance in their organization. Many employers, however, feel that making training as brief as possible is in their interest; they have made only a minimum investment in employees who can be lured away by other companies, and replacement employees can be trained more quickly.

There will also be a continuation of the strong trend of organizations to externalize training costs and to use *lateral recruitment*. Companies prefer hiring individuals who already have training from a college or trade school to providing training for new employees, because historically they have found it much more cost effective. Hiring from the outside on the management level is another practice that is becoming more common than the practice of advancing people from lower levels within the organization.

The Office of Technology Assessment discussed whether office jobs will be enhanced by office automation. Automation can be used to standardize and routinize tasks so that the amount of human input or judgment needed is very low. The computer's programs direct and control what the individual does and, in some cases, are even used to pace the employee. This process can result in a dramatic decrease in job interest and satisfaction, and a great increase in the amount of job stress. Organizations that use office automation only in this manner may end up with factorylike offices, which experience problems similar to those of manufacturing assembly lines.

In contrast, office automation can be used to enhance job quality, and it is being used by some companies, according to the Office of Technology Assessment, deliberately for this purpose. Individual employees can be relieved of routine repetitive steps and work instead on fewer, broader tasks, thereby having more of a sense of the purpose and outcome of their work. Office automation can also result in making available to lower-level employees information that was previously used only by persons in higher level jobs. For example, information previously known only to lawyers, medical doctors, or biologists can now be searched for by clerks using databases that contain the information.

The Office of Technology Assessment's report noted that office automation can be used either to enhance job quality or to decrease the importance of skill and routinize individual work. Management has a substantial amount of responsibility regarding the purpose for which automation will be used. The Office did not specifically predict whether the overall impact of office automation on job quality over the next 15 years will be positive or negative.

The seventh possible consequence of office automation pointed out by the Office of Technology Assessment was its impact on employees' health. Three problem areas were addressed, in particular with relation to the use of VDTs (video display terminals): *visual and musculoskeletal problems, reproductive processes,* and *stress.*

For years now, people have raised questions about the long-term health effects of using VDTs. Many individuals using terminals during most of the workday have increased complaints about eyestrain and musculoskeletal problems such as backaches. According to the Office, there is no evidence as yet that problems like these (although serious in terms of day-to-day discomfort), lead to any organic deterioration or chronic disease or illness. Evidence from other occupations with a heavy workload and repetitive tasks, however, does suggest that musculoskeletal strain resulting from VDT work may lead to chronic health effects. The Office therefore pointed out that better workstation design, improved human/computer interfaces, and work breaks during long periods of VDT work can greatly alleviate visual and musculoskeletal problems.

There has been serious concern over reports of clusters of reproductive failures and accidents among clerical VDT employees. To date, these clusters have not been fully explained, but the Office of Technology Assessment reviewed current information and ongoing research in this area and concluded that, at this time, there is no good basis for the fear of VDT effects on reproductive processes. This conclusion, however, does not necessarily apply to the future. The Office recommended that new findings from scientific research be considered as they are reported.

Office automation does result in an atmosphere of increased stress. To some individuals this is seen as a challenge, but some forms of continuing, unrelieved stress are clearly harmful. Computer pacing and computer monitoring, which result in an employee having less autonomy or control over his or her work and in a decrease in his or her performance level, significantly add to stress. Individuals experience anxiety over being able to learn and over being able to do well at their new jobs, and this feeling of job insecurity also increases stress. The Office of Technology Assessment pointed out that there is increasing evidence that long-term high levels of stress are conducive to several kinds of chronic illnesses, such as heart attacks. Because stress-related illness is difficult to control, serious health problems may arise among office personnel of the future.

The information currently available regarding the effect of office automation (in particular the use of VDTs) on employees' health, then, caused the Office of Technology Assessment to draw three conclusions. First, visual and musculoskeletal problems currently can be alleviated through appropriate office and workstation design. Second, at this time there is no basis for worrying about VDT effects on reproductive processes. And third, stress-related illness or disease may emerge as the greatest public health problem among office employees in the future.

Data security and the *confidentiality* of data in computers and databases will also be affected by office automation. The Office of Technology Assessment indicated that greater usage of decentralized or end-user computing increases concern over these issues, because it allows wider access to data and to the means of manipulating it. For example, microcomputer disks used to store data are more easily lost, destroyed, and copied than disks used on the mainframes or central computers. Small computers are not usually monitored or physically guarded, and most end-users are not as well informed about the requirements of confidentiality for client and employee data as computer professionals are. Office automation also often allows work to be done away from the office—in airplanes and homes—which also increases vulnerability. For these and many other reasons, office automation can lead to problems regarding data security and confidentiality.

The Office of Technology Assessment indicated that most organizations have implemented technological and/or procedural means for protecting data with regard to their central computing operations, but the vulnerability of data processed by end-user devices is often overlooked. Organizations moving into office automation for the first time may not realize the threats until serious problems arise.

The ninth possible consequence of office automation covered by the Office of Technology Assessment is its impact on the amount of home-based office work to be done in the near future. One important capability of office automation technology is to allow work to be done at physical locations quite removed from the organizations' primary offices. An individual's home can become the primary work site. The Office predicts that home-based clerical work, with the work performed on a piece-rate or hourly basis, could increase significantly over the next few years.

Office automation, and in particular the increasing trend to capture data at the point of entry and transfer it via telecommunications lines, has already had an effect on the amount of *data entry* work performed "off-shore," or outside of the United States. According to the Office of Technology Assessment, some American firms have already relocated their data entry operations to other countries to take advantage of low labor costs. Entrepreneurs who act as intermediaries also make off-shore data entry services available to U.S. organizations. This type of activity seems to be increasing because advances in communications technology are making it more cost effective, and the Federal Government is encouraging it as a mechanism for assisting economic development in Caribbean countries. If the predicted developments in input technology (such as the improvement of optical scanners and the development of speech recognition) occur, then the need for data entry services will decrease, and as a result, the amount of off-shore data entry will stop increasing. Meanwhile, however, the increase in off-shore performance of this type of work represents a direct loss of U.S. data entry jobs.

There is presently very little empirical evidence regarding one possible consequence of office automation. The Office of Technology Assessment pointed out that government offices in small cities and rural counties are not making much use of office automation, in spite of the opportunities presented by microcomputers. This may be due to a lack of access to qualified personnel or consultants who could help the offices select office equipment and train employees to support it. There is at this stage little information about the aggregate effect of office automation on local and State government offices across the country.

The twelfth possible effect of office automation that concerned the Office of Technology Assessment was its impact on working women and minorities. The Office noted that most clerical jobs are now held by women and that one-third of all the women in the United States are in clerical occupations; they are vulnerable to displacement. In addition, women have less seniority than men in managerial and professional occupations that may be affected by office automation. Office automation is also of particular interest to minorities, because clerical jobs have often been the first step to white-collar employment for these groups. The Office of Technology Assessment concluded that minorities, and in particular black and Hispanic women, are disproportionately represented in jobs likely to be directly affected by office automation.

Chapter 10

How To Get Your First Computer Job

Two other chapters that you should be sure to read are Chapter 2, "Should You Work in Computers?," and Chapter 4, "Changing Your Career to a Computer Career." The information appearing below supplements the discussion of job-hunting that appears in these earlier chapters.

FINDING THE OPENINGS

Geographically, certain areas of the country are known to be major centers for computing and computer jobs. These areas have changed somewhat over recent years, and new areas are said to be of growing importance to people who are working in DP. The standard areas, which have been computer job centers for some time, include the New York metropolitan area, the greater Boston area, and California's "Silicon Valley," which is located south of San Francisco. Washington, D.C. has long been a good area for computer job-hunters because of the extensive use of computers by government agencies and offices. In general, larger companies in larger cities offer the best prospects for job seekers.

If you know you will be located in a particular area, how do you zero in on the openings that are available locally? Want ads are helpful, and they should be checked regularly in computer trade publications (see the list of publications in Appendix B), directories, and local newspapers. If you are now attending a college or trade school, the career services department will be a helpful source of information about local companies. The library and the Chamber of Commerce may be able to supply you with a list of local companies that have computer job openings.

Be sure to talk with friends and relatives who are working in DP in your area. You may also want to attend area meetings of some of the computer trade organizations, such as the American Federation of Information Processing, the Data Processing Management Association, and the Association for Computing Machinery. For information about area or student chapter meetings, write or call the organization at the address or phone listed under Associations in Appendix A. Registering with employment or personnel agencies is also an effective means of securing computer employment. Employment counselors will interview you, and quite often, they will ask you to write up a new resume in a specific format. Then they will send you out on several job interviews. For a list of computer employment agencies, see Chapter 7.

YOUR RESUME

Use standard 8 1/2-inch-by-11-inch paper, either white or ivory, for your resume. It should be typed, with no errors, and preferably one page long, although it can extend to a second page if necessary. When writing your resume, be positive and emphasize your best characteristics, but only use information which is relevant. Be brief, and use facts. If you are interested in more than one particular job, prepare a different resume for each position in which you are interested.

Never list your desired salary or past salaries on your resume. Omitting personal data, unless it is unusually relevant, is recommended by experts in the field. The description of your work experience should not include any personal pronouns, e.g., "I," but instead should start with a verb such as "initiated . . ." or "developed . . ." Do not include a photograph with your resume, and do not include the specific names of your references or former or current employers.

There are certain pieces of information that should be included in your resume. They are, first of all, your name, address, and a telephone number where you can be reached during the day. Second, your career objective should appear, described very succinctly. Then work experience should be described in reverse chronological order, that is, with the most recent employment described first. For each job, be sure to include the name and location of your employer, the dates of your employment, your job title, and specific responsibilities and accomplishments. Describe your education next, with the name and location of your college or university included, as well as your degree, year, major, and extracurricular activities. Following your education information, note that references are available upon request.

Some personnel agencies recommend that

along with this information you include a detailed explanation of your experience with specific types of hardware and software, which would appear with the description of each job you have held.

Most experts in the field recommend that you include a cover letter when you mail out a resume. The cover letter should be brief, and include three kinds of information. In the first paragraph, there should be an explanation of how you discovered the opening for which you are applying. In the following paragraph, indicate specifically what you have to offer that will meet the company's needs. The final paragraph should include a request for an interview, with a sentence similar to: "I will call you early next week to see when you would have a few minutes to meet with me."

INTERVIEWING

Once you've set up an interview, there are a number of things you need to know about what you should do before, during, and after the interview. Whether or not you receive a job offer will depend in part on how well-prepared you are for the interview and how knowledgeable you are about the interviewing process.

This is one time, however, when persistence and patience are very important. Keep in mind that usually a person will have at least several interviews before he or she if offered a job. Even at that point, the individual may decide to interview a little longer if the job opportunity offered to him or her is not exactly what he or she wants. The interviewing process can take weeks or months, depending on the individual.

How to Prepare for Your Interview

Before you go to your interview, do preliminary research on the company and, if possible, the particular position for which you will be interviewing. Call the company's public relations department and ask them to send you a copy of the latest annual report, or go to the local library to read it. Check with your librarian for additional information; some libraries have files of newspaper clippings and other information on companies in their area. Knowing some facts about the company is a good way to demonstrate your interest in the job.

Try to schedule interviews for jobs in which you are less interested first, so you will have some practice before going to interviews for more exciting positions. Keep in mind that in order to do well in your more interesting interviews, you need to approach each one positively, as an opportunity to learn new things, meet new people, and increase your self-confidence.

Talk with the people you would like to use as references before giving their names to an interviewer. Usually, the people you're hoping to use as references will be more than accommodating, but some may feel they need to talk with you first to get more specific information about your present interests and goals. Even the best of references may leave a negative impression if he or she is unaware that you are interviewing and is startled to receive a phone call about you.

Make a list of what you consider to be the important points that you want to bring up at the interview. Include in the list information regarding your experience and how it uniquely qualifies you for the position in which you're interested. Review this list the morning before going to the interview, but not right before the interview, because it will make you more nervous than you would be otherwise.

Prepare your answers to the usual interview questions, many of which appear below. Use the questions to bring out the important points you want to cover. You may find it useful to role-play the interview situation with a friend or to jot down your thoughts on how you would answer each question. Do not take the time to write out the answers and do not memorize your answers; there is a fine line between being well-prepared and being overly prepared. Memorized answers will make you appear unnatural and will make the interviewer feel as if there's something you want to avoid discussing. Typical interview questions include:

- [ ] Tell me about yourself. (Other versions of this question include: What are your principal strengths and limitations? Do you think you are qualified for this job?)

- [ ] Why are you leaving the job you have now?
- [ ] What did you especially like and especially dislike about your last job?
- [ ] What results or duties did not meet your expectations?
- [ ] What type of position would you like to have?
- [ ] What are your career goals? What do you expect to be doing five years from now?
- [ ] How do you feel your career progress has been until now?
- [ ] In what ways have you improved over the last few years?
- [ ] What have you done to enhance your skill development over the last few years?
- [ ] Would you rather do a job, design it, evaluate it, or manage others who are doing it?

As you go to more interviews, you may find that certain questions particular to your own case come up fairly regularly. These should not be problematic unless there is something in your background that is not easy to understand. If this is the case, plan ahead what you will say as an explanation. Be honest, but do not berate yourself. Instead, explain the situation in a way that does not reflect negatively on either you or the other parties involved, especially if the other parties are former employers. Give a concise and to-the-point explanation rather than a lengthy one. Be sure not to try to gloss over the problem area, though, because the interviewer may sense or assume that you are trying to hide something.

What to Bring to Your Interview

Bring several extra copies of your resume and transcript to the interview. You may carry them in a briefcase or a file folder, as long as they are neat.

If you have a sample of work that you have completed that is directly related to an entry-level position for which you are applying—for example, a program you have written—you may want to bring it to your interview. If the position is not an entry-level one, it is probably in your best interest to discuss your projects rather than bring them with you, because each manager often has his or her own preferred style of working.

What to Wear to Your Interview

Look professional and ready for business at your interview. Business suits in quiet or conservative colors are usually appropriate dress. It is also recommended that you wear clothes that are not brand new—especially shoes—so you are comfortable enough with what you're wearing to concentrate on what you're saying.

Personnel Interviews

You may be interviewed by someone in the personnel department before you are interviewed by your prospective boss. If this happens, you will probably be asked some of the questions noted above as well as questions of a more general nature, because the interviewer will be more interested in how you will fit into the company than what your technical abilities are like. He or she will also be interested in whether or not you would stay with the company for an extended period of time, so you may want to point out the specific reasons (based on your research) that you plan to do so.

The impression you make on the personnel interviewer will be one of the factors which determine whether or not a job offer is made to you, but not the sole factor.

What to Say and Do in Your Interview

The first impression you give the interviewer is affected a great deal by whether or not you arrive on time. Find out before you leave the exact directions to the company and allow enough time for traffic and other possible distractions. Plan to arrive at the company about ten minutes early. Always carry the phone number of the person you are to see, and if some major unforeseen problem occurs that will force you to be even a little late, call and explain the situation.

Do not, on the other hand, be extremely early (more than 15 or 20 minutes) for an interview, because it will suggest that you have time on your hands or that you are desperately interested in the job.

Have good posture during your interview. Either sit forward in your chair to demonstrate your interest in the discussion or sit straight up in the chair. And keep your hands and feet still unless you are gesturing to make a point.

Look your interviewer in the eyes during most of the interview. If you wish to break eye contact, do so when you are thinking about answering a question, but meet the interviewer's eyes again as you deliver the response to his or her question. This will affect his or her view of the sincerity of your response, among other things. If you normally are uneasy with this much eye contact, practice beforehand with a friend who is asking you some of the common interview questions.

Do not smoke during your interview, even if your interviewer does.

Show your respect for your interviewer by addressing him or her formally, as Mr. or Ms. Use his or her first name only if he or she specifically asks you to do so.

Be alert, and act reserved and businesslike. Speak up, speak clearly, and do not rush through your sentences.

Expect to be nervous for your interview. Everyone else is—especially when they're very interested in the position. As long as your nervousness does not interfere with your general manner and your response to the interviewer's questions, it may be seen as a positive indication of your excitement about and interest in the job.

Establish rapport with your interviewer. Show an interest in him or her as a person by listening carefully to everything he or she says. Point out any similarities you may have with him or her.

Take an active and not a passive role in your interview. Answer the questions with more than a simple yes or no answer. Remember the list of important points you wanted to cover and bring them up for discussion when the opportunity presents itself. Ask questions about the position for which you are applying—exactly what the responsibilities and duties of the position are and what specific projects you will be working on, for example. One thing the interviewer will be interested in is your ability to ask intelligent questions. This will indicate to him or her that you will need less guidance—and less of his or her time—to get a job done. Do not, however, talk too much, and do not bring up questions regarding vacation time, company benefits, and salary until after you have received a firm job offer.

When you're interviewing for a job, you're actually in a sales situation. You're selling your interviewers on your abilities to do the job well. Be confident. Believe that you are right for the job and an asset to the company. Be enthusiastic about your talents, but be sincere. Do not exaggerate what you have done or what you are capable of doing, because doing so will only present problems for you at a later time. Instead of just claiming certain attributes, bring up your accomplishments in the field and point out how they indicate that you have the right attributes for the job. If you do not understand a buzzword that the interviewer uses, admit it. He or she is more interested in your understanding of concepts rather than buzzwords, anyway.

There are two common kinds of interviews that you may encounter and of which you should be aware: an interview that puts you under a seemingly inordinate amount of stress, and an interview in which many aspects of the company and the job are presented in a negative light.

The stressful interview is one which is run at high speed and in which you are expected to answer all questions quickly, concisely, and in a literate manner. If this seems too much to ask of a person in an evaluative situation like a job interview, that is because it is meant to be too much. The interviewer is interested in testing the interviewee's ability to remain calm and lucid under unfriendly circumstances, probably because this is an important part of the job for which he or she is applying. For example, some computer careers (see Chapter 5) involve interaction with demanding users who are interested only in getting the job done and not necessarily in understanding what is involved in the implementation of a large project. The technical people who interface with the user must be able to work well under pressure, stay calm, and keep the user reasonably satisfied with the project's progress.

The best thing to do when you are in the middle of a high-stress interview is to recognize it for what it is. The important thing is to stay calm and answer the questions as best you can.

The second type of interview to watch for is an interview in which the company and the position are described very negatively. All of the difficult responsibilities of the position are stressed, and several reasons you probably do not want the job are discussed.

When you find yourself in a negative interview, try to understand why the job is presented as it is. Did the last several people who took the job leave the company after only a short time? Occasionally, the interviewer is testing the applicant's interest, and sometimes he or she may feel that the best way to find a person who will stay in a certain job is to describe the job as realistically as possible in order to avoid any surprises. Even if the job as it is now described sounds like it is not for you, concentrate on getting the offer.

After the interview, think about whether the job could provide an exceptional opportunity for you. Will you be promoted more quickly if you start at the company in this position instead of an easier one? Will you be able to work on interesting projects sooner than you would be able to in another job or at another company? Sometimes situations described very negatively can be a real opportunity for entry-level individuals. In some cases, however, the job is being accurately described, and an offer should not be accepted by an individual who feels he or she would not enjoy the position. The decision is up to you.

Regardless of the type of interview you have, you may find part of the way through the interview that the job is not exactly what you had expected. Many entry-level positions, in particular, can involve some boring or routine work. But your goal in the interview is always to get the job offer. You may decide later that it would be a good starting point for you, or you may be able to use it as leverage to help you firm up an offer at another company. Before the end of the interview, ask for the job by saying, for example, "Do you think I can have the job?"

Many tips regarding what to say and do in your interview have been discussed in the previous pages. They are all important, but perhaps the most important tip is to be yourself, believe in yourself, and do not forget to ask for the job. And again, usually job offers do not result from every interview, so be patient and persistent.

The Job Offer

A few follow-up phone calls may be necessary after an interview in order to obtain a written job offer. Never assume that an offer is firm until you have it in writing.

WHAT TO EXPECT
WHEN YOU BEGIN THE JOB

There are distinct differences between computer jobs in larger DP departments and jobs in smaller DP departments. Companies with larger departments usually offer more opportunity to advance. Even though junior programmers, for example, may work only on maintenance projects and not on development, they have more of a chance of progressing into development work than if they were part of a small DP department. Often, DP professionals in large departments work on a small part of a project for quite a long period of time.

Many large departments offer some kind of structured training program, whether the program includes self-instructional audiovisual cassettes or time spent working with a senior DP individual.

There are different drawbacks and advantages to working in a small DP department. Jobs are often broader in scope and definition, so programmers, for example, may deal directly with users and may redefine and sometimes help to develop the systems analyst's specs. Often programmers and other DP professionals work on a number of different systems and/or applications. In some cases, however, they do not have an opportunity to develop systems, but instead spend their time customizing software packages for their installation (or fitting it to their installation's needs). Training, if it exists in a smaller DP department, is usually very unstructured, so it is difficult to tell which senior person should be asked for help with questions on a particular project.

Work in a medium-sized computer installation can offer the advantages of both larger and smaller shops and the disadvantages of neither. Entry-level positions in medium-sized shops are difficult to find, however.

Chapter 11

Long-Range
Computer Career Planning

Long-term computer career planning can be very time-consuming. Often, there is so much to do at your present job that there never seems to be enough time to investigate other opportunities or to take classes to upgrade your skills. Long-term career planning is necessary, though, for a satisfying career, and in order to be effective, career planning must be an ongoing activity. But why is long-term planning so important to a successful and fulfilling career?

First, good long-range planning will not restrict an individual's ability to change and take risks. Each plan should include checkpoints at six-month or twelve-month intervals, at which time the computer professional should allocate a substantial amount of his or her private time to the reevaluation of his or her long-term career plan. New on-the-job experience and recent training may result in substantial revisions of a long-term plan. The checkpoints are also a time for evaluating whether or not the expected progress has been made in the past six months or year. If progress is slower than

expected, you may want to revise your plan to make it more realistic, or you may want to get additional information from a career counselor or other sources, which are discussed below.

Long-range career planning is important to computer professionals partly because technology is changing so rapidly that some skills are outdated in as little as three years. So, the training that you need to reach a certain goal may differ greatly from what you thought you would need when you first set down your plan two or three years ago.

Without a long-term career plan that you review periodically, it is possible for computer professionals to get very involved with solving a particular problem. While that person is concentrating on putting out those particular fires, he or she may be bypassed for opportunities that arise and that may be in line with his or her long-term goals.

Computer professionals working in research and development departments, whether on software or hardware, sometimes run into the problem of investing a great deal of time and energy on a project that dies before coming to fruition. There are a number of reasons that not every system that is developed is a success—occasionally, the senior executives at a company change their minds (or sometimes they are replaced by individuals who want to follow a different course of action), or sometimes a project is dropped because a critical detail comes to light. Whenever this happens, the people working on the project feel that they have wasted a lot of time, but they also may have acquired skills from working on the dead project that are not easily transferable to other projects. Keeping long-term goals in mind can help a computer professional lessen the impact of a cancelled project on his or her career.

A computer programmer or systems analyst who is concentrating on short-term goals and rewards may become too specialized. This problem is difficult to avoid, because the rewards of specialization may be very high. For example, a junior programmer might start his or her computer career at a large company that is about to implement a billing system for internal computer usage. With tight deadlines on the system's implementation, it is easy for the programmer to spend all of his or her time learning about the product and solving problems that occur in trying to interface the product with other software that the company is currently using. Soon the programmer has detailed knowledge about the billing system, but little understanding of other products used in the company and other projects underway in his or her department. Once the billing system has been fully implemented, the person who installed the system is often made the "expert" for the system. He or she will continue to upgrade the system by applying updates. The programmer will be consulted whenever problems arise and will be held responsible for fixing them. Because the knowledge that this one person has is critical to the smooth running of the billing system, he or she may be paid handsomely in order to continue work on that one project. Sometimes, even if a programmer is no longer challenged by the project, he or she will continue to work on it—to the exclusion of other projects—because of job security, knowing that they and their highly specialized

knowledge cannot be easily replaced, and because of the sizeable paycheck. But a person who has become this specialized will eventually be overlooked at promotion time, because his or her skills are not very general. Sometimes, programmers in this position have to change companies in order to avoid a dead end in their career paths, and sometimes they have to take a cut in salary because they were being paid more than the market value for their skills. The frustration experienced in over-specialization can be avoided by formulating a long-term career plan and then consistently evaluating your progress toward your goals.

It is clear, then, that a number of problems can be avoided by taking time out early in your career to put together a long-range computer career plan.

DEVELOPING YOUR OWN LONG-RANGE COMPUTER CAREER PLAN

Many career counselors recommend a five-year personal career plan. There are three basic steps you need to follow to devise your own plan, but before you work on your plan, decide how you will keep tabs on your career development. Do you want to set aside time for a personal career planning session every six months or every year? Make a note of your next planning session on a calendar you always use. When you've put together your initial plan, date it and file your notes away in a place you'll be able to find in six months or a year.

Following are the three steps to follow to come up with your personal career plan.

First, determine what your goals are. In order to do this, you should be aware of what opportunities are available. Read Chapter 5 thoroughly so you are knowledgeable about the different computer careers that exist. Deciding what you want to do with your life also depends on knowing who you are and where your interests and talents lie.

Take the time to discuss with your spouse and write down what you want to do with your life, how much money you would like to make, and what kind of lifestyle you want. Set a tentative time frame for your goals over the next five years. Try to set some intermediate goals as well as some longer-term goals. Note what progress you expect to have made toward your career goals by the time you sit down to think about your career plan again.

Step two involves deciding what you need to do to achieve the goals you defined in step one. Make a list of ten things that you can do to start getting closer to your goals. Be very specific as to when you plan to do these things. For example, think about the training that might be required to reach your goals (see Chapter 12 on Training and Education) and set a time frame for taking one class or course. Advanced degrees are sometimes a big plus for higher-level careers. In particular, an M.B.A. is seen in today's market as evidence of a business management orientation that is much broader than particular computer skills. If not an entire degree, you may want to take a special seminar or workshop to help you keep up with new developments in your present or intended field. Besides providing current technical information, seminars can provide opportunities for meeting other people who work in or are interested in your field. Another source of information, as well as professional contacts, is meetings, trade shows, and exhibitions. If you are not interested in traveling, you can upgrade or increase your skills by reading trade publications and books. Or you may want to join a professional association in your field (see Appendix A).

Part of your list of things to do to achieve your goals may be a job change. How do you know when it's time for a change in positions? One good indication is a loss of whatever drew you to the job in the first place, for example, a sense of challenge. Make a list of your job change priorities, such as challenge, responsibility, and money. But remember that going through a job change is traumatic for many people. If you are sure it's time to switch, it is important to leave on the right note, so you will have good references for the future. Give your employer adequate notice and provide enough documentation for a smooth replacement for your position. Experts differ on how often individuals can job-hop without becoming stigmatized. See Chapter 5 regarding the outlook or demand for people working in your field. In general, prospective employers for higher-level computer jobs usually want to see from three to five years on a job. A shorter term of employment might require an explanation. Again, this varies with the position, the employer, and the individual being interviewed for the job.

The third step to follow regarding your personal career plan is to keep to your schedule for re-evaluating your plan. Ever six or twelve months, look over your plan and update it based on the experience and information you have recently accumulated. Are your goals still the same? Are other measures needed to ensure that you reach your goals? How well did you estimate your progress, by this time, toward your intermediate and longer-term goals?

SUMMARY

To summarize: to have an effective long-range computer career plan, determine what your goals are, decide what you need to do to achieve your goals, and keep to a schedule for a periodic re-evaluation of your career plan. Careful and consistent long-range computer career planning can help ensure your success and fulfillment in a computer career.

Chapter 12

Training and Education

Many different types of training and education are available today. Before deciding on the training you need, study Chapter 5's description of computer careers and decide what kind of computer career you want. How much and what type of education you need also depends on how far you would like to progress on either the DP or your company's management ladder. Many people decide to get a bachelor's degree because it opens the door to so many opportunities.

Six different sources of education and training are discussed in this chapter. They are, in alphabetical order:

- [ ] Armed Forces training (Air Force, Army, Marine Corps, Navy).
- [ ] Colleges and universities (Undergraduate and graduate colleges).
- [ ] Community colleges.
- [ ] Corporate training programs.
- [ ] Home study courses.
- [ ] Trade and technical schools.

ARMED FORCES TRAINING

Included in this section are descriptions of many of the computer careers training programs available through or from the Air Force, Army, Marine Corps, and Navy. Further information can be obtained from your local recruiter.

Air Force[8]

Individuals enlisted in the Air Force may qualify for specialization in the *computer systems occupation*. The job involves the collection, processing, recording, preparation, and submission of data to various automated systems. In addition, the individual will do some programming, operate some computer systems, and analyze the systems' design. The background desirable for this specialization is business math, algebra, and geometry. Examples of civilian jobs which are similar includes computer operator,

[8]Source: Community Relations Division, Secretary of the Air Force, Office of Public Affairs, Room 4A120, The Pentagon, Washington, DC 20330.

printer operator, and programmer. For the most current information, call your local Air Force recruiter.

Navy[9]

Individuals enlisted in the Navy may qualify for training as a *data processing technician* or a *data systems technician*. Appearing below are a description of the two programs: what the personnel do, their working environment, qualifications and interests, the career path after recruit training, opportunities, and related civilian jobs. For further information, check with your local Navy recruiter.

Data processing technicians. *Data processing technicians* operate a wide range of equipment required to keep personnel records (such as health, pay, qualifications, assignments, and promotions), to maintain supplies and disbursement records, and to keep track of all the equipment the Navy owns.

What they do:

☐ Operate data processing equipment such as sorters, collators, reproducers, interpreters,

☐ Perform systems analyst functions.

Data processing technicians usually work in a clean, comfortable office or computer room. Sometimes they work alone; sometimes they work with others. They are generally closely supervised and do mostly mental work.

Writing ability, creativity, curiosity, a good memory, and an orientation toward ideas and information are all very important qualifications for success in this rating. Other important qualities are the ability to do detailed work and keep records, and some degree of manual dexterity. It is helpful, too, if candidates work efficiently with others as a team, get along well with people, and are able to express themselves clearly verbally. Competence with tools, machines, and equipment is a useful quality in this rating.

The enlistee is taught the fundamentals of this rating through on-the-job training or formal Navy schooling. Advanced technical and operational training is available in this rating during later stages of career development.

School	Present Location	Approximate Training Time	Subjects	Training Methods
Class "A" Technical School	San Diego, CA	8 weeks	Basic data processing	Group Instruction

accounting machines, and electronic data processing systems.
☐ Write programs for controlling electronic data processing operations.
☐ Establish and maintain controls on data processing machines.
☐ Determine cause of operational failure of data processing machines.
☐ Design card layouts and report forms.
☐ Prepare procedure manuals.
☐ Perform office management functions.

Graduates of "A" school may be assigned to ships or shore stations in the United States or overseas. During a 20-year period in the Navy, DPs usually spend approximately 40 percent of their time assigned to fleet units and 60 percent assigned to shore stations.

Except for highly qualified applicants, opportunities for placement in this rating are limited. At present, over 3,800 men and women are performing work in the data processing rating.

The following are related job titles: *systems analyst, data entry, computer programmer, supervisor of computer operations, computer operator, peripheral equipment operator.*

[9]Source: Department of the Navy, Chief of Naval Education and Training, Public Affairs Office, Naval Air Station, Pensacola, FL 32508.

Data systems technicians. *Data systems technicians* are electronics technicians who specialize in computer systems. They service, maintain, adjust, and repair digital computers, video processors, tape units, buffers, key sets, digital display equipment, data link terminal sets, and related equipment.

What they do:

☐ Perform a variety of functions relating to operation and maintenance of computers and other electronic digital data systems.

☐ Establish and administer safety precautions in dealing with electrical equipment and radioactive material.

People who want to enter the data systems technician rating should have good arithmetic ability and the ability to speak and write well, do detailed work, and keep accurate records. They should be idea and information oriented, resourceful, curious, and have a good memory. Manual dexterity is important. It is also helpful if they are able to do repetitive tasks, perform well as team members, work with tools, equipment, and machines, and have physical strength.

The enlistee is taught the fundamentals of this rating through on-the-job training or formal Navy schooling. Advanced technical and operational training is available in this rating during later stages of career development.

School	Present Location	Approximate Training Time	Subjects	Training Methods
Basic Electricity and Electronics	Great Lakes, IL, Orlando, FL, or San Diego, CA	9-10 Weeks (individualized)	Basic Technical knowledge and skills of electricity and electronics	Individualized instruction
Class "A" Technical School	San Francisco, CA (Vallejo)	22 weeks	Basic computer maintenance and theory	Group instruction, lab

☐ Operate electronic test equipment.
☐ Maintain inventory of tools and equipment.
☐ Compile data for reports.
☐ Establish and administer maintenance systems.

People in this rating usually work in clean, comfortable shop situations. They perform site adjustments and repairs on large pieces of digital equipment scattered throughout shipboard and shore installations. They perform most of their work as part of a team under close supervision. Their work is mostly mental, with physical strength required for some maintenance tasks.

Graduates of "A" school continue on for advanced training at "C" school. DSs may be assigned to any ship, submarine, or shore station equipped with electronic computers. During a 20-year period in the Navy, DSs usually spend approximately 60 percent of their time assigned to fleet units and 40 percent assigned to shore stations.

Opportunities for placement in this rating are limited to highly qualified applicants. Currently, there are over 2,600 men and women performing work in the DS rating.

The following are related civilian job titles: *electronics mechanic, hardware service technician.*

Army[10]

Individuals enlisted in the Army may qualify for Information Systems Management training, which is administered by the Information Systems Command. For further information about this program, see or call your local Army recruiter or, if you are in the Army, the officer to which you report.

A computer training program for civilians is available to qualified Department of Army civilians who are hired into the field of data processing. The two-year career program for these federal civil service workers is called the *Automatic Data Processing (ADP) Career Intern Plan.*

A college degree is not necessary for participation in the program, but it is desirable. Typically, beginning career interns earn about $14,000 annually; at the completion of two years of training they make about $22,000 annually.

A general description of the program, which is administered by the United States Training and Doctrine Command (TRADOC), appears below. Also shown are a description of the plan's two phases and its 18 courses.

Summary of ADP Career Intern Plan

Participants in the program are designated as *TRADOC ADP Career Interns.* They will receive training for eventual advancement to GS-334 positions in the ADP Civilian Career Program.

Intern training will be accomplished by on-the-job training (OJT), self-study training courses, formal classroom training, and Temporary Duty (TDY) training. Additionally, college level courses at local universities may be made available. On-the-job training provides for the acquisition of necessary knowledge, skill, and understanding in the environment of an ADP computer specialist while under competent supervision. On-the-job training and classroom/self-study experiences involve progressively more difficult and complex assignments until, at the end of the scheduled training, the intern is fully qualified to function as an ADP computer specialist.

This is a two-year training program with training accomplished the first year at Fort Monroe and assignment the second year at the intern's assigned Permanent Duty Location (PDL). This program may be expanded to include additional training due to changes in technology.

The training for the first year includes rotational OJT at Fort Monroe and attendance in designated training courses designed to provide the intern with a thorough introduction to as many ADP topics as possible. Those interns who complete required training early may be selected to attend advanced training classes and/or advanced OJT.

The training for the second year includes attendance in designated training courses and continuing OJT at the PDL.

Facilities available to the intern include two large-scale IBM computers, several different minicomputers, office automation network of processors, and a data graphics system.

Because of the changing staffing needs within TRADOC, the PDL for a particular intern can seldom be identified until the latter part of the first year of training. An agreement for DA CTED Interns, DA form 5227-R, Jun 83 (Enclosure 2), must be signed by every intern. Permanent Duty Location determinations are based primarily on long-range command-wide staffing requirements, the immediate needs of the location, academic performance of the individual trainee, and the preferences of the intern. Such determinations will be made and communicated to the intern as early as possible. Exceptions to this rule are those interns hired at TRADOC installations to fill existing vacancies and sent TDY or moved Permanent Change of Station (PCS) to Fort Monroe for training. In all cases, the TRADOC ADP Career Program Manager will make final determinations of the PDL for a particular intern based upon information supplied by the DPFO Commander to include intern academic performance and intern PDL preference.

Areas of Concentration

Applied Systems Analysis and Design (520 hrs.). Trainee will work under the direction of an experienced computer system analyst. Proj-

---

[10]Source: Department of the Army, Headquarters TRADOC.

ect will involve the analysis and design of a functional system to operate on the DPFO mainframe or the office automation network of processors. As part of the normal analysis and design environment, there will be involvement with Army regulations and procurement policies.

Applied FORTRAN Programming (520 hrs.). Trainee will work under the direction of an experienced computer specialist. Project will involve the use of FORTRAN capabilities in solving scientific problems. Work will be performed on DPFO mainframe or the office automation network of processors. There may be extensive use of vendor developed statistical packages.

Computer Graphics (520 hrs.). Trainee will work under the direction of an experienced computer programmer. Project will involve the use of several different processors in the practical application of graphic solutions to business problems. There will be extensive use of vendor developed graphics packages.

Advanced Data Communications (520 hrs.). Trainee will work under the direction of an experienced computer specialist. Project will involve additional training courses to include advanced data communication concepts and a thorough introduction to data communication hardware.

Advanced Database Management (520 hrs.). Trainee will work under the direction of an experienced computer specialist who serves as the DPFO database administrator. Project will involve additional training in advanced database concepts. Work may involve using a microdatabase on one of the office automation network processors.

Applied Assembler Programming (520 hrs.). Trainee will work under the direction of an experienced computer specialist. Project will involve working with the DPFO Executive Support Group on the IBM mainframes or any of the office automation network processors in an effort to integrate software from various vendors.

Extended COBOL Application (520 hrs.). Trainee will work under the direction of an experienced computer specialist. Project will be similar to the basic COBOL OJT, but will be more extensive.

Management of Standard Army Systems (520 hrs.). Trainee will work under the direction of an experienced computer specialist. Project will involve additional training, to be conducted by HQ TRADOC Staff ADP personnel who are involved in ADP system Acquisition and approval, as well as the overall monitoring of processing in TRADOC. Temporary Duty (TDY) to Forts Eustis and Lee may be involved in order to obtain a thorough background in the day-to-day operation/maintenance of standard Army systems.

Information Systems Management (520 hrs.). Trainee will work under the direction of the Commander, DPFO or the Deputy Commander, DPFO. Project will involve a study of the practical application of management theories and strategies in the area of business data processing.

ADP Procurement Policies and Procedures (520 hrs.). Trainee will work under the direction of the Commander, DPFO, or Deputy Commander, DPFO. Project will involve a study of Army ADP procurement policies and procedures. Additional training will be provided by in-house personnel.

Course Objectives

Overall course descriptions and course objectives are listed below for each course identified in the ADP Career Intern Training Plan. ADP training vendors provide detailed course objectives at the start of each course. Courses normally will be studied in the sequence listed below.

Data Processing Concepts—Control Data Corporation—PLATO. Course provides an introduction to basic ADP concepts and vocabulary. Upon successful completion of the course with a grade of 80 or better, the student will be able to:

- ☐ List the five functions of a computer system.
- ☐ Define applications in terms of input, processing, and output.
- ☐ Explain the importance of accuracy and control in business.
- ☐ List the phases of a system development life cycle.

- [ ] Describe the work performed by each data processing job title.
- [ ] Describe the functions of the arithmetic/logic unit, unit, storage, and control.
- [ ] Describe how data is read to and written from each of the common input/output devices.
- [ ] Contrast byte and word storage.
- [ ] Trace the flow of data through a multiprogramming computer.
- [ ] Describe sequential, indexed sequential, and random file organization.
- [ ] Explain the seven steps of the program development cycle.

Note: This course has several subparts, each of which has a test which must be passed with a grade of 80 or better. The final grade is the average of all the subpart test grades.

Program Logic and Techniques—Advanced Systems; Inc.—(ASI). Course provides practical understanding of problem solving techniques used in computer programming. Upon successful completion of this course with a grade of 80 or better, the student will be able to:

- [ ] Develop computer flow charts.
- [ ] Describe the programing task in terms of input processing and output.

Note: This course has several subparts, each of which has a test which must be passed with a grade of 80 or better. The final grade is the average of all the subpart test grades.

Out in DPFO Operations. On-the-job training assignment in DPFO operations will provide the intern with a practical understanding of the functions of the DPFO Production Branch. Upon successful completion of the OJT with a supervisory rating of average or better (ATDP Form 139), student will be able to:

- [ ] With guidance and assistance, function as an entry level operator of the DPFO computers.
- [ ] With guidance and assistance, function as

an assistant to the DPFO tape librarian.

BASIC—PLATO. BASIC is a business data processing program language used on mini- and microcomputers. Course will provide a detailed understanding and practical application of the essentials of BASIC. Upon successful completion of the course with a grade of 80 or better and execution of four problem programs (see below), the student will be able to design, flow chart, code, test, and debug business-oriented BASIC programs involving:

- [ ] Listing with heading, labeled information, and final totals.
- [ ] Calculation requiring counters, truncation, rounding, accuracy vs. precision.
- [ ] Two-way, three-way, and complex multiple decisions.
- [ ] Use of strings, subscripted variables, tables and table lookup methods.

Note: This course has four subparts, two of which have a test which must be passed with a grade of 80 percent or better. The final grade is the average of both the subpart test grades.

There are four BASIC problem programs which must be correctly written and successfully run in order to complete the course. General guidance for the amount of time allotted to complete the four BASIC problem programs is detailed below. Prior to programing, flow charts must be approved by an advisor.

- [ ] Program 1 should be completed five working days after start of course.
- [ ] Program 2 should be completed eight days after start of course.
- [ ] Program 3 should be completed 12 working days after start of course.
- [ ] Program 4 should be completed 15 working days after start of course.

Points are awarded, as detailed below, only for the successful completion of the four BASIC problem programs within the time constraints. Any time saved at the beginning of the course may be used at the end.

Program 1-2 20 points each
Program 3-4 30 points each

Programs 1-2 must be completed by the end of ten working days. Points are deducted for each program (1-2) not completed at the end of ten working days, but these programs must still be completed by the end of 15 working days.

Programs 3-4 must be completed by the end of 15 working days. Points are deducted for each program not completed at the end of 15 working days; however, work on the incomplete programs must continue until all programs are complete. Practical exercise portion of course must be completed with a total of 80 points or greater at the end of 15 working days.

Note: A walkthrough of programs 2 and 4 will be conducted. In the walkthrough process, a selected trainee must explain the logic of the program flowchart. Additionally, the selected trainee must explain the step-by-step flow of the problem program itself and respond to questions from other interns and/or the course advisor. The interns selected to explain the flowcharts and the problem programs will be notified at least one day prior to the walkthrough. For the selected interns, specific comments on the walkthrough will be made on the semi-annual appraisal, DA Form 4969.

File Organization and Accessing Methods/VSAM Concepts—ASI. Course will provide a practical application of methods and procedures for organizing and accessing data files. Upon successful completion of this course with a grade of 80 or better, the student will be able to:

☐ Develop the logic flow of a complete file maintenance system including the application of record changes, deletions, and additions.

☐ Name and describe the four most common forms of data file organization.

☐ Create, load, and process and VSAM data set.

Note: This course has several subparts, each of which must be passed with a grade of 80 or better. The final grade is the average of all the subpart test grades.

Structured COBOL—ASI. COBOL is a business data processing language. Course will provide a detailed understanding and practical application of IBM COBOL. Upon successful completion of this course with a grade of 80 or better and execution of 11 problem programs (see below), the student will be able to:

☐ List the rules for forming each of the following:

    (a) Literals
    (b) External names
    (c) Section names
    (d) File names
    (e) Condition names
    (f) Data names
    (g) System names
    (h) Paragraph names
    (i) Record names

☐ Write an Identification Division containing all required and optional entries.

☐ Write an Environment Division, Configuration Section, for a program which creates reports, from sequential file input.

☐ Write an Environment Division, Input/Output Section containing SELECT clauses and ASSIGN clauses.

☐ Write a Data Division, File Section, describing the characteristics of a sequential file and its records, including REDEFINES clauses and FILLER.

☐ Write a Data Division, Working-Storage Section, including VALUE clauses.

☐ Write descriptions of numeric data fields whose data representations are the following: External (Zoned) Decimal, Internal (Packed) Decimal, and Binary.

☐ Write a Procedure Division which accomplishes a two-file merge using the following statements: OPEN, CLOSE, READ,

WRITE, MOVE, ADD, SUBTRACT, MULTIPLY, DIVIDE, COMPUTE, STOP, PERFORM, and IF.
- [ ] Write a Data Division entry to describe the horizontal formatting of a printed report.
- [ ] Write Environment and Procedure Division entries to create vertical formatting of a printed report.
- [ ] Write routines to detect and process single and multiple control breaks.
- [ ] Use pseudocode to help design the logic flow of a program.

There are 11 COBOL programs which must be correctly written and successfully run in order to complete the course. General guidance for the amount of time allotted to complete the 11 COBOL problem programs is detailed below:

- [ ] Program 1 should be completed two working days after start of course.
- [ ] Program 2 should be completed four working days after start of course.
- [ ] Program 3 should be completed six working days after start of course.
- [ ] Program 4 should be completed eight working days after start of course.
- [ ] Program 5 should be completed ten working days after start of course.
- [ ] Program 6 should be completed 12 working days after start of course.
- [ ] Program 7 should be completed 16 working days after start of course.
- [ ] Program 8 should be completed 20 working days after start of course.
- [ ] Program 9 should be completed 30 working days after start of course.
- [ ] Program 10 should be completed 30 working days after start of course.
- [ ] Program 11 should be completed 45 working days after start of course.

Points are awarded only for the successful completion of the 11 COBOL problem programs within the time constraints as detailed below. Any time saved at the beginning of the course may be used at the end.

Program 1-6 and 8-9	5 points each
Program 7	10 points
Program 10-11	25 points each

Note: Submission of an incomplete/incorrect problem will result in point deductions as detailed below for each incomplete/incorrect submission.

Program 1-6 and 8-9	1 point
Program 7	2 points
Program 10-11	3 points

Programs (1-4) must be completed by the end of ten working days. Points are deducted for each program (1-4) not completed at the end of ten working days, but these programs must still be completed by the end of 45 working days.

Programs (1-7) must be completed by the end of 20 working days. Points are deducted for each program (1-7) not completed at the end of 20 working days, but these programs must still be completed by the end of 45 working days.

Programs (1-11) must be completed by the end of 45 working days. Points are deducted for each program not completed at the end of 45 working days; however, work on the incomplete programs must continue until all programs are completed. Practical exercise portion of the course must be completed with a total of 80 points or greater at the end of 45 working days. Note: Course test is given at the end of 45 working days (see below).

Each section of the course text (1-11), has a quiz to be completed. All quizzes must be passed with a grade of 80 percent or better. In addition, there is a final end-of-course test which must be passed with a final grade of 80 percent or better.

Note: A walkthrough of program 4, 9, and 11 will be conducted. In the walkthrough process, a selected trainee must explain the logic of the program flowchart. Additionally, the selected trainee must explain the step-by-step flow of the problem program itself and respond to questions from other interns and/or the course advisor. The interns selected to explain the flowchart and the problem program will be notified at least one day prior to the walkthrough. For the selected interns, specific comments on the walkthrough will be made on the semiannual appraisal, DA Form 4969.

Advanced COBOL—Deltak. Course will provide a detailed understanding and practical application of advanced data handling/manipulation features of COBOL. Upon successful completion of this course, which is the execution of two programs (see below), the student will be able to:

☐ Code statements used for subroutine and subprogram linkage.
☐ Code statements to build and use two- and three-dimensional tables.

There are two COBOL programs which must be correctly written and successfully run in order to complete this course. General guidance for the amount of time allotted to complete the two COBOL problem programs is detailed below:

☐ Program 1 must be completed 5 working days after start of course.
☐ Program 2 must be completed 10 working days after start of course.

Points are awarded only for the successful completion of the two COBOL problem programs within the time constraints as detailed below. Any time saved at the beginning of the course may be used at the end.

Program 1   40 points each
Program 2   60 points each

Note: Submission of an incomplete/incorrect problem will result in point deductions as detailed below for each incomplete/incorrect submission.

Program 1   10 points
Program 2   10 points

Program 1 must be completed by the end of five working days. Points are deducted for the failure to complete program 1 by the end of five working days, but this program must still be completed by the end of ten working days.

Programs 1 and 2 must be completed by the end of the ten working days. Points are deducted for each program not completed at the end of ten working days; however, work on the incomplete programs must continue until all programs are completed. Practical exercise portion of the course must be completed with a total of 80 points or more at the end of ten working days. There is no final test.

Note: A walkthrough of program 2 will be conducted. In the walkthrough process, a selected trainee must explain the logic of the program flowchart. Additionally, the selected trainee must explain the step-by-step flow of the problem program itself and respond to questions from other interns and/or the course advisor. The interns selected to explain the flowchart and the problem program will be notified at least one day prior to the walkthrough. For the selected interns, specific comments on the walkthrough will be made on the semiannual appraisal, DA Form 4969.

COBOL OJT. The COBOL OJT will allow the student to put book theory into practice. Upon successful completion of the OJT with a supervisory rating of average or better Intern Weekly Progress Report (ATDP Form 139) the student will be able to:

☐ Effectively and efficiently use TSO to manipulate COBOL program statements.
☐ Develop detailed program flow charts from information provided by the OJT supervisor as follows:

(a) Record layouts, input/output.
(b) Written description of what the program is to do.
(c) General, nonspecific program flow charts.

☐ Write moderately complex COBOL program.
☐ Write a COBOL program that conforms to

structured guidelines presented in ASI COBOL Course.

☐ Document the completed OJT COBOL program(s) according to Computer Systems Command documentation procedures.
☐ Effectively use DPFO Executive Support Group data manipulation utility E01CTU.
☐ Write a COBOL program that has two input data files.
☐ Write COBOL program that effectively and efficiently uses:

    (a) Two- or three-dimensional tables.
    (b) Manipulation of COMP or COMP-3 data.
    (c) Editing procedures.
    (d) Redefine clause(s).
    (e) Error handling procedures.

Note: The OJT will have milestones to be met by the trainee. An In Progress Review (IPR) will be conducted at each milestone date. Failure to meet milestone dates, as identified through the Intern Progress Review (IPR), will result in a termination of the OJT with a Marginal rating.

Job Control Language—PLATO. Course provides basic background in the MVS operating system prior to providing a detailed overview of MVS job control statements. Upon successful completion of the course with a grade of 80 or better, the student will be able to:

☐ Specify the difference between previous OS and VS operating systems and the MVS operating system.
☐ State the general functions of the Job Control Language in a MVS system.
☐ Describe the rules for valid JCL format and syntax.
☐ Code multiple-step job streams incorporating conditions execution.

Note: this course has several subparts, each of which has a test which must be passed with a grade of 80 or better. The final grade is the average of all the subpart test grades.

FORTRAN—Deltak. FORTRAN is a scientific data processing language. Course provides for practical, but limited experience in FORTRAN programming—coding, compiling, testing, and debugging. Upon successful completion of the course with the grade of 80 and execution of 10 problem programs (see below), the student will be able to:

☐ Read, process, and write arrays of one or more dimensions.
☐ Read, process, and write sequential and random access files.
☐ Control program execution using IF, GO TO, CALL, and DO statements.

There are ten FORTRAN problem programs which must be correctly written and successfully run in order to complete the course. General guidance for the amount of time allotted to complete the 10 FORTRAN problem programs is detailed below:

☐ Program 1 should be completed two working days after start of course.
☐ Program 2 should be completed three working days after start of course.
☐ Program 3 should be completed four working days after start of course.
☐ Program 4 should be completed five working days after start of course.
☐ Program 5 should be completed six working days after start of course.
☐ Program 6 should be completed seven working days after start of course.
☐ Program 7 should be completed eight working days after start of course.
☐ Program 8 should be completed ten working days after start of course.
☐ Program 9 should be completed 12 working days after start of course.
☐ Program 10 should be completed 14 working days after start of course.

Points are awarded only for the successful completion of the 10 FORTRAN problem programs within the time constraints as detailed below. Any time saved in the beginning of the course may be used at the end.

Program 1-3	5 points each
Program 4-9	10 points each
Program 10	25 points

Note: Submission of an incomplete/incorrect problem will result in point deductions as detailed below for each incomplete/incorrect submission.

Program 1-3	1 point
Program 4-9	2 points
Program 10	5 points

Programs 1-3 must be completed by the end of the four working days. Points are deducted for each program (1-3) not completed at the end of five working days, but these programs must still be completed by the end of 15 working days.

Programs 1-7 must be completed by the end of ten working days. Points are deducted for each program (1-7) not completed at the end of ten working days, but these programs must still be completed by the end of the 15 working days.

Programs 1-10 must be completed by the end of 15 working days. Points are deducted for each program not completed at the end of 15 working days; however, work on the incomplete programs must continue until all programs are completed. Practical exercise portion of the course must be completed with a total of 80 points or more at the end of 15 working days. Note: There is no final test.

Business Systems Analysis and Design—PLATO. Course provides a complete curriculum on all of the essential skills necessary for successful systems design and analysis—to include interpersonal skills. Upon successful completion of the course with a grade of 80 or better, the student will be able to:

☐ List three reasons for using a phased approach to the development, modification, and enhancement of data processing systems.
☐ Explain the key difference between the systems analyst job and other data processing jobs such as systems design and programming.
☐ Describe the working relationship between the systems analyst and the user.

Note: This course has several subparts, each of which has a test which must be passed with a grade of 80 or better. The final grade is the average of all the subpart test grades.

ADP Systems Analysis For Computer Programmer—Office of Personnel Management. Course is designed to produce ADP personnel, functional analysts, system users, and managers who are capable of utilizing structured design and analysis techniques in the development of ADP systems. Detailed course objectives and grading scheme will be provided students at the beginning of the course.

Data Communications Transmission Requirements—ASI. Course provides a basic understanding of the technology underlying the marriage of telecommunications and the computer. Also discussed is the design process that should be used in developing communication networks. Upon successful completion of the course with a grade of 80 or better, the student will be able to:

☐ Demonstrate an understanding of data communication concepts and terminology.
☐ Demonstrate an understanding of communication line/channel concepts and terminology.
☐ Demonstrate an understanding of communication network concepts terminology.
☐ Give descriptions of network requirements, draw a diagram showing the locations of contractors, multiplexors, and circuit switches that would be necessary to implement the required network.
☐ Demonstrate an understanding of both local area and nationwide network design techniques.

Note: This course has several subparts, each of which has a test which must be passed with a grade of 80 or better. The final grade is the average of all the subpart test grades.

Database Concepts and Fundamentals—ASI. Course will provide a generic, basic understanding of the organization, operation, and concepts and database information systems to include a data dictionary. Upon successful completion of the course with a grade of 80 or better, the student will be able to:

☐ Differentiate between database and traditional batch processing.
☐ Explain the difference between schema and subschema.
☐ Discuss what factors are considered in making a decision to use a query language.

Note: This course has several subparts, each of which has a test which must be passed with a grade of 80 or better. The final grade is the average of all the subpart test grades.

Meeting Leading—Professional Development, Inc. The course will provide a basic understanding of when, why, and how to conduct effective, efficient meetings. Upon completion of the course, the student will be able to:

☐ Determine effective meeting leadership techniques.
☐ Identify the qualities of a good meeting leader.
☐ Identify the problems associated with planning a meeting and offer suggestions on how to avoid these pitfalls.

Note: There is no final test. Discussion between the student and the ADP Training Officer will reflect student understanding of the topic.

Effective Presentations—ASI—Practical Management Associates, Inc. Course is designed to provide a thorough understanding of exactly what to do in order to conduct an effective presentation. Upon successful completion of the course, the student will be able to:

☐ Describe the unique qualities and charac-

teristics of presentations distinguishing between the two major forms: informative and persuasive.
☐ Adapt content, delivery, presentation style, and material to the needs of different audiences.

Note: There is no final test. Discussion between the student and the ADP Training Officer will reflect student understanding of the topic.

Microprocessors—Human Technology, Inc. Course is designed to give a broad overview of the impact and application of microprocessors. Fundamental hardware and software concepts are developed and reinforced with hands-on exercises. There is no test. Upon successful completion of the course the student will be able to:

☐ Identify suitable and unsuitable applications.
☐ Discuss the future of 8-, 16-, and 32-bit micros.
☐ Differentiate among the following memory concepts and list their characteristics: SOS, MSI, ROM, MOS, and PROM.
☐ Make an oral presentation in which at least one software package is demonstrated and reviewed. Guidelines for the presentation will be made available at the start of the course.

ADP Security—ASI. Courses provide a basic understanding of the requirement for security in the ADP arena. Topics include physical security of the overall environment as well as security of the hardware and software.

Note: There is no final test. Discussion between the student and the ADP Training Officer will reflect student understanding of the topic.

Marine Corps[11]

The computer science school for the Marine Corps

---

[11]Source: United States Marine Corps, Computer Sciences School, Education Center, Marine Corps Development and Education Command, Quantico, VA 22134.

is located in Quantico, Virginia. Eighteen different courses are taught at the school, which is attended by men and women enlisted in the Army, Navy, and Air Force, as well as in the Marine Corps. Attendees must be in the data processing occupational specialty.

The courses cover a very broad range of computer topics, from COBOL and assembly language (BAL) to operations to systems analysis. They range in length from two weeks to 13 weeks; each class has different prerequisites. The titles of the 18 classes, the length of the class, its purpose, and the prerequisites are shown below.

Marine Corps members should address their requests, as appropriate, to the Manpower Section Headquarters, U.S. Marine Corps, Washington, DC 20380. Request for training quotas for non-Marine Corps activities should be directed to Commandant of the Marine Corps (TPI-40), Headquarters, U.S. Marine Corps, Washington, DC 20380. If you would like additional information, please call or write Training Operations Section, Computer Sciences School, MCDEC Quantico, VA 22134; (703) 640-2891; or ask your local Marine Corps recruiter.

Advanced MARK IV File Management System Course. The length of the course is two weeks (10 days). The course's purpose is to provide knowledge of the advanced techniques and special features of the MARK IV File System to practicing MARK IV users. Application is provided for special features of the MARK IV File Management System, and one year's experience using the MARK IV File Management System is required before beginning the course.

Assembler Language Code Programming (ALC) (Combination) Course. The length of this course is eight weeks (40 days). Its purpose is to provide technical education to personnel to prepare them for duties as an IBM programmer.

This course of instruction offers a comprehensive introduction to assembler language coding as a second programming language for experienced programmers. Within the course are the following: ALC directives, standard instruction set, input and output processing, decimal and floating point features, logical instructions, macro construction, and subprogramming and parameter-passing techniques.

To be eligible for the course, one must have the rank of Corporal through Gunnery Sergeant, with MOS 4063 or equivalent, and six months' programming experience.

Automated Data Processing Equipment for the Fleet Marine Force (ADPE-FMF) Programming Course. The course's length is four weeks (20 days). Its purpose is to provide technical training to COBOL programmers to enable them to perform duties as applications programmers.

The course is designed as a basic introduction to computer programming with emphasis on supervised practical application. Instruction includes technical characteristics, programming techniques, EDL and COBOL coding using structured design, subprogramming, static screen interface, and utilization of the inquiry/retrieval and report generator program.

An MOS 4063 rating is a prerequisite for the course.

Automatic Data Processing Orientation (ADPO) Course; SSC 393. The length of the course is two weeks (10 days). Its purpose is to teach nondata processing personnel the use of high-level, query languages, data processing equipment, and procedures used to communicate requirements for information.

This course includes a basic introduction to data processing; report generation using MARK IV, NATURAL, Statistical Analysis System, and ADPE-FMF; and information system development. Emphasis is placed on using the computer and computer systems to satisfy the informational requirements of the commander and his staff.

A rank of Gunnery Sergeant through Major is required; no data processing training or experience is necessary.

COBOL Programming Course; SSC 395. Eight weeks (41 days) are required to complete the course. Its purpose is to provide technical education to prepare personnel for duties as applications

COBOL programmers.

The course is designed as a basic introduction to computer programming, with emphasis on supervised practical application. Instruction includes computer concepts, basic job control language (JLC), utilities, technological characteristics, programming techniques, and COBOL coding using structured techniques.

The prerequisites include two years' active duty remaining upon course completion; sergeant and below; waivers on career and reenlistment options; GT: 110; EDPT: 61; for Navy students—combined GCT/ARI: 110.

COBOL Programming (Specialist) Course; SSC T2K. The length of the course is two weeks (10 days). Its purpose is to provide technical education to personnel to prepare them for duties as programmers using COBOL as a second programming language or as a refresher course for the experienced COBOL programmer.

The emphasis of the course is on supervised practical application using all of the MVT access methods. Prerequisites include programming MOS/AFSC/NEC and six months' programming experience.

Computer Operator Course; SSC 40L. Four weeks (20 days) are required for the course. Its purpose is to provide technical education to enlisted personnel in order to prepare them for duties as operators for the current automated data processing (ADP) equipment inventory.

This course will provide the entry-level student with the basic concepts of data processing. Hands-on experience is provided for the operating of IBM-type peripherals and MVS/JES2 commands. Prerequisites include a rank of sergeant and below; waivers on career and reenlistment options; GT: 110 or above; and EDPT: 61 or above.

Data Control Techniques (DCT) Course; SSC 39G. The course length is seven weeks (33 days). Its purpose is to provide data control techniques training to prepare enlisted personnel for duty as data controllers for the current Marine Corps ADP inventory.

The course is designed to provide operations personnel with a working knowledge of data control practices and procedures. MVS job control language, utility programs, JCL procedure optimization, and principles of data control techniques are emphasized. Throughout the course, data processing administrative procedures are introduced.

Prerequisites include ranking of Corporal through Master Sergeant, MOS 4034; at least two years' experience in operating a computer system which utilizes the IBM/S370 instruction set immediately preceding assignment to this course; and two years' obligated service upon graduation.

Data Management Course; SSC DAB. The course length is two weeks (10 days). The purpose is to provide technical education to personnel in the specialized area of data management access methods using assembler language.

This course of instruction deals with various access methods and file organizations, which includes the definitions and uses of QSAM and BSAM. Partitioned, indexed, and direct-access methods are also discussed, and practical applications of each are provided. Prerequisites are programmers MOS/AFSC/NEC; six months' programming experience; and completion of ALC Course (38R).

Data Processing Management Seminar; SSC 39A. The course's length is two weeks (10 days). Its purpose is to provide advanced-level education to prepare senior Marine Corps staff noncommissioned officers, serving in the data systems occupational field, for assignment to intermediate management billets.

A nontechnical, executive-level similar for senior staff noncommissioned officers serving in the data systems field, the course includes a broad spectrum of fiscal, administrative, personnel, and logistical management techniques as applied to Marine Corps data processing. The course is intended to train current and prospective senior staff data processing managers in current requirements, administrative skills, and data processing problem-handling techniques.

Prerequisites include Occupational Field (OF) 40; Gunnery Sergeant through Master Gunnery Sergeant; and two years' active duty remaining upon completion of course.

Data Systems Officer (DSO) Course; SSC 399. The length of the course is thirteen weeks (65 days). Its purpose is to provide technical education in data processing to Warrant Officers through Captains to prepare them for basic- and intermediate-level data systems automation officer billets in Marine Corps data processing activities. The course includes lectures, practical applications, and laboratory sessions, which provide the student with an introduction to data processing and the current Marine Corps ADP inventory. Other subjects covered are the use of the OS/VS2 MVS job control language and utilities; the use of the data management techniques; programming training in COBOL, the MARK IV File Management System, and NATURAL; an introduction to teleprocessing concepts, systems analysis, and database management systems; and the structure and function of Marine Corps data processing.

A rank of Warrant Officer through Captain is required; no security clearance is required; two years' obligated service must be remaining upon completion; GT: 120 or higher; and EDPT: 70 or higher.

FORTRAN Programming (Specialist) Course; SSC T2H. The course length is two weeks (10 days). Its purpose is to provide technical education to Armed Forces personnel to prepare them for duties as FORTRAN programmers.

This course of instruction provides training in the concepts and techniques of coding FORTRAN programs to solve scientific problems. This course of instruction includes defining, designing, coding, testing, and correcting FORTRAN programs; and providing guidelines to be used to distinguish between degrees of efficiency in FORTRAN programs.

Prerequisites are programming MOS/AFSC/NEC; and six months' programming experience.

Multiple Virtual Storage (MVS) Diagnostics Course; SSC D2H. The course is completed in three weeks (13 days). Its purpose is to provide the experienced data processor the basic knowledge and skills required to isolate problems to a component level.

This course is designed to provide a working knowledge of MVS diagnostics to include problem-identification procedures and case studies relating to SVC dumps, stand-alone dumps, LOGREC, system trace data, and other techniques necessary to identify problems at the MVS component level.

An MOS 4069 or equivalent is required.

Multiple Virtual Storage (MVS) Fundamentals and Logic Course; SSC D2C. The course length is eight weeks (40 days). Its purpose is to provide the experienced data processor knowledge of the multiple virtual storage (MVS) operating system.

This course is designed to develop a working knowledge of the MVS operating system to include its structure, components, programs, and utilities which the systems programmer will utilize for the tasks and duties to be accomplished.

Prerequisites include a rank of Sergeant through Gunnery Sergeant (civilians and officers may attend); two years' experience in MOS's 4063 or 4065 or one year's on-the-job training in a systems programming shop; two years' experience working on an IBM or IBM-compatible operating system; and two years' active duty remaining at completion of course.

Multiple Virtual Storage (MVS) Performance and Tuning Course; SSC D2J. The course length is three weeks (13 days). Its purpose is to provide the basic knowledge and skills to generate and fine tune an MVS operating system, through performance-oriented reports, to the experienced MVS systems programmer.

This course is designed to provide a working knowledge of the MVS operating system performance and tuning through the extensive use of SMF, RMF, and OMEGAMON data and reports. Case studies will be used to permit the student to code an IPS, ICS, and validate the performance of SRM.

An MOS 4069 or equivalent is required.

Systems Analysis and Design I (SA&D I) Course; SSC 39B. Course length is two weeks (10 days). Its purpose is to provide orientation to analysis and design of automated information systems utilizing procedures compatible with the guidance in MCO P5231.1, Life Cycle Management for

Automated Information Systems.

This course exposes students to the mission analysis and/or project initiation and concept development phases of life cycle management for automated information systems (AISs). Emphasis is on team synthesis of the Mission Element Need Statement (MENS), Requirements Statement, Feasibility Study, and portions of high-level design documents.

The student must be serving in or be pending assignment to a billet involving the management or development of automated information systems.

Systems Analysis and Design II (SA&D II) Course; SSC D2D. The course length is two weeks (10 days). The purpose is to provide personnel performing either functional computer-related analyst functions involved with the development of Marine Corps automated information systems (AISs) with an orientation as to the concepts, methodologies, and techniques required to conduct such functions as set forth in DoD Standard 7935.1-S and MCO P5231.1 (Life Cycle Management for Automated Information Systems).

Major topics include review of system development life cycle, structured walkthrough of systems development documents, and structured design methodology applied to the system development process. Other topics include system documentation using Hierarchy plus Input-Process-Output (HIPO) and other charting techniques; review of a sample functional description, systems specification, database specification, and program specifications using structured design, HIPO techniques, and other charting techniques; and system user, operator and program maintenance manuals, the test and implementation plans.

The student must be serving in or be pending assignment to a billet involving the management and/or development of automated information systems; he must have completed SA&D I—no waivers.

Systems Control Course; SSC T2G. The length of the course is two weeks (10 days). Its purpose is to provide technical education to personnel in the specialized functions systems control and

selected IBM utility programs.

This block of instruction is devoted to system control with heavy emphasis on system resources and job control language (JCL). Utilities and linkage editor usage are also covered, including IEBUPDTE, IEHPROGM, IEHLIST, and IEBPTPCH. Prerequisites are programming MOS/AFSC/NEC and six months' programming experience; Air Force personnel should consult AFM 50-5.

COLLEGES AND UNIVERSITIES

Many colleges and universities throughout the nation offer courses specifically geared toward various aspects of computer work. In addition, business and management courses are also of great help in establishing a base for a successful career in computers.

Undergraduate Education

In 1982-83, the most recent year for which statistics were available at the time this book went to press, 24,506 individuals in the United States were awarded bachelor's degrees in computer and information sciences at colleges and universities across the country. The titles of the programs varied, including computer and information sciences, information sciences and systems, data processing, computer programming, and systems analysis as well as some others. Of the graduates, 15,603 were men and 8,903 women; 17,624 attended public institutions and 6,882 attended private schools.

Clearly, the field of computers has gained tremendously in popularity since 1978-79, when 8,719 persons (or 64 percent less) received bachelor's degrees in computer and information sciences, and even since 1980-81, when 15,121 individuals (or 38 percent fewer) were awarded the degrees. The 1982-83 figure represents a 17 percent increase over the bachelor's degrees in computer and information science awarded the year earlier.

To find out if a college education is required

for you to begin working in the computer career of your choice, consult Chapter 5 carefully. A bachelor's degree is preferred for the majority of computer careers today, although it is not essential that a person major in computer science in order to work in a computer career. Many employers are looking for evidence of high communications skills in addition to technical ability. In rare cases in which a college degree is not a must for a certain job, then it is still a good foundation for advancement into supervisory positions.

There is little standardization among schools regarding their computer science or data processing curricula. As mentioned above, even the name of the program varies from school to school. When you are deciding upon a college, look carefully through the course descriptions in the catalogs. Before making your choice, you may want to compare the school's curriculum to the "Curriculum Recommendations for Undergraduate Programs in Computer Information Systems," published by the Data Processing Management Association. The recommendations can be ordered from DPMA, 505 Busse Highway, Park Ridge, IL 60068, for a prepaid fee of $5.50. For an additional $3, you may also want to order the "Directory of Adopting Colleges," which lists the colleges that have adopted at least part of the recommended curriculum. The Association for Computing Machinery, Inc., 11 West 42nd Street, New York, NY 10036, also has curriculum recommendations available for $7 to members and $10 to non-members.

Many books that can be found in your local library or bookstore provide information about four-year colleges and universities. They include *The Comparative Guide to American Colleges*, published by Harper & Row; *Lovejoy's College Guide,* published by Simon & Schuster; *The College Handbook*, from the College Entrance Examination Board; *Barron's Profiles of American Colleges*, published by Barron Educational Series, Inc.; and *Peterson's Guide to Four-Year Colleges*, from Peterson's Guides, Inc. The Association for Computing Machinery, Inc. has an *Administrative Directory* of Computer Science departments in the United States, which is available for $9 to members and $12 for non-members.

Graduate Education

In 1982-83, the most recent year for which statistics were available at the time this book went to press, 5,321 master's degrees were awarded by U.S. colleges and universities to individuals in computer and information science programs. This was 20 percent more than in 1981-82. Three thousand, eight hundred thirteen degrees went to men and 1,508 went to women; private institutions awarded 2,602 degrees and public schools awarded 2,719 degrees.

In the same year, 262 individuals received doctoral degrees in computer and information sciences from American colleges and universities. This represents a four percent increase over 1981-82. Thirty-four women and 228 men earned the degree; 69 of these individuals attended private colleges and 193 went to public schools.

With the exception of the M.B.A. (Master of Business Administration), graduate degrees are required only for researchers and university faculty in the computer fields. For people expecting to be employed in these two areas, a master's or doctorate degree can substantially increase their starting salary. The M.B.A., on the other hand, is recommended for a number of different computer careers (see Chapter 5) and improves an individual's chances for progressing into a position with quite a bit of managerial responsibility.

If you are considering graduate training, read the program's description and the school catalog carefully. The Data Processing Management Association is presently drafting curriculum recommendations for graduate programs in computer fields. The information is expected to be available to the public for a minimal fee in the near future. The recommendations can be ordered from DPMA at the address shown above. It may be helpful to compare the courses in the suggested curriculum to those in the program you are considering.

The local library and bookstore carry a number of books describing graduate programs in the

U.S., including the *Directory of Graduate Programs*, from the Graduate Record Examinations Board and the Council of Graduate Schools in the United States; *A Guide to American Graduate Schools*, published by Viking Press; and *Peterson's Annual Guides to Graduate Study,* from Peterson's Guides, Inc. The Association for Computing Machinery, Inc. publishes a *Graduate Assistantship Directory in the Computer Sciences* which members can order for $7.50 and non-members for $10.

COMMUNITY COLLEGES

Community colleges are two-year schools which receive funding from a county, city, or state government. They usually cost less than private trade or technical schools. The training available at community colleges is less intensive than training received from private trade schools. For example, a student usually takes business courses as well as computer technology, and the courses offered do not meet every weekday. Classes in community colleges are offered during three different semesters—fall, spring and summer. Community colleges offer two types of programs, *associate degrees* and *certificates of proficiency*.

Usually two different associate's degree programs are available: an A.A.S. or an Associate of Applied Science and an A.S. or an Associate of Science. Both are two-year programs. The A.A.S. program is a career program; it prepares a student for the working world, and the credits from the program are not transferable to other degrees, such as a Bachelor of Science. In rare cases, partial credit is allowed, for example, if a student transfers to another program at the same school. This is the exception to the rule.

The A.S. degree prepares a student for further study—for example, a B.S.—and credit for the courses is transferable. For example, one typical community college offers an A.A.S. degree in data processing (which is basically computer programming) and computer operations, and an A.S. degree in computer science. Computer-related courses included in the A.A.S. program in data processing are: introduction to computer and business data processing, introduction to COBOL programming,

intermediate COBOL programming, job control language (JCL), advanced COBOL programming, assembler programming I, operating systems, assembler programming II, and data processing management. In contrast, in the A.S. program in computer science, the computer-related courses are: introduction to computers for scientists and engineers, FORTRAN or Pascal programming, numerical analysis, assembler programming I, computer applications field project I, computer applications field project II, assembler programming II, and a DP elective. In both programs, courses in other areas, such as English, math, and the social sciences, are included in the curriculum.

There is no standard curriculum for an associate's degree, although the Data Processing Management Association has a recommended curriculum for the degree. It may be helpful to compare the DPMA-recommended curriculum to that of the community college you are thinking about attending. Generally, the recommendations have been well received. They can be ordered for the prepaid price of $5 from the Data Processing Management Association, 505 Busse Highway, Park Ridge, IL 60068.

The two-year associate's degree (the A.A.S.) is often exactly the training that an employer is expecting, because the degree is so practical. The careers for which it is the required training are described in Chapter 5.

Certificates of Proficiency are also available from most community colleges. They are often acquired by persons who already have a degree—a B.S. or even an M.S.—who are interested in training which specializes in the technical skills needed for a particular job. The length of the programs normally varies from three months to one year. Usually the courses offered in certificate programs carry credit which is transferable to other degree programs. In one typical program, certificates are offered in data processing (or programming) and computer operations. The data processing program includes the following computer-related courses: introduction to computers and business data processing, introduction to COBOL programming, intermediate COBOL programming, job control language (JCL), advanced COBOL programming, and operating systems. One course in English composition and three electives—one in business, one in math, and one free elective—are also included in the certificate program. In rare cases, a community college may offer a shortened certificate program in which no academic credit is given. Such programs are sometimes part of the continuing education department or another similar department rather than an academic department.

Certificate programs, like associate's degree programs, are never exactly the same. When considering one for yourself, be sure to find out first exactly what kind of training is required for the position in which you are interested.

Community colleges and trade schools both offer hands-on experience with computers, but there are a number of differences between the two types of programs which can help you decide which one is better for you. Would you prefer paying tuition by the semester rather than once for the whole program? How much funding do you have available for this training? Would a broader and more well-rounded education be more useful to you in the long run? Do you plan on attending a four-year college to study toward and complete your bachelor's degree? How interested are you in getting a certain credential versus getting a certain job? By considering these and related questions and by studying the parts of Chapter 5 that describe the careers in which you are interested, you will be able to decide whether you would rather attend a community college or a private trade or technical school.

If you decide to opt for a community college education, be sure to get school catalogs from the colleges in your area. The catalogs include information about tuition and faculty qualifications as well as course descriptions. Check with your local library to see what information they have about the community college. And then look around carefully. Make sure the school's computer equipment is up-to-date. Check into the amount of assistance you will get in finding a job after you've completed the program and even while you're taking courses. Ask whether or not the tuition includes charges for books and equipment and if there are any additional fees. Find out how many students enrolled last year in the associate's degree or certificate program in which you plan to enroll, how many students dropped out or transferred to another program before completing all the courses, and how many of the graduates are now employed in the area in which they were trained. Most schools will make available to you the names and addresses of its graduates; call at least several and discuss your questions and reservations with them. Ask them about their experience with the community college. Ask the college for the names of some of the companies at which graduates were placed, and call to ask for their evaluation of the training offered at the school. Finally, ask for a tour of the college's equipment and facilities, and check to see if you can sit in on one or two of the classes that you would be taking once you enrolled.

If you have trouble locating a community college in your area, the public library or a local bookstore will have a copy of *The College Handbook*, published by the College Entrance Examination Board, which includes detailed information on two-year and four-year colleges.

CORPORATE TRAINING PROGRAMS

One recent study found that corporate training programs for computer programmers often involve a combination of in-house and out-of-house training (Fig. 12-1). The *in-house training* ranges from classes taught by consultants or company employees to instruction using audiovisual aids or the computer (computer-aided instruction). *Out-of-house training* usually involves courses given by hardware or software manufacturers, training institutes, or trade schools. The subjects taught vary from an introduction to computing to programming with COBOL or assembly language (BAL) to the fundamentals of the operating system. Some companies set up a definite order in which the classes should be taken; the CAI courses are sometimes used in between more formal classroom or out-of-house instruction, because they allow for more flexibility in the individual's training schedule.

The individual is expected to apply the infor-

Fig. 12-1. Corporate training programs for computer programmers, according to one recent study, often involve a combination of in-house and out-of-house training. (Photograph courtesy of Applied Data Research, Inc., Princeton, NJ 08540.)

mation he or she is learning to his or her work on a day-to-day basis. In fact, some smaller organizations, instead of relying on a formal training program, use informal instruction by the employee's peers and instruction and/or close supervision by his or her manager. The individual is often shown how to perform certain tasks or work with a system and then is expected to perform the job by himself or herself after several weeks of guidance. In the ideal situation, the employee doing the training is still available for questions for a period of time.

Corporate training programs for computer careers are not limited to programming. Some large companies, in particular banks and insurance companies located in or near big cities, have formal training programs that require a substantial investment on the trainee's part in time and energy but which groom the individual for management positions. For example, one large investment banking firm's program begins with a two-week introduction to the company and its information systems department. For the next six months, trainees work 40 hours weekly as computer operators, on various shifts, and spend 20 hours weekly in classroom instruction. The instruction covers a broad range of computing topics. During the following six months, the trainee works either as a programmer or a shift supervisor in the computer room and spends time in the evenings and on weekends at training sessions and seminars. At the end of one year, trainees who have done very well are given more responsibility.

Training programs vary a great deal from company to company. One major bank, for example, has its trainees gain experience in a staff position, a labor-intensive position that allows for management experience, and a technology-intensive position before giving them positions of significant management responsibility.

There are both advantages and disadvantages to participating in a corporate training program. The disadvantages include the overtime that is sometimes required and for which the trainee is not always directly compensated. Another problem stems from the fact that, once you're trained for a specific position, your employer may be happy to have to stay in that position longer than you would like. In order to advance, you may need additional training, and you may even need to change employers. Some companies recognize this problem and have designed a career path for trainees to help them avoid getting stuck in a rut.

The advantages of being trained by a corporation usually outweigh the disadvantages. For one thing, your employer is allowing you to start your computer career by gaining experience as you train. In addition, your employer pays for your training, and you earn a salary while you are being trained. Also, the training is specifically designed to prepare you for a particular computer job.

Five years ago, corporate training programs in DP were plentiful due to a lack of personnel with experience in computing. Today, fewer organizations are willing to invest the money in a formal training program when they can hire persons with some experience. One recent study showed, however, that over 35 percent of the organizations surveyed offer training in computer programming.

Because of the reduction in the number of training programs available, higher qualifications are required for today's trainees. Whether or not an applicant is accepted depends on the company and on the individual. One major financial services organization without a formal training program, for example, recently hired a person with very good communication skills and a background in accounting but little or no DP experience for an information center position (For a description of information center positions, see Chapter 5). They had decided he was the right person for the job.

To find corporate training programs near you, watch the newspaper want ads carefully. Call any nearby state departments with computer installations and ask if they have a DP training program. There are also several books which describe corporate training programs, including the *Directory of Career Training and Development Programs,* published by Ready Reference Press (Santa Monica, CA); and *Breaking In: The Guide to Over 500 Top*

Corporate Training Programs, from Morrow.

HOME STUDY[12]

Each year, an estimated three million Americans study by correspondence. They study to improve themselves and to get ahead, and they study by correspondence because they have found it to be a practical, convenient, and economical way to get the kind of training and education they need and want.

Home study institutions provide a second opportunity to many who have not acquired all of the education they need and who, for many reasons, are unable to take advantage of residential educational opportunities.

Home study students can progress at their own pace—as fast as they can master the assignments or as slowly as their schedule permits.

Good home study courses are streamlined and include only essential subject matter. Home study students studying with quality institutions learn what they need to know. Their training is practical. If they are taking a course related to their work, it is likely they can apply today what they learned last night.

What Is Home Study?

Home study is enrollment and study with an educational institution which provides lesson materials prepared in a sequential and logical order for study by students on their own. When each lesson is completed, the student mails the assigned work to the school for correction, grading, comment, and subject matter guidance by qualified instructors. Corrected assignments are returned immediately to the student. This exchange provides a personalized student-teacher relationship.

If a student slows pace or fails to send assignments, the school sends letters of encouragement. Although many schools provide employment placement information and assistance, no reputable

school ever guarantees a job to the student or graduate.

Some home study institutions have combination courses which provide training-in-residence for students who complete their home study lessons. In-service or on-the-job training is required or provided with other courses and is a feature of many industry-related home study programs.

Quality correspondence institutions screen prospective students to ensure that only those who can benefit from the courses are enrolled. While there are educational prerequisites for some academic subjects, interest and aptitude are the primary factors leading to success in most home study courses. Because they provide alternative educational opportunities, correspondence institutions try not to deny a prospective student the opportunity to succeed in a course—interest and experience can make up for the failure to fulfill all formal requirements for admission.

Home study courses vary greatly in scope, level, and length. Some have a few lessons and require only weeks to complete while others have a hundred or more assignments requiring three or four years of conscientious study.

Acceptance of students and awarding of academic credit is the prerogative of the receiving academic institution. Also, the employing organization may set its own admission or employment standards.

Selecting a School

For persons selecting a correspondence school, like selecting a residential school, they are building a part of their life plan. Tuition is one consideration, but the time and energy of ambitious students are the real investments. Selecting the right school and the right course is most important, and selecting a home study institution is not difficult if reliable standards are applied. Important factors to be considered are:

☐ How long has the school been established?
☐ What is its past record for teaching satisfied students who attribute much of their success to the school?

---

[12]From *You and Home Study*, by William A. Fowler, Executive Director, National Home Study Council. Permission to reproduce granted by the National Home Study Council, 1601 18th St., NW, Washington, DC 20009.

- [ ] Are its courses up to date?
- [ ] Does it maintain a competent staff of instructors?
- [ ] Is the school truthful in its advertising and promotional methods?
- [ ] Does it adhere strictly to ethical standards in its relationships with students?
- [ ] Does it render full educational service for tuition it receives?
- [ ] Is it financially responsible so that it can continue to meet its obligations to students?
- [ ] Is it accredited by a nationally recognized accrediting agency?

Answers to these questions are not always readily available. It is difficult to tell the quality of a school by its advertising copy. It is desirable to find out about the courses, staff, services, general reputation, and practices of the school to see whether it lives up to its objectives and reflects what the promotional material says.

COLLEGE AND UNIVERSITY HOME STUDY COURSES

The Independent Study Division of the National University Continuing Education Association is the professional organization of colleges and universities offering correspondence courses. All of the member institutions of NUCEA are members of their respective regional educational accrediting associations, and courses offered for degree credit by correspondence are accredited as a part of the institution.

The *NUCEA Guide To Independent Study Through Correspondence Instruction* lists courses available through regionally accredited colleges and universities which are members of the independent Study Division of NUCEA. The Guide may be purchased from Peterson's Guides, Book Order Department, Box 978, Edison, NJ 08817.

TRADE AND TECHNICAL SCHOOLS

Private trade and technical schools, which are sometimes referred to as occupational schools, are often seen advertised on television, in the phone book, and in newspapers. These schools offer condensed training that can last up to two years but frequently lasts only six to 12 months. The length of the program depends on the specific skills being learned. Usually, the skills taught are only those required for employment in a certain area; students are not required to take English classes as part of their instruction in programming, for example. Typically, classes meet every weekday for two or three hours, either during the day or evening. Sometimes homework assignments are given that must be completed by the next day's class.

Typically, trade schools employ a hands-on approach so students get experience in programming or hardware repair. Some schools provide internships with certain companies in their area as a part of their program. Trade schools are generally much more expensive than community colleges. Many of the schools work to place individuals who have completed their program in a job in their field, but no school can really guarantee employment upon completion of a certain program of instruction.

Most occupational schools do not offer certificates as evidence of the completion of a certain program of instruction. Colleges and universities generally do not offer credit for technical school training, although it depends on the individual technical school and college involved.

There are a number of issues to keep in mind when choosing a trade or technical school, because the quality of the available training varies widely. Get a copy of the school's catalog and look through it carefully. Check to see if the trade school is licensed by the state postsecondary school licensing bureau. (If this is not indicated in the catalog, call the Department of Education in your state.) Several states do not require trade or technical schools to be licensed, but most states do. Find out if the school is accredited by the National Association of Trade and Technical Schools. (Further information on accreditation appears below.) Accreditation is one indication of the school's quality. Read the course descriptions and decide whether they will prepare you for the computer career you have chosen. Find out if the instructors have experience in the careers they are teaching.

Ask about the school's equipment and facilities. Is the hardware up-to-date? How much hands-on experience does a student get by the completion of the program? Sometimes this valuable experience, if it is extensive enough, will be substituted by an employer for actual work experience. Look into the placement assistance available and ask about the types of jobs that are found for graduates. Check the total cost of attending the school. Are there other charges besides tuition and supplies? What is the school's refund policy if you decide to leave the program before completing it? How long would you have to wait to take the program again—that is, how frequently is it offered?

Be sure to visit the school and sit in on one or two classes, if possible. Ask the students what they think of the school's program, and ask specific questions about the use of the hardware. For example, in a programming class, how much access does each person have to the computer? What is the average turn-around time (the time required for your job to be processed and its output to be printed and returned to you)?

Finally, ask the school for a list of its graduates and their addresses and the names of some of the companies presently employing its graduates. Call several graduates and several employers and ask them what they think of the school's program.

Accreditation . . . Why It's Important To You[13]

Accreditation is your assurance that a school has met national standards of educational performance that have been established by an impartial non-government agency. The Accrediting Commission of the National Association of Trade and Technical Schools evaluates private schools offering occupational education at the postsecondary level. Although an accrediting agency is not part of the government, the U.S. Department of Education has officially recognized several agencies. The NATTS Commission is one such nationally recognized accrediting agency under the provisions of Chapter

33, Title 38, U.S. Code and subsequent legislation. Because it is recognized by the Department of Education, students attending an accredited school may be entitled to participate in scholarship, grant, financial aid, and other assistance programs.

Once begun, the process of accreditation generally takes a year to complete. It includes a visit to the school by a team of specialists in education and the career being taught by the school. The team asks the same questions a prospective student should:

- ☐ Does the school clearly state its objectives and demonstrate overall ability to meet them?
- ☐ Does it have a qualified administrative staff and faculty?
- ☐ Does it have fair and proper admissions and enrollment practices in terms of educational benefits to the students?
- ☐ Does it provide educationally sound and up-to-date courses and methods of instruction?
- ☐ Does it demonstrate satisfactory student progress and success to include acceptance of graduates by employers?
- ☐ Is it fair and truthful in all advertising, promotional, and other representations?
- ☐ Does it reflect financial business soundness of operation?
- ☐ Does it provide and maintain adequate physical facilities, classrooms, and laboratories?
- ☐ Does it provide student and administrative accounting?

The NATTS Commission admits only those schools which give evidence that they meet accreditation standards. Schools listed in the next section have demonstrated they have met these standards. The Commission meets quarterly to review schools applying for accreditation or reaccreditation and may add schools to its accredited list or delete others from it. An accredited school is reviewed every five years to ensure it continues to meet the Commission's standards.

Communications regarding the Commission

---

[13]Source: National Association of Trade and Technical Schools, 2251 Wisconsin Ave., NW, Washington DC 20007.

should be addressed to Dorothy C. Fenwick, PhD, Executive Secretary, Accrediting Commission, National Association of Trade and Technical Schools, 2251 Wisconsin Avenue., N.W., Washington, DC 20007.

Appearing below is a list of the private trade and technical schools accredited by the National Association of Trade and Technical Schools, and which offer training in computer careers.

ALABAMA

Herzing Institute
1218 South 20th Street
Birmingham, AL 35205
(205) 933-8536
Word processing, computer programming, computer operations, computer technology.

National Education Center—
National Institute of Technology Campus
1900 28th Avenue, South
Homewood, AL 35209
(205) 871-2131
Electronic engineering technology; information systems.

R.E.T.S. Electronic Institute
2812 12th Avenue, North
Birmingham, AL 35234
(205) 251-7962
Electronic engineering technology; dc and ac theory and circuit analysis; solid state devices and circuits; digital logic devices and circuits; microprocessors; industrial electronics, microprocessor applications, and robotics.

ARIZONA

ABC Technical and Trade Schools
3781 East Technical Drive
Tucson, AZ 85713-5375
(602) 748-1762
Electronics communications; computer electronics technicians; computer/robotics technician.

Academy of Drafting
1131 West Broadway Road
Tempe, AZ 85282
(602) 967-7813
Computer aided design; robotics.

Al Collins Graphic Design School
605 East Gilbert Drive
Tempe, AZ 85281
(602) 966-3000
Computer graphics.

DeVry Institute of Technology
2149 West Dunlap Avenue
Phoenix, AZ 85021
(602) 870-9222
Electronics; electronics engineering technology; digital electronics; computer information systems.

High-Tech Institute
4021 North 30th Street
Phoenix, AZ 85016
(602) 954-9400
Computer/electronics technology; drafting CAD technology.

Miller Institute—
Tucson Campus (Extension)
1840 East Benson Highway
Tucson, AZ 85714
(602) 294-2944
Electronics drafting/CAD; computer science.

Miller Institute—Main Campus
4837 East McDowell Road
Phoenix, AZ 85008
(602) 252-2331
Electronics; drafting/CAD; computer science.

Mountain States Technical Institute
3120 North 34th Drive
Phoenix, AZ 85017
(602) 269-7555
Computer programming, word processing.

**National Education Center—
Arizona Automotive Institute Campus**
6829 North 46th Avenue
Glendale, AZ 85301
(602) 934-7273
Computer aided drafting.

**National Education
Center—Bryman Campus**
9215 North Black Canyon Highway
Phoenix, AZ 85021
(602) 861-9200; (602) 258-5901
Computer information systems.

Phoenix Institute of Technology
2555 East University Drive
Phoenix, AZ 85034
(602) 244-8111
Computer aided design and drafting.

ARKANSAS

**National Education Center—
Arkansas College of Technology Campus**
9720 Rodney Parham Road
Little Rock, AR 72207
(501) 224-8200
Electronics/electronic technician; computer science/informational systems; secretarial science.

CALIFORNIA

Academy International
Post Office Box 90859
Santa Barbara, CA 93190
(805) 965-5264
Computer business applications.

**Academy Pacific
Business and Travel College**
6253 Hollywood Boulevard
Hollywood, CA 90028
(213) 462-3211
Computer and word processing careers.

**American Business
College—Technical Division**
5952 El Cajon Boulevard
San Diego, CA 92115
(619) 582-1319
Data processing; word processing; data entry operator (keypunch); drafting, (CAD/CAM), and electronic technician.

**American Business College—
Technical Division (Branch)**
1541 Broadway
San Diego, CA 92101
(619) 239-4138
Drafting and (CAD/CAM); electronic technician.

**American Technical
College for Career Training**
191 South "E" Street
San Bernardino, CA 92401
(714) 885-3857; (714) 783-2322
Computer.

American Technical Institute
6843 Lennox Avenue
Van Nuys, CA 91405
(818) 988-7054
Electronic, computer, and VCR technology; industrial computer technology.

**American Technical
Institute—Orange County (Branch)**
15062 Jackson Street
Midway City, CA 92655
(714) 891-9211
Electronic/computer technology; industrial computer technology.

AMS College
10025 Shoemaker Avenue
Santa Fe Springs, CA 90670
(213) 944-0121
Computer programming; computer technology.

Associated Technical College
1670 Wilshire Boulevard
Los Angeles, CA 90017
(213) 484-2444
Telecommunications; computer technology.

Associated Technical College—Anaheim (Extension)
1101 South Anaheim Boulevard
Anaheim, CA 92805
(714) 520-9701
Telecommunications.

Associated Technical College—San Diego (Extension)
1415 Sixth Avenue
San Diego, CA 92101
(619) 234-2181
Telecommunications.

Bay-Valley Tech
2550 Scott Boulevard
Santa Clara, CA 95050
(408) 727-1060
Electronics; drafting; computer programming.

California Paramedical and Technical College
3745 Long Beach Boulevard
Long Beach, CA 90807
(213) 426-9359
Computer operator; word processing; programming.

California Paramedical and Technical College (Branch)
4550 La Sierra Avenue
Riverside, CA 92505
(714) 687-9006
Computer operator; word processing; computer technician.

Computer Learning Center (Branch)
1240 South State College Boulevard
Anaheim, CA 92806
(714) 956-8060
Computer programming and operations.

Computer Learning Center of Los Angeles
3130 Wilshire Boulevard
Los Angeles, CA 90010
(213) 386-6311

Computer programming; computer operations; computer electronics and technology.

Control Data Institute
1780 West Lincoln Avenue
Anaheim, CA 92801
(714) 635-2770
Computer programming operations; computer technology; office technology.

Control Data Institute
5630 Arbor Vitae
Los Angeles, CA 90045
(213) 642-2345
Computer technology; computer programming and operations; office technology and word processing.

Control Data Institute (Branch)
5206 Benito Street
Montclair, CA 91763
(714) 621-6867
Computer technology.

Control Data Institute (Extension)
660 J Street
Sacramento, CA 9514
(916) 447-5282
Electronic technician; microprocessor.

Control Data Institute
1930 Market Street
San Francisco, CA 94102
(415) 864-1156
Computer technology; computer programming and operations; word processing (office technology).

Control Data Institute (Branch)
20301 Ventura Boulevard
Suite 330
Woodland Hills, CA 91364
(213) 992-3344
Computer programming and operations; automated office technology.

DeVry Institute of Technology (Extension)
12801 Crossroads Parkway South
City of Industry, CA 91744
(213) 699-9927

> *Electronics technician; digital electronics technician; electronics engineering technology; computer information systems.*

Edison Technical Institute
4629 Van Nuys Boulevard
Sherman Oaks, CA 91403
(818) 788-7141

> *Electronics technology; business data processing; microelectronic technician training; computer technology.*

Golden State School, Bakersfield Extension
3916 South Chester
Bakersfield, CA 93307
(805) 833-0123

> *Electronics technology; advanced electronics technology.*

Golden State School, Oxnard Extension
1910 Sunkist Circle
Post Office Box 5098
Oxnard, CA 99303
(805) 487-3975

> *Electronics technology; advanced electronics technology; and electronics assembly.*

Golden State School
Post Office Box 5807
195 West Bernedict Street
San Bernadino, CA 92408
(714) 884-0479

> *Electronics technology; advanced electronics technology; and electronics assembly.*

Institute for Business and Technology
801 Hibiscus Lane
San Jose, CA 95177
(408) 246-9120

> *Computer programming/systems analysis; BASIC programming; BASIC/Pascal programming; electronics drafting; electromechanical*

drafting; computer aided drafting; computer accounting specialist; information processing specialist.

Institute of Computer Technology
3200 Wilshire Boulevard
Los Angeles, CA 90010
(213) 381-3333

> *Computer programming; computer operator; programmer analyst; data entry.*

ITT Technical Institute (Extension)
7100 Knott Avenue
Buena Park, CA 90620
(714) 523-9080

> *Electronics; engineering technology.*

ITT Technical Institute
8374 Hercules Street
La Mesa, CA 92041
(619) 462-0682

> *Electronics engineering technology; engineering graphics technology.*

ITT Technical Institute (Extension)
6723 Van Nuys Boulevard
Van Nuys, CA 91405
(818) 989-1177

> *Electronics engineering technology.*

ITT Technical Institute
1530 West Cameron Avenue
West Covina, CA 91790
(213) 960-8681

> *Electronics; engineering technology; and automated manufacturing technology.*

Maric College of Medical Careers
San Diego Campus
7202 Princess View Drive
San Diego, CA 92120
(619) 583-8232

> *Computerized medical office administration.*

Maric College of Medical Careers
(Extension) North County Campus
1300 Rancheros Drive
San Marcos, CA 92069
(619) 747-1555

> *Computerized medical office administration.*

Masters Design and Technical Center
3350 Scott Boulevard
Building 46
Santa Clara, CA 95054
(408) 727-1955
Electronic drafting; computer aided design.

Med-Help Training School
1079 Boulevard Way
Walnut Creek, CA 94595
(415) 934-1947
Medical office computer.

Microwave Training Institute
444 Castro Street
Mountain View, CA 94941
(415) 969-7363
Word processing.

National Education Center
1380 South Sanderson
Anaheim, CA 92806
(714) 758-0330
Information systems management; electronic engineering technician.

National Technical Schools
4000 South Figueroa Street
Los Angeles, CA 90037
(213) 234-9061
Electronics.

**North-West College of
Medical and Dental Assistants**
134 West Holt Avenue
Pomona, CA 91768
(714) 623-1552
Medical computer specialist.

**North-West College of
Medical and Dental Assistants**
2121 West Garvey Avenue
West Covina, CA 91790
(213) 962-3495
Medical computer specialist.

Pacific Coast College
323 West Eighth Street
Los Angeles, CA 90014
(213) 622-2371
Computer concepts and applications.

**Pacific Coast College
—Garden Grove Campus**
6562 Stanford Avenue
Garden Grove, CA 92645-2296
(714) 898-5669
Medical computer and legal computer.

Pacific Coast College—Los Angeles
198 South Alvarado Street
Los Angeles, CA 90057
(213) 413-3390
Microcomputer skills.

Pacific Coast Technical Institute
1740 Orangethorpe Park
Anaheim, CA 92801
(714) 879-1053
Computer tech repair.

Pacific Coast Technical Institute
14620 Keswick Street
Van Nuys, CA 91405
(213) 781-9500
Computerized office administration; computer technician.

Polytechnical Institute
890 Pomeroy Avenue
Santa Clara, CA 95051
(714) 630-9614
Electronic engineering technology; electronic technology; computer technician.

Practical Schools
3290 East Carpenter Avenue
Anaheim, CA 92806
(714) 630-9614
Electronic engineering technology; electronic technology; computer technician.

San Joaquin Valley College
4706 West Mineral King Avenue
Visalia, CA 93291
(209) 732-6426
Computer programming; computer business (word processing and computer accounting).

San Joaquin Valley College
211 South Real Road
Bakersfield, CA 93309
(805) 834-0126
Computer programming; computer business (word processing and computer accounting.

San Joaquin Valley College (Extension)
3333 North Bond
Fresno, CA 93726
(209) 229-7800
Computer programming; computer business (word processing and computer accounting.

Southwest Trade School
334 Rancheros Drive
San Marcos, CA 92069
(619) 774-8730
Electronic assembly; electronic test technician; electronic technician; electronic technology; computer laboratory technician; robotics technician.

Systems and Programming Development Institute
5525 Wilshire Boulevard
Los Angeles, CA 90036
(213) 937-7734
Computer programming; computer operations; data entry operations.

Technical Training Center
One West Campbell Avenue
Campbell, CA 95008
(408) 374-8324
Computer hardware technology.

Total Technical Institute (Extension)
3180 Newberry Drive
San Jose, CA 95118
(408) 978-8787
Computer hardware technology.

Travel and Trade Career Institute
3635 Atlantic Avenue
Long Beach, CA 90807
(213) 426-8841
Computer careers.

Western Technical College
5434 Van Nuys Boulevard
Van Nuys, CA 91401
(818) 783-6520
Telecommunications.

COLORADO

Control Data Institute (Extension)
720 South Colorado Boulevard
Denver, CO 80220
(303) 691-9756
Computer technology; computer programming and operations; office technology.

Denver Institute of Technology
The Educational Plaza
7350 North Broadway
Denver, CO 80221
(303) 426-1808, (800) 874-6163
Electronics technology with specialties in computer service; architectural/structural, civil and machine drafting with computer assisted design and drafting (CAD/D).

Denver Technical College
5250 Leetsdale Drive
Denver, CO 80222
(303) 329-3000
Computer information systems and electronics engineering technology.

Electronic Technical Institute
1070 Bannock Street
Denver, CO 80204
(303) 629-6225
Electronics technician; electronics technology with specialties in computer, digital microprocessing and microcomputer systems.

ITT Technical Institute (Extension)
2121 South Blackhawk Street
Aurora, CO 80014
(303) 695-1913
Electronics engineering technology.

Rocky Mountain College of Art and Design
1441 Ogden Street
Denver, CO 80218
(303) 832-1557
Commercial art in illustration and graphic design; fine art in drawing and painting; signs and outdoor advertising.

Technical Trades Institute
2315 East Pikes Peak Avenue
Colorado Springs, CO 80909
(303) 632-7626
Electronic engineering technology; engineering design/drafting.

Technical Trades Institute (Extension)
772 Horizon Drive
Grand Junction, CO 81506
(303) 245-8101
Electronic engineering technology.

CONNECTICUT

Connecticut School of Electronics
Post Office Box 7308
586 Boulevard
New Haven, CT 06519
(203) 624-2121
Electronic technology/electronic technician.

Porter and Chester Institute (Branch)
138 Weymouth Street
Enfield, CT 06082
(203) 741-3561
Electronic engineering technology and computer electronics.

Porter and Chester Institute
Post Office Box 330
2139 Silas Deane Highway
Rocky Hill, CT 06067
(203) 529-2519

Engineering technology; computer electronics; executive secretary.

Porter and Chester Institute
670 Lordship Boulevard
Post Office Box 364
Stratford, CT 06497
(203) 375-4463
Electronic engineering technology; engineering technology; computer electronics.

Porter and Chester Institute
625 Wolcott Street
Waterbury, CT 06705
(203) 575-1244
Electronic engineering technology; computer electronics.

Technical Careers Institute
11 Kimberly Avenue
West Haven, CT 06516
(203) 932-2282
Computer repair and electronics.

Technical Careers Institute (Branch)
605 Day Hill Road
Windsor, CT 06095
(203) 688-8351
Electronic technology; computer technician; drafting (CAD).

DISTRICT OF COLUMBIA

Academy of Business Careers
825 15th Street, N.W.
Washington, DC 20005
(202) 737-4200
Information processing.

FLORIDA

Central Florida Computer Institute
7129 University Boulevard
Winter Park, FL 32792
(305) 671-2272
Computer operator/microcomputer programmer; word processor.

Datamerica Institute
1101 South West 27th Avenue
Miami, FL 33135
(305) 649-8227
Word processing; data entry CRT.

International Technical Institute
8407 Laurel Fair Circle
Tampa, FL 33610
(813) 621-3566
Computer programming; data processing management.

ITT Technical Institute
11211 North Nebraska Avenue
Tampa, FL 33612
(813) 977-2700
Electronic engineering technology.

Keiser Institute of Technology
4861 North Dixie Highway
Fort Lauderdale, FL 33334
(305) 776-4456
Computer operator; computer programming; computer repair technician.

Martin Technical College
1901 North West Seventh Street
Miami, FL 33125
(305) 541-8140
Electronics.

Miami Technical College
1001 South West First Street
Miami, FL 33130
(305) 324-6831
Computer business application; electronic technician; electronic engineering technician; computer technology; computer programming.

National Education Center—Bauder
Fashion College Campus
4801 North Dixie Highway
Fort Lauderdale, FL 33334
(305) 491-7171
Business administration/computer information systems.

National Education Center—Brown Institute Campus
111 North East 44th Street
Fort Lauderdale, FL 33334
(305) 772-0280
Electronics technology.

National Education Center—Tampa Technical Institute Campus
3920 East Hillsborough Avenue
Tampa, FL 33610
(813) 238-0455
Computer engineering technology.

National Institute of Technology
12th Avenue at North G Street
Lake Worth, FL 33460
(305) 586-2593
Electronic engineering technology; microprocessors; computer programming.

National School of Technology
16150 North East 17th Avenue
North Miami, FL 33162
(305) 949-9500
Medical data processing; computer programmer; microcomputer operator; data entry operator.

New England Institute of Technology at Palm Beach
1126 53rd Court
West Palm Beach, FL 33407
(305) 842-8324
Electronics; administrative secretarial technologies.

Porter and Chester Institute (Extension)
19914 Northwest 2nd Avenue
Miami, FL 33269
(305) 652-9323
Electronics; engineering technology; computer electronics.

R.E.T.S. Technical Training Centers
201 West Sunrise Boulevard
Fort Lauderdale, FL 33311
(305) 764-3432

Electronic engineering technology; microcomputer/microprocessor technology.

R.E.T.S. Technical Training Centers (Branch)
1 North East 19 Street
Miami, FL 33132
(305) 573-1600

Electronic engineering technology; computer service technician; microcomputer/microprocessor technology.

Total Technical Institute
2880 North West 62nd Street
Fort Lauderdale, FL 33309
(305) 973-4760

Computer hardware technology; applied computer electronics technology.

United Electronics Institute
4202 Spruce Street
Tampa, FL 33607
(813) 875-3717

Electronic engineering technology; computer and digital electronics.

GEORGIA

Balin Institute of Technology
1359 B Spring Street, North West
Atlanta, GA 30309
(404) 874-5278

Computer assisted drafting (CAD).

Control Data Institute
3379 Peachtree Road, North East
Suite 400
Atlanta, GA 30326
(404) 261-7700

Computer technology; computer programming and operations; office technology (word processing).

DeVry Institute of Technology
250 North Arcadia Avenue
Decatur, GA 30030
(404) 292-7900

Electronics; electronics engineering technology; computer information systems.

Total Technical Institute (Extension)
6185-C Jimmy Carter Boulevard
Norcross, GA 30071
(404) 449-9012

Computer hardware technology; computer programming and operations.

IDAHO

Link's School of Business
970 Lusk Street
Post Office Box 7567
Boise, ID 83707
(208) 344-8376

Electronics engineering technology.

ILLINOIS

Airco Technical Institute
1201 West Adams
Chicago, IL 60607
(312) 666-5590

Comprehensive computer aided drafting (CAD).

American Vocational School
102 North Center
Bloomington, IL 61701
(309) 828-5151

Computer aided drafting; computer repair.

Control Data Institute (Branch)
1072 Tower Lane
Bensenville, IL 60106
(312) 595-2805

Computer technology; computer programming and operations; office technology (secretarial and word processing).

Control Data Institute
200 North Michigan Avenue
Chicago, IL 60601
(312) 454-6888

Computer technology; computer programming

and operations; office technology (secretarial and word processing).

Coyne American Institute
1235 West Fullerton Avenue
Chicago, IL 60614
(312) 935-2520

Microcomputer technician; computer programming.

DeVry Institute of Technology
3300 North Campbell
Chicago, IL 60618
(312) 929-8500

Electronics engineering technology; electronics technician; digital electronics technician and computer programming for business; computer information systems.

DeVry Institute of Technology (Extension)
2000 South Finley Road
Lombard, IL 60148
(312) 953-1300

Computer programming for business; digital electronics technician; electronics engineering technology; electronics technician; computer information systems.

Illinois Technical College
506 South Wabash Avenue
Chicago, IL 60605
(312) 922-9000

Electronics engineering technology.

INDIANA

Acme Institute of Technology
504 West Calvert Street
South Bend, IN 46613
(219) 233-5792

Numerical control programming; electronics engineering technology; computer service technician.

ITT Technical Institute
5115 Oak Grove Road
Evansville, IN 47715
(812) 479-1441

Electronics engineering technology.

ITT Technical Institute
4919 Coldwater Road
Fort Wayne, IN 46825
(219) 484-4107

Electronics engineering technology.

ITT Technical Institute
9511 Angola Court
Indianapolis, IN 46268
(317) 875-8640

Electronics engineering technology; electronics technology.

Professional Careers Institute
2611 Waterfront Parkway
East Drive
Indianapolis, IN 46224
(317) 299-6001

Computer programming.

IOWA

Hamilton Technical College
425 East 59th Street
Post Office Box 2674
Davenport, IA 52807
(319) 386-3570

Electronics technology; computer maintenance.

National Education Center—
National Institute of Technology Campus
1119 5th Street
West Des Moines, IA 50265
(515) 223-1486

Electronics (with additional specialties in digital, microprocessing, and computer technician).

KANSAS

Bryan Institute (Extension)
9400 Nall Avenue
Overland Park, KS 66207
(913) 341-9201

Computer programming.

Control Data Institute (Extension)
Tower II, Gateway Centre
4th and State Avenue
Kansas City, KS 66101
(913) 321-3400
Computer service technician; data processing; electronics; office technology; word processing.

Electronic Computer Programming Institute
401 East Douglas
Lower Level Suite One
Wichita, KS 67202
(316) 263-0276
Computer programming and data processing.

Topeka Technical College
3600 South Topeka Boulevard
Topeka, KS 66611
(913) 266-3180
Computer programming and data processing; electronic technician.

Wichita Automotive and Electronics Institute
4011 East 31st Street
Wichita, KS 67210
(316) 682-6548
Digital computer; electronics; microcomputer technician.

Wichita Technical Institute
942 South West Street
Wichita, KS 67213
(316) 943-2241
Electronics technology; computer and digital electronics.

KENTUCKY

Institute of Electronic Technology
509 South 30th Street
Post Office Box 1113
Paducah, KY 42001
(502) 444-9676
Electronic engineering technology.

Louisville Technical Institute
3901 Atkinson Drive
Louisville, KY 40218
(502) 456-6509
Drafting and engineering technology.

**National Education Center—
Kentucky College of Technology Campus**
3947 Park Drive
Louisville, KY 40216
(502) 448-5304
Electronic engineering technology; business information systems.

R.E.T.S. Electronic Institute
4146 Outer Loop
Louisville, KY 40219
(502) 968-7191
Electronics engineering technology.

LOUISIANA

Baton Rouge School of Computers
9255 Interline Drive
Baton Rouge, LA 70809
(504) 923-2525
Computer programming; computer operations; data entry/keypunch; computer secretary with word processing and computer accounting; computer electronics technician.

International Technical Institute
13944 Airline Highway
Baton Rouge, LA 70817
(504) 292-4230
Computer service technician.

R.E.T.S. Training Center
3605 Division Street
Metairie, LA 70002
(504) 888-6848
Electronics and engineering technology.

MARYLAND

Arundel Institute of Technology
1808 Edison Highway
Baltimore, MD 21213
(301) 327-6640
Communications and computer electronics.

Control Data Institute
1718 East Northern Parkway
Baltimore, MD 21239
(301) 323-7780
> *Computer technology; computer programming operations.*

PSI Institute of Washington (Extension)
1310 Apple Avenue
Silver Spring, MD 20910
(301) 589-0900
> *Data processing technology (computer programming).*

R.E.T.S. Electronic School
511 Russell Street
(Baltimore-Washington Parkway)
Baltimore, MD 21230
(301) 727-6863
> *Electronic engineering technology; microcomputer/microprocessor technology; automation robotics technology; practical electronic servicing; computer aided design drafting.*

TESST Electronic School
5122 Baltimore Avenue
Hyattsville, MD 20781
(301) 864-5750
> *Electronic engineering technology, including electronics, communications, digital logic microprocessors.*

MASSACHUSETTS

Associated Technical Institute
345 West Cummings Park
Woburn, MA 01801
(617) 935-3838
> *Electronics/computer technology; computer programming, data processor.*

Control Data Institute
One Alewife Place
Cambridge, MA 02140
(617) 876-1155
> *Computer technology; computer programming/operations; office technology.*

GTE Sylvania Technical School
95 Second Avenue
Waltham, MA 02254
(617) 890-7711
> *Computer electronics; telecommunications electronics.*

**Northeast Institute
of Industrial Technology**
41 Phillips Street
Boston, MA 02114
(617) 523-2813
> *Industrial electronics with specialties in computer servicing and maintenance; communications; electronics instrumentation; computer aided drafting (CAD).*

R.E.T.S. Electronics School
965 Commonwealth Avenue
Boston, MA 02215
(617) 783-1197
> *Electronics technology, including communications; robotics; microprocessors.*

MICHIGAN

Control Data Institute
Suite 1401
21700 Northwestern Highway
Southfield, MI 48075
(313) 552-6600
> *Computer technology; computer programming and operations; office technology.*

ITT Technical Institute
3013 Eastern Avenue, South East
Grand Rapids, MI 49508
(616) 452-1458
> *Electronics engineering technology.*

Lansing Computer Institute
913 West Holmes Road
Suite 255
Lansing, MI 48910
(571) 332-3024

Word processing; computer programming and operations.

National Education Center—National Institute of Technology Campus (Branch)
15115 Deerfield
East Detroit, MI 48021
(313) 779-5530
Electronics; electronic engineering technology; specialized electronic servicing (computer technician); industrial electronic technology.

National Educational Center— National Institute of Technology Campus
18000 Newburgh Road
Livonia, MI 48152
(313) 464-7387
Electronic engineering technology; applied electronics technology; specialized electronic servicing; industrial electronics; microprocessor technology.

National Education Center— National Institute of Technology Campus
2620 Remico Street, South West
Wyoming, MI 49509
(616) 538-3170
Electronic engineering technology; applied electronic technology; microprocessors.

MINNESOTA

Control Data Institute
1001 Washington Avenue North
Minneapolis, MN 55401
(612) 339-8282
Computer technology; computer programming and operations; office technology.

Control Data Institute (Branch)
245 East Sixth Street
St. Paul, MN 55101
(612) 292-2699
Computer technology.

Dunwoody Industrial Institute
818 Wayzata Boulevard
Minneapolis, MN 55403
(612) 374-5800

Computer and digital systems technology; industrial electronics technology.

National Education Center—Brown Institute Campus
3123 East Lake Street
Minneapolis, MN 55406
(612) 721-2481
Electronics (with specialties in computer; communications); management information systems.

Northwest Technical Institute
11995 Singletree Lane
Eden Prairie, MN 55344
(612) 944-0080
CADD (computer aided drafting and design).

Northwestern Electronics Institute
825 41st Avenue
(41st and Central North East)
Minneapolis, MN 55421
(612) 781-4881
Electronics technology with specialties in computer, microprocessors, lasers, and robotics.

MISSOURI

Bailey Technical School
3750 Lindell Boulevard
St. Louis, MO 63108-3483
(314) 533-8700
Electronics engineering technology.

Basic Institute of Technology
4455 Chippewa
St. Louis, MO 63116
(314) 771-1200
Electronic engineering technology; computer engineering technology.

Bryan Institute
12184 Natural Bridge Road
Bridgeton, MO 63044
(314) 291-0241
Computer technology.

Bryan Institute
103 East Lockwood
Webster Groves, MO 63119
(314) 962-9111
Data processing.

Control Data Institute
3694 West Pine Boulevard
Des Peres Hall
St. Louis, MO 63108
(314) 534-8181
Computer technology; computer programming and operations; office technology.

DeVry Institute of Technology
11224 Holmes Road
Kansas City, MO 64131
(816) 941-0430
Electronics engineering technology; electronics technician; digital electronics technician; computer information systems.

Electronic Computer Programming Institute
611 West 39th Street
Kansas City, MO 64111
(816) 561-7758
Data processing; computer programming; microcomputer technology.

Electronic Institutes
5605 Troost Avenue
Kansas City, MO 64110
(816) 361-5656
Communications; microprocessor and industrial technology; microprocessor technology; digital electronics.

Missouri Technical School
9623 Saint Charles Rock Road
St. Louis, MO 63114
(314) 428-7700
Basic electronics; electronic service technician; digital/microprocessor/microcomputer.

Ranken Technical Institute
4431 Finney Avenue
St. Louis, MO 63113
(314) 371-0233
Computer technology; communication electronics technology.

St. Louis Tech
4144 Cypress Road
St. Ann, MO 63074
(314) 427-3600
2D/3D computer aided drafting.

Vatterott and Sullivan Educational Centers
3929 Industrial Drive
St. Ann, MO 63074
(314) 428-5900
Electronics/computer repair; computer operations.

Vocational Training Center
5027 Columbia Avenue
St. Louis, MO 63139
(314) 776-3302
Word processing data entry operator.

NEBRASKA
Electronic Computer Programming Institute
The Center—4th Level
42nd and Center
Omaha, NE 68105
(402) 345-1300
Data processing and computer programming.

Gateway Electronics Institute
4001 South 24th Street
Omaha, NE 68107
(402) 734-4420
Electronics, including computer maintenance.

Institute of Computer Science
808 South 74th Plaza
Suite 200
Omaha, NE 68114
(402) 393-7064
Computer programming; word processing.

NEVADA

Education Dynamics Institute
2635 North Decatur Boulevard
Las Vegas, NV 89108
(702) 648-1522
Computer programming; electronic engineering technology.

NEW HAMPSHIRE

New England Technical Institute
750 Massabesic Street
Manchester, NH 03103
(603) 669-1231
Electronic engineering technology; electronic computer technician; computer data processing (business secretarial division).

Polytechnic Institute of New England
546 Amherst Street
Nashua, NH 03063
(603) 881-8277
Electronics technology (digital, special, servicing).

NEW JERSEY

Academy of Business Careers
One Ronson Road
Post Office Box 519
Woodbridge, NJ 07095
(201) 750-1530
Word processing; computer programming; computer operations.

Berdan Institute
265 Route 46 West
Totowa, NJ 07512
(201) 256-3444
Word processing specialist.

Brick Computer Science Institute
525 Highway 70
Brick, NJ 08723
(201) 477-0975
Data processing with specialties in keypunch, data entry, computer operations, programming, CICS, systems analysis; computer repair.

Chubb Institute for Computer Technology
8 Sylvan Way
Post Office Box 342
Parskippany, NJ 07054-0342
(201) 285-9700
Computer programming.

DeVry Technical Institute
479 Green Street
Woodbridge, NJ 07095
(201) 634-3460
Electronics engineering technology; electronics technician; digital electronics technician; computer information systems; telecommunications installer.

Electronic Computer Programming Institute
152 Market Street
Paterson, NJ 07505
(201) 523-1200
Data processing; data entry; computer programming; computer operations.

Empire Technical Schools of New Jersey
576 Central Avenue
East Orange, NJ 07018
(201) 675-0565
Computer programming; word processing.

HCA Institute
Cherry Hill Executive Campus
430 Cherry Hill Mall
Cherry Hill, NJ 08002
(609) 663-8500
Word processing/secretary.

Lincoln Technical Institute
Haddonfield Road and U.S. 130 North
Pennsauken, NJ 08110
(609) 665-3010
Mechanical drafting and design, including CAD; electronics; computer technology; computer systems technology.

Lyons Institute
16 Springdale Road
Cherry Hill, NJ 08003
(609) 424-5800
Digital computer electronics.

Lyons Institute
10 Commerce Place
Clark, NJ 07066
(201) 574-2090
Digital and microprocessor technology.

Lyons Institute
320 Main Street
Hackensack, NJ 07601
(201) 488-3790
Digital and microprocessor technology.

Metropolitan Technical Institute
400 Lyster Avenue
Saddle Brook, NJ 07662
(201) 843-4004
Electronics technology; electronics engineering technology; computer science; general electronics; digital integrated circuits; linear integrated circuits; memories and microprocessors; interfacing and robotics.

**National Education Center—
R.E.T.S. Electronic School Campus**
103 Park Avenue
Nutley, NJ 07110
(201) 661-0600
Electronic engineering technology; computer/electronic technician; digital electronics; microprocessors.

Pennco Tech
Post Office Box 1427
Erial Road
Blackwood, NJ 08012
(609) 232-0310
Electronics engineering technology; computer programming.

Plaza School of Drafting
Garden State Plaza—Routes 4 and 17
Paramus, NJ 07652
(201) 843-0344

Computer aided drafting.

Star Technical Institute
Cinnaminson Mall
Route 130 South
Cinnaminson, NJ 08077
(609) 786-8836
Interactive graphics-CAD; electronic computer technology; computer programming/accounting applications; word processing/secretarial.

Star Technical Institute
Road 5, 617A Blackhorse Pike
Williamstown, NJ 08094
(609) 629-0550
Electronic computer technology.

Star Technical Institute (Extension)
1386 South Delsea Drive
Vineland, NJ 08360
(609) 696-0500
Computer programming/accounting applications; word processing/secretarial.

Union Technical Institute
1117 Green Grove Road
Neptune, NJ 07753
(201) 922-1100
Computer systems technician; electronics; computer aided drafting; systems technician.

NEW YORK

**Advanced Training
Center—Kenmore Branch**
c/o Advanced Training Center
2829 Sheridan Drive
Tonawanda, NY 14150
(716) 835-4410
Data processing technician; information processing.

Advanced Training Center
2829 Sheridan Drive
Tonawanda, NY 14150
(716) 835-4410

Computer programming; CRT/data entry; data processing technician; information processing.

Albert Merrill School
21 West 60th Street
New York, NY 10023
(212) 246-7130
Computer programming and operations; data processing technician.

Center for the Media Arts
226 West 26 Street
New York, NY 10001
(212) 807-6670
Computer graphics.

Control Data Institute (Branch)
1325 Franklin Avenue
Garden City, NY 11530
(516) 294-8100
Computer technology; computer programming operations.

Control Data Institute
11 West 42nd Street
New York, NY 10036
(212) 944-4400
Computer technology; computer programming and operations.

Empire Technical School
350 Fifth Avenue
New York, NY 10118
(212) 563-3100
Data processing.

Hausman Computer School
500 Eighth Avenue
New York, NY 10018
(212) 736-1117
Data processing.

International Career Institute
120 West 30th Street
New York, NY 10001
(212) 244-5252
Word processing.

Island Drafting and Technical Institute
128 Broadway
Amityville, NY 11701
(516) 691-8733
Computer aided drafting; digital computer electronics (including microprocessors).

Lehigh Technical School
91-14 Merrick Boulevard
Jamaica, NY 11432
(212) 297-2722
Electronic technician; digital computer technician.

Manhattan Career Institute
351 East 61st Street
New York, NY 10021
(212) 593-1231
Computer programming; word processing secretary; computer service technician.

Manhattan Technical Institute
154 West 14 Street
New York, NY 10011
(212) 989-2662
CAD (computer aided drafting).

Metropolitan Career Institute
203 Jackson Street
Hempstead, NY 11550
(516) 538-0996
Word processing; electronic and computer technology.

Midland Career Institute
175 Fulton Avenue
Hempstead, NY 11550
(516) 481-2774
Word processing; word processing secretary.

Midland Career Institute (Branch)
40 Kings Park Road
Commack, NY 11725
(516) 543-3066
Word processing; word processing secretary.

National Electronic Technical School
24 Montcalm Avenue
Buffalo, NY 14609
(716) 835-2033
Electronic technology; microcomputer technology.

Printing Trades School
229 Park Avenue South
New York, NY 10003
(212) 677-0505
Computerized typesetting.

PSI Institute
269 West 40th Street
New York, NY 10018
(212) 944-9200
Data processing and computer programming; computer technology.

SCS Business and Technical Institute
1472 Broadway
New York, NY 10036
(212) 921-5000
Word processing operation; data entry/accounting specialist (CRT); CRT operator; data entry operations.

SCS Business and Technical Institute (Brooklyn)
57 Willoughby Street
Brooklyn, NY 11201
(718) 237-3730
Digital electronics and computer technology; data entry/accounting specialist; computer entry operator.

Suburban Technical School
175 Fulton Avenue
Hempstead, NY 11550
(516) 481-6660
Electronic technology; digital computer technology; microprocessor applications; telecommunications.

Suburban Technical School (Branch)
40 Kings Park Road
Commack, NY 11725
(516) 543-3990

Electronic technology; digital computer technology; microprocessor applications; telecommunications.

Suffolk Technical Institute
28 West Street
Bay Shore, NY 11706
(516) 665-8030
Computer programming; computer operations.

SYRIT Computer School Systems
5220-13th Avenue
Brooklyn, NY 11219
(718) 853-1212
Electronics technician; computer programming; computer operator.

Technical Career Institutes
320 West 31st Street
New York, NY 10001
(212) 594-4000
Electronics engineering technology; technical secretary (including word processing).

OHIO

ACA College of Design
2528 Kemper Lane
Cincinnati, OH 45206
(513) 751-1206
Computer graphics.

A.T.E.S. Technical Institute
2076-86 Youngstown-Warren Road
Niles, OH 44446
(216) 652-9919
Electronic engineering technology; computer programming.

Columbus Paraprofessional Institute
4820 Indianola Avenue
Columbus, OH 43214
(614) 885-9460
Data processing and computer programming.

Columbus Paraprofessional Institute—East (Branch)
70 Robinwood Avenue
Columbus, OH 43213
(614) 221-4481
>*Secretarial with word processing; word processing specialist; word processing for secretaries.*

Control Data Institute
6701 Rockside Road
Suite 102
Independence, OH 44131
(216) 447-1095
>*Computer technology; computer programming and operations.*

Control Data Institute
1946 N. 13th Street
Suite 392
Toledo, OH 43624
(419) 255-5969
>*Computer technology.*

DeVry Institute of Technology
1350 Alum Creek Drive
Columbus, OH 43209
(614) 253-7291
>*Electronics engineering technology; electronics; computer information systems; computer programming for business.*

Electronic Servicing Institute
3030 Euclid Avenue
Cleveland, OH 44115
(216) 391-5500
>*Electronics technician with specialties in computers, robots.*

Electronic Servicing Institute (Branch)
1875 North Ridge Road East
Lorain, OH 44055
(216) 277-8832
>*Electronics technician with specialties in computers, robots.*

Electronic Technology Institute
4300 Euclid Avenue
Cleveland, OH 44103
(216) 391-9696
>*Electronic engineering technology.*

Hickok Technical Institute
2012 West 25th Street
Cleveland, OH 44113
(216) 696-2626
>*Electronics technician; microprocessor/computer repair; drafter/computer aided drafting.*

McKim Technical Institute
1791 South Jacoby Road
Akron/Copley, OH 44321
(216) 666-4014
>*Electronics technology.*

National Education Center—National Institute of Technology Campus
1225 Orien Avenue
Cuyahoga Falls, OH 44221
(216) 923-9959
>*Electronics with specialties in applied or engineering electronics technology; digital and microprocessors.*

Northwestern Business College—Technical Center
1441 North Cable Road
Lima, OH 35805
(419) 227-3141
>*Computer programming; word processing.*

Ohio College of Business and Technology
415 West Court
Cincinnati, OH 45203
(513) 421-6797
>*Data entry/operations specialist; business computer programming; electronics technology.*

Ohio College of Business and Technology (Branch)
7601 Harrison Avenue
Mt. Healthy, OH 45231
(513) 424-3205

Data entry/operations specialist; business computer programming; electronics technology; data processor; word processor.

Ohio College of Business and Technology (Extension)
992 Lila Lane
Milford, OH 45150
(513) 831-6940
Word processing; electronics.

PSI Institute of Cleveland (Extension)
1858 Euclid Avenue
Cleveland, OH 44115
(216) 771-6680
Data processing and computer programming; computer technology.

RETS Institute of Technology
1606 Laskey Road
Toledo, OH 43612
(419) 478-7387
Electronic engineering technology; electronics with specialties in computer repair; microprocessor technology.

R.E.T.S. Tech Center
116 Westpark Road
P. O. Box 130
Centerville, OH 45459
(513) 433-3410
Electronic engineering technology; fiber-optics communications; robotics; computer science technology; computer programming; word processing.

Technichron Vocational Institute
4040 Spring Grove Avenue
Cincinnati, OH 45223
(513) 541-8111
Robotics technician; microprocessor technician; electronics.

Total Technical Institute
13505 West 130th Street
North Royalton, OH 44133
(216) 237-0288

Computer hardware technology; applied computer electronics technology.

OKLAHOMA

Bryan Institute
2843 East 51st Street
Tulsa, Ok 74105
(918) 749-6891
Computer programming.

National College of Technology
3020 North Stiles Avenue
Oklahoma City, OK 73105
(405) 528-2731
Electronic technology; business computer programming.

Sooner Mechanical Trade School
1100 West Main Street
Oklahoma City, OK 73106
(405) 235-8683
High-tech electronics.

Southwest Technical College
1520 South Central
Oklahoma City, OK 73129
(405) 632-7785
Electronic technology.

United Technical Institute
4533 Enterprise Drive
Oklahoma City, OK 73128
(405) 942-7700
Word processing specialist; word processing specialist-secretary/stenographer; computer office specialist; data processing specialist; electronics basic/digital, micro, communications; robotics.

OREGON

Computer Career Institute
2104 Southwest Fifth
Portland, OR 97201
(503) 226-1241
Business data processing and computer technician.

ITT Technical Institute
10822 Southeast Bush Street
Portland, OR 97266
(503) 760-5690
Electronic engineering technology.

Oregon Polytechnic Institute
900 Southeast Sandy Boulevard
Portland, OR 97214
(503) 234-9333
Electronic engineering technology.

PENNSYLVANIA

American Institute of Drafting
1616 Orthodox Street
Philadelphia, PA 19124
(215) 288-8200
Computer assisted design.

Berean Institute—Technical Division
1901 West Girard Avenue
Philadelphia, PA 19130
(215) 763-4833
Electronic technology; advanced electronics; data processing; word processor.

Computer Learning Center
3607 Rosemont Avenue
Camp Hill, PA 17011
(717) 761-1481
Word processor; computer operator/programmer.

Computer Learning Center/Maxwell Campus
2860 DeKalb Pike
Norristown, PA 19401
(215) 277-7920
Computer operations; computer programming; microcomputer career program.

Control Data Institute
4 Penn Center Plaza
Suite 600
Philadelphia, PA 19103
(215) 854-1370

Computer programming; computer technology; office technology.

Control Data Institute (Extension)
1 Allegheny Center Mall
Pittsburgh, PA 15212
(412) 321-1300
Computer service technician; data processing; electronics.

Dean Institute of Technology
1501 West Liberty Avenue
Pittsburgh, PA 15226-9990
(412) 531-4433
Drafting, including computer aided drafting; electrical technician.

Electronic Institutes
#19 Jamesway Plaza
Middletown, PA 17057
(717) 944-2731
Electronic and computer technology.

Electronic Institutes
4634 Browns Hill Road
Pittsburgh, PA 15217
(412) 521-8686
Electronic and computer technology.

Erie Institute of Technology
2221 Peninsula Drive
Erie, PA 16506
(814) 838-2711
Microcomputer electronics; electronic engineering technology.

FPM Data School
1704 Fourth Avenue
Arnold, PA 15068
(412) 339-3571
Business computer specialist; data entry preparation; concentrated computer programming; business administration with option in business computer sciences.

Gateway Technical Institute
100 Seventh Street
Pittsburgh, PA 15222
(412) 281-4111

Drafting and design technology with computer aided drafting.

Greensburg Institute of Technology
302 West Otterman Street
Greensburg, PA 15601
(412) 837-3330
Microcomputer repair; computer aided mechanical drafting technology; computer aided architectural drafting technology; electronic technology; electronics.

Information Computer Systems Institute
2201 Hangar Place
Allentown, PA 18103
(215) 264-8029
Computer programming specialist; computer operations/word processing.

J.H. Thompson Academics
2910-11 State Street
Erie, PA 16508
(814) 456-6217
Computer operator/word processing specialist.

Lehigh Data Processing Institute
833 North Park Road
Wyomissing, PA 19610
(215) 372-1722
Computer programming; computer operations/word processing.

Lincoln Technical Institute
5151 Tilghman Street
Allentown, PA 18104
(215) 398-5300
Electronics; computer technology.

Lyons Technical Institute
"D" Street and Erie Avenue
Philadelphia, PA 19134
(215) 426-5500
Electronics; computer technology.

Lyons Technical Institute
67 Long Lane
Upper Darby, PA 19082
(215) 734-1250

Digital computer electronics; electronics engineering technology.

Penn Technical Institute
110 Ninth Street
Pittsburgh, PA 15222
(412) 355-0455
Electronics technology.

Pennco Tech.
3815 Otter Street
Bristol, PA 19007
(215) 824-3200
Drafting/CAD; electronics; computer programming.

Pennsylvania Institute of Technology
Rose Valley-Notre Dame Campus
800 Manchester Avenue
Media, PA 19063
(215) 565-7900
Engineering technology; computer electronics; technology.

Pittsburgh Technical Institute
635 Smithfield Street
Pittsburgh, PA 15222
(412) 471-1011
Computer graphics (CADD).

PSI Institute of Philadelphia (Extension)
219 North Broad Street
Philadelphia, PA 19107
(215) 567-3104
Business administration/computer science; computer programming; computer operations; data entry operator.

R.E.T.S. Electronic Schools
West Chester Pike and Malin Road
Broomall, PA 19008
(215) 352-5586
Electronic engineering technology; basic electronics and solid-state technology; microprocessor and computer technology; advanced microcomputer technology; electronic communications; data communications.

Triangle Tech
2000 Liberty Street
Erie, PA 16502
(814) 453-6016
Architectural and mechanical drafting with CAD systems.

Triangle Tech
Triangle Tech Plaza
Blank School Road
Greensburg, PA 15601
(412) 832-1050
General drafting with specialties in architectural drafting and construction with computer aided drafting technology and mechanical drafting and design with computer aided drafting technology.

Triangle Tech
1940 Perrysville Avenue
Pittsburgh, PA 15214
(412) 359-1000
Architectural with CAD; mechanical with CAD.

Triangle Tech
I-80
Exit 16
P. O. Box 551
DuBois, PA 15801
(814) 371-2090
Mechanical drafting and design with CAD; architectural drafting and construction with CAD.

Washington Institute of Technology
82 South Main Street
Washington, PA 15301
(412) 222-1942
Electronic technology.

Wilma Boyd Career School
One Chatham Center
Pittsburgh, PA 15219
(412) 456-1800
Word processing.

York Technical Institute
3351 Whiteford Road
York, PA 17402
(717) 755-1100
Electronics technology.

PUERTO RICO

Instituto Superior Electronico
Kennedy Avenue Km 34
Apartado 4379
Hato Rey Station, Puerto Rico 00919
(809) 781-3865
Electronics.

Liceo de Arte y Tecnologia
405 Ponce de Leon Ave.
Hato Rey, Puerto Rico 00917
(809) 754-8250
Word processing clerk.

Metropolitan Institute of Science and Technology
359 San Claudio Street
Cupey Mall
San Juan, Puerto Rico 00926
(809) 755-7795
(809) 755-7284
(809) 755-7947
Electronics engineering technology.

San Juan City College
818 Ponce de Leon Avenue
Miramar
Santurce, Puerto Rico 00907
(809) 725-4949
Electronics (engineering); computer programming.

RHODE ISLAND

Allied Technical Institute
20 Marblehead Avenue
North Providence, RI 02904
(401) 353-8800
Computer programmer; computer service technician; electronic technician.

Hall Institute
120 High Street
Pawtucket, RI 02860
(401) 722-2003
(401) 461-6000
Computer aided drafting.

New England Institute of Technology
184 Early Street
Providence, RI 02907
(401) 467-7744
Electronics technology; drafting/CAD technology; computer programming technology.

RISE Institute of Electronics
14 Third Street
Providence, RI 02906
(401) 861-9664
Electronics technician; service technician; digital technician; engineering technology; computer technology; digital electronics technology; electronics servicing technology; engineering technology accelerated.

SOUTH CAROLINA

Medical Training Center
4949 Two Notch Road
Columbia, SC 29204
(803) 754-5580
Electronics/microcomputer technician.

Nielsen Electronics Institute
1600 Meeting Street
Charleston, SC 29405
(803) 722-2344
Electronics technology.

SOUTH DAKOTA

Nettleton College
P.O. Box 924
9th and Spring Avenue
Sioux Falls, SD 57102
(605) 336-1837
Computer science.

TENNESSEE

Control Data Institute
5100 Poplar Avenue
Suite 132
Memphis, TN 38137
(901) 458-0088
Computer technology; computer programming and operations; office technology.

Electronic Computer Programming Institute
3805 Brainerd Road
Chattanooga, TN 37411
(615) 624-0077
Data processing and computer programming; micro-systems programming and operations; word processing; data entry.

ITT Technical Institute (Extension)
441 Donelson Pike
Nashville, TN 37214-3526
(615) 889-8700
Electronic engineering technology.

Tennessee Institute of Electronics
3203 Tazewell Pike
Knoxville, TN 37918
(615) 688-9422
Electronic technology.

TEXAS

American Trades Institute (Extension)
11034 Shady Trail
Suite 117
Dallas, TX 75229
(214) 350-7853
Computer programming.

Bryan Institute (Extension)
1719 West Pioneer Parkway
Arlington, TX 76103
(817) 265-5588
Computer programming.

CBM Education Center
406 West Durango
San Antonio, TX 78207
(512) 224-9286
Computer programming and operations; data entry; electronic technician; microprocessing.

CBM Education Center (Extension)
2550 West Highway 83
San Berito, TX 78586
(512) 399-4007
Data entry.

CBM Education Center (Extension)
1002 Corpus Christi Street
Laredo, TX 78040
(512) 726-4676
Data entry; word processing specialist.

Computer Learning Center of Houston
11200 Westheimer Road
Houston, TX 77042
(713) 781-6800
Computer programming; computer operator.

Control Data Institute
8585 North Stemmons Freeway
Dallas, TX 75247
(214) 688-5900
Computer technology; computer program-ming/operations; office technology (word processing).

Control Data Institute (Extension)
2990 Richmond Avenue
Suite 600
Houston, TX 77098
(713) 522-6115
Data processing; computer technology; computer programming; office technology.

DeVry Institute of Technology
4250 North Beltline Road
Irving, TX 75038
(214) 258-6767 Administration
(214) 258-6330 Admissions
Electronics engineering technology; computer science for business.

Durham Nixon-Clay College—Technical Division
119 West 8th Street
P.O. Box 1626
Austin, TX 78767
(512) 478-3446
Electronics; drafting.

El Paso Trade School
1000 Texas
El Paso, TX 79901
(915) 532-3737
Electronics; microcomputer technology.

Elkins Institute in Dallas
2603 Inwood Road
Dallas, TX 75235
(214) 350-1212
Electronics (digital-microprocessing); computer aided drafting.

Elkins Institute of Houston
7322 West Freeway
Suite 1450
Houston, TX 77074
(713) 271-7722
Electronic technology.

Fort Worth Trade Schools
3617 Collinwood
Fort Worth, TX 76107
(817) 731-8423
Electronics technology.

Hallmark Institute of Technology
1130 99th Street
San Antonio, TX 78214
(512) 924-8551
Electronics.

Hallmark Institute of Technology (Extension)
10401 I-10 West
San Antonio, TX 78230
(512) 690-9000
Electronics and computer technician.

ITT Technical Institute
2202 Road to Six Flags
Arlington, TX 76011
(817) 640-7100
Electronics engineering technology.

ITT Technical Institute (Extension)
9421 Roark Road
Houston, TX 77099
(713) 270-1634
Electronics engineering technology.

Microcomputer Technology Institute
6116 Windswept Lane
Houston, TX 77057
(713) 974-7181
Microcomputer electronics technology; computer aided business technology; digital technician; electronics technician.

National Education Center—Bryman Campus
9724 Beechnut
Suite 300
Houston, TX 77036
(713) 776-3656
Information systems; electronics.

National Education Center—National Institute of Technology Campus
3040 North Buckner Boulevard
Dallas, TX 75228
(214) 324-2811
Electronic engineering technology; computer programming and operations.

National Education Center—National Institute of Technology Campus
401 West Byrd Street
Universal City, TX 78148
(512) 658-7078
Computer programmer/operator; electronic engineering technology.

Southwest School of Electronics
5424 Highway 290 West
Suite 200
Austin, TX 78735
(512) 892-2640
Electronics.

Texas Institute
1820 Regal Row
Dallas, TX 75235
(214) 637-5211

Data processing; computer operations; micro/mini systems programming/word processing; office systems management.

Total Technical Institute (Extension)
9205 Skillman Street
Suite 116
Dallas, TX 75243
(214) 340-9922
Computer hardware technology.

**Video Technical Institute
Computer Business School (Branch)**
2201 North Collins
Suite 305
Arlington, TX 76011
(817) 860-0741
Computer office technology.

UTAH

The Bryman School
445 South Third East
Salt Lake City, UT 84111
(801) 521-2830
Word processing.

ITT Technical Institute
4876 West North Temple
Salt Lake City, UT 84116
(801) 537-5003
Electronic engineering technology.

VIRGINIA

Control Data Institute
3717 Columbia Pike
Arlington, VA 22204
(703) 553-2050
Computer programming and operations; computer repair; word processing.

Electronic Computer Programming Institute—Main Campus
3661 East Virginia Beach Boulevard
Norfolk, VA 23502
(804) 461-6161

Data processing and computer programming; computer technology; computer maintenance; computer electronics; electronics-computer technology; computer service technician; office technology/word processing; electronics technology; word processing.

Electronic Computer Programming Institute—Richmond Campus (Extension)
4303 West Broad Street
Richmond, VA 23230
(804) 359-3535

Data processing and computer programming; computer technology; computer maintenance; computer service technician; computer electronics; electronics-computer technology; office technology; word processor; electronics technology.

Virginia Institute of Technology (Branch)
1118 B West Mercury Boulevard
Hampton, VA 23666
(804) 827-5000

Computer programming specialist; electronics technician.

Virginia Institute of Technology
5425 Robin Hood Road
Norfolk, VA 23513
(804) 855-9300

Computer programming; electronics technician.

WASHINGTON

ITT Peterson School of Business— Technical Division
130 Nickerson Street
Seattle, WA 98109
(206) 285-2600

Data processing and computer programming; electronics engineering technology; business applications and information systems.

ITT Technical Institute (Extension)
North 1050 Argonne Road
Spokane, WA 99212
(509) 926-2900

Computer technician; computer-aided drafting; electronics engineering technology.

Miller Institute— Spokane Extension Campus
801 East Second Avenue
Spokane, WA 99202
(509) 535-3535

Electronics and drafting/CAD.

Perry Technical Institute
P.O. Box 9457
Yakima, WA 98909
(509) 453-0374

Telecommunications technology.

Seattle/Opportunities Industrialization Center
315-22nd Avenue South
Seattle, WA 98144
(206) 223-6258

Computer operations/applications; data entry; electronics technician; word processing.

Spokane Technical Institute
East 5634 Commerce
Spokane, WA 99212
(509) 535-7771

Computer programming; electronic technician; microprocessor technology.

WEST VIRGINIA

National Education Center— National Institute of Technology Campus
5514 Big Tyler Road
Cross Lanes, WV 25313
(304) 776-6290

Electronics engineering technology; computer programming.

WISCONSIN

Control Data Institute
804 North Milwaukee Street
Milwaukee, WI 53202
(414) 223-0223

Computer programming and operations; computer technology; office technology.

Wisconsin School of Electronics
1601 North Sherman Avenue
Madison, WI 53704
(608) 249-6611

Electronic engineering technology; electronic service engineering; electronic/electrical drafting.

ACCREDITATION

Accreditation by a nationally recognized accredited agency, such as the Accrediting Commission of the National Home Study Council, provides assurance that a school meets high standards and offers quality educational materials and services.

Schools which are not accredited should be carefully checked. Here are ways that the prospective student can do this:

- ☐ Study the institution's catalogs and brochures carefully.
- ☐ Compare the descriptions of the course offerings to other similar correspondence courses.
- ☐ Investigate the institution's reputation with the State Department of Education, Better Business Bureau, and Chamber of Commerce.
- ☐ Ask the school for specific answers to questions.

Success with a home study course depends as much on the determination and ability of the student as it does on the course materials and the educational services of the home study school. The school provides the student with encouragement and the opportunity to learn, but it is up to the student to succeed.

What Does Accreditation Mean To You?[14]

If someone asked you if the school you're taking a home study course from is accredited, what would

you say? What does accreditation mean to you as a student?

Basically, accreditation is a process that gives public recognition to schools that meet certain standards. It is a promise that a school will provide the quality of education it claims to offer. Accreditation assures the student that the school operates on a sound financial basis, has an approved program of study, qualified instructors, adequate facilities and equipment, and approved recruitment and admissions policies.

The U.S. Department of Education lists a number of accrediting agencies which determine the reliability and quality of education or training offered by schools and colleges. The National Home Study Council's Accrediting Commission is the only U.S.D.E. listed agency solely accrediting home study schools.

Application for accreditation is voluntary. However, only bona fide correspondence institutions with two years operating experience may apply. Once application is made, the school must write a Self Evaluation Report. This report includes the analysis of pertinent data on all aspects of the school and its operation. Courses offered by the school are submitted to the Commission, which in turn sends them to subject specialist experts for review. After these reports are received, an examining committee is assigned to visit the school. The committee studies the entire operation of the school and verifies the information in the Self Evaluation Report. State Departments of Education, federal agencies, Better Business Bureaus, and other official bodies are surveyed to obtain pertinent information about the school's overall reputation. A confidential survey of students selected at random also provides helpful information for the Accrediting Commission.

After all reports and surveys are in, the nine-member Accrediting Commission reviews them in terms of the published standards and determines whether or not to accredit the school. If a school is accredited, it must conform to all educational and business standards of the National Home Study Council's Accrediting Commission, submit annual reports, and be re-examined every five years. The

---

[14] *What Does Accreditation Mean To You?*, by Sally R. Welch, Director of Publications for the National Home Study Council. Permission to reproduce granted by the National Home Study Council.

Commission may also call for special reports or examinations when changes at the school make them necessary.

Accreditation is also important when it comes to federal programs for educational grants and loans. Eligibility for federal financial assistance can be limited to students who are enrolled with qualifying accredited schools.

Standards for Accrediting Home Study Schools[15]

Standards for accrediting home study schools serve as guideposts in helping the school's staff and faculty evaluate important aspects of their program. The main values of the accrediting process result from continuous growth and improvement through self-evaluation. Constructive self-evaluation is the basis for the improvement of educational services and selective administrative practices.

These standards have been developed by the Research and Education Standards Committee, the Business Standards Committee, officials and other members of the National Home Study Council, with the advice and cooperation of outstanding authorities on accrediting in the United States. All standards have been approved and adopted by the National Home Study Council, the Board of Trustees, and the Accrediting Commission. These same standards provide a guide for the examiners and Commissioners when they in turn evaluated the school as part of the accrediting program.

Accredited home study schools possess the following characteristics:

Educational Objectives. Educational objectives are clearly defined and simply stated. They indicate what the educational program can do for reasonably diligent students. The character, nature, quality, value, and source of the instruction and educational service are set forth in language understood by the types of students enrolled. If a course prepares for an occupation or field of occupations, the objectives clearly state the types of occupations for which preparation is given.

---

[15]Permission to reproduce granted by the Accrediting Commission of the National Home Study Council.

The objectives of the school must be of such a nature that they can be achieved through correspondence study. The educational objectives are reasonably attainable. Appropriate objectives include the development of skills, the provision of job-related training, the imparting of information, training in the application of knowledge, and the development of desirable habits and attitudes. Evaluation of the educational program is based on the announced course objectives and the success with which the objectives are fulfilled.

Educational Materials. Instructional materials are sufficiently comprehensive to achieve the announced objectives. Instructional materials are accurate and reflect current knowledge and practice. Instructional materials are prepared by qualified persons competent in their field. Materials other than standard textbooks produced by recognized publishers are prepared by correspondence educators skilled in preparing materials for home study use.

The reading difficulty of the instructional materials is keyed to the reading competence of the average enrollee in the course.

Suitable instructions on how to study the course clearly indicate to the students what to do and how to learn effectively.

The organization and presentation of the instructional materials are in accord with the sound psychological principles of learning.

Instructional programs make effective use of appropriate teaching devices and supplemental instructional aids.

Illustrations are used intelligently and they have educational and/or inspirational value.

Instructional materials are legibly reproduced, well manufactured, suitably bound, and attractive in layout and format.

Educational Services. The submission of examinations which adequately cover the materials is required. Adequate evaluation, correction services, and necessary counseling by the instructor are provided for examinations.

A *resident course* (terminal training) should supplement the home study course whenever it is necessary to attain the stated educational objectives.

Relevant inquiries from students are welcome and are answered promptly and satisfactorily with due regard for any legal and professional restrictions.

Adequate provisions are made to meet the individual differences of students and to provide counseling and guidance as required to assist the student to attain his educational goals.

Students who fail to do satisfactory work are encouraged to continue until they either show inability to do satisfactory work, or until they demonstrate satisfactory progress.

A constructive program is followed to encourage students to start, continue, and finish the courses in which they have enrolled.

Reactions of students are sought as one basis for evaluating and improving instructional materials and services.

Student Services. Minimum student services include prompt return of accurately graded examinations.

Ample study materials should be provided at all times to the student. Essential student records should be adequately maintained.

Competent counseling should be available to students on request. If employment assistance and other services for alumni are offered, they should be as purported.

Student Success and Satisfaction. A high proportion of students are satisfied with the training and educational services.

A satisfactory percentage of enrolled students start the course, continue their studies, and finish. A sample checking of the students in a school must indicate a reasonable achievement in, and completion of, their course and satisfaction with the services which the school is rendering.

Qualifications of Faculty. A qualified person serves as the educational director. He has overall administrative responsibilities for the educational program and a policy-making voice in advertising, sales, and collections.

In large schools, department heads or other qualified persons are delegated educational, editorial, and research responsibilities within subject fields.

The school has a sufficient number of qualified instructors to give individualized instructional service to each student.

Admission Practices and Enrollment Agreements. An accredited school exercises care to enroll only students who can reasonably be expected to benefit from the instruction.

The written enrollment agreement and/or written documents left with the student specify clearly the nature and scope of the course, the services and obligations to which the school is committed, and the privileges and obligations, financial and otherwise, of the student. Any changes in tuition, procedures, or rates must be made applicable to all future enrollees.

Advertising and Promotion. Advertising, promotional literature, and field representatives of home study schools make only clear and provable statements fully within the spirit of the Trade Practice Rules for Private Home Study Schools as approved by the Federal Trade Commission. Advertising in magazines, newspapers, on the radio, or on television must be ethical in every respect. Flamboyant statements, emphasis on shortcuts, or any statement in fact or by inference which is offensive to public educational authorities or to the general public are not to be employed in advertising or selling.

Methods of selecting, training, supervising, terminating, and compensating field representatives assure representatives who reflect credit upon the home study field. Field representatives, when used, must be directly responsible to the school. The school must give supervision to its representatives, and orientation or pre-employment training must be provided before permitting them to solicit enrollments. A current list of field representatives and their supervisors shall be available; the address of each field representative shall be available through the usual reference sources such as the telephone book, the local credit bureau, and bank. A school under indictment by a State or Federal government agency for any deviation from good ethical practice shall not be accredited until cleared of all charges.

Financial Responsibility. The school can

show, by financial statement, that it is financially responsible and that it can meet its financial obligations to provide service to its students.

The school can show two years of sound and ethical operation. Schools which are branches or affiliates of established schools may be accredited after fewer than two years of operation.

Tuition Policies. The amount of tuition charges is reasonable in light of the educational services rendered and the school's operating costs.

Tuition collection practices and procedures are fair. They encourage the progress of students and seek to retain their good will. The right to protect its financial interests is inherent with any accredited school. Its tuition collection practices are in keeping with sound ethical business standards.

The school recognizes that there are legitimate reasons why an enrolled student may not be able to complete his training with benefit to himself. Accordingly, the school has a policy for equitable tuition adjustment in such cases. Records should be maintained on tuition refunds and enrollment cancellations to provide a reference source for management analysis.

Plant and Equipment. The building, workspace, and equipment comply with the local fire, building, health and safety requirements and are adequately equipped to handle the educational program of the institution.

Educational records of all students are maintained in a safe, fireproof, and reasonably accessible place as long as they are likely to be needed. Other records are maintained in accordance with current educational, administrative, business, and legal practice.

Research and Self-Improvement. An accredited school shows evidence of progressiveness and of effort to improve operating efficiency and service. Sound research procedures and techniques are used to measure how effectively the announced course objectives are being met.

Effective procedures are utilized to constantly improve materials and keep them current and up-to-date.

Interest in improving the course of instruction and in the upgrading of personnel and faculty is demonstrated through membership in professional associations, review and application of research, and practical experience in general field of education and the specific field of home study.

An accredited school has an established program or plan reflecting a desire to improve its services to the student and to provide for the growth of the school and its staff and faculty.

Accredited Home Study Schools[16]

The following 11 schools are accredited home study schools which offer courses in one or more of the following categories: computer programming, computer repair technician, computer technology, data processing, electrical engineering technology, electronics, microcomputers, microcomputer repair and service, and robotics.

AMS College

10025 Shoemaker Avenue
Sante Fe Springs, CA 90670
Founded: 1976
Computer programming.

Cleveland Institute of Electronics, Inc.

1776 East 17th Street
Cleveland, OH 44114
Founded: 1934
Degree and non-degree courses in electronics technology.

Grantham College of Engineering

10570 Humbolt Street
Los Alamitos, CA 90720
Founded: 1951
Associate and bachelor degrees in electronics engineering technology.

Granton Institute of Technology

263 Adelaide Street West
Toronto, Canada M5H 1Y3
Founded: 1934

---

[16]From *NHSC 1985-86 Directory of Accredited Home Study Schools,* copyright © 1985 by National Home Study Council. Reprinted by permission.

Engineering and technology, electronics and mechanics, repair and installation.

Halix Institute
1543 West Olympic Boulevard
Suite 226
Los Angeles, CA 90015
Founded: 1984
   Computer programming (English and Spanish).

Heathkit/Zenith Educational Systems
Hilltop Road
Saint Joseph, MI 49085
Founded: 1975
   Electricity and electronic fundamentals, advanced electronics, digital electronics, microprocessors and microcomputers, robotics, computer programming.

Hemphill Schools
1543 West Olympic Boulevard
Suite 226
Los Angeles, CA 90015
Founded: 1920
   Computer programming courses available in English language.

ICS—International Correspondence Schools
Scranton, PA 18515
Founded: 1891

Courses at the secondary and postsecondary level in technology and engineering.

ICS Center for Degree Studies
Scranton, PA 18515
Founded: 1974
   Associate degree programs in engineering and electronics.

McGraw-Hill Continuing Education Center
3939 Wisconsin Avenue, NW
Washington, DC 20016
Founded: 1971
   Computers and electronics.

NRI Schools
3939 Wisconsin Avenue, NW
Washington, DC 20016
Founded: 1914
   Microcomputers, electronic communications, and robotics.

National Technical Schools
4000 South Figueroa Street
Los Angeles, CA 90037
Founded: 1905
   Robotics, microcomputers and digital logic electronics.

Chapter 13

Women and Minorities in Computing

A computer career is a good choice for women and individuals of minority races (Fig. 13-1). They are paid better salaries than in the overall work force where, for example, women's pay is only about 60 percent of men's pay. In addition, the recent need for experienced workers in computer fields is expected by some to result in even fewer barriers to women and minorities.

Part of the reason that individuals in these minority groups fare better in computing than in other fields may be the quantitative nature of the work performed. Subjectivity plays a large role in the evaluation of someone's work when it is more quantitative in nature, but in computers the bottom line, the last question, is often: "Does it work?," "Does the program run?," or "Is it ready for me to use?."

The future of computing is bright for women and persons of minority races because of the number of new jobs that are being created in the field. Employers can afford to be a little choosier than they were five years ago, but even now technological careers dominate the Bureau of Labor Statistic's list of fastest-growing jobs from 1984 to 1995; programmers are among the top five on the list.

In recent years, more women and members of minority races are getting their education in computer fields. For example, in 1980-1981, 33 percent of persons receiving bachelor's degrees in computer and information science were women, while 36 percent were women in 1982-1983 (the most current information available at press time). The percent of women awarded master's degrees in the same field rose from 23 percent in 1980-1981 to 29 percent in 1982-1983. Ten percent of the Ph.Ds in computer and information science awarded to Americans in 1980-1981 went to women, while 13 percent went to women in 1982-1983.

Even though progress is being made, and even though the field of computers is a promising one for women and minority groups, the data available in sex and race differences does indicate some disappointing patterns. For example, women and members of minority races tend to occupy more lower-level computer jobs than men do. The 1980 census (one of the most current surveys available

Fig. 13-1. A computer career is a good choice for women and individuals of minority races partly because of the recent need for experienced workers in computer fields. (Photograph courtesy of Honeywell, Inc.)

regarding this information, because questions regarding sex and race were no longer asked in most government surveys after the early 1980s) shows that while 31 percent of computer programmers in the country were women, only 23 percent of systems analysts were female.

Some studies have shown that women do not get promoted as quickly as men. Other research indicates that women and members of minority groups tend to stay on the same job longer than white men and also make fewer company changes.

Women and minority group members working in computing should keep several tips in mind: Do not be afraid of changing jobs in order to get out of or avoid a rut or a dead-end position. Concentrate on the additional training necessary to advance from your present job (see Chapter 4). Consider the possibility of self-employment in sales or consulting once you have developed enough expertise to make this possible. You may want to stay in touch with or join several associations or organizations for support and also as a source of information. See Appendix A; included in this list of associations are groups specializing in minority group interests.

For more general statistics and information regarding computer careers, see the Introduction.

Appendix A

Associations

The following list of associations can be helpful in obtaining more information about in general and specific aspects of particular careers.

Accountants Computer Users Technical Exchange
6081 East 82nd Street
Suite 110
Indianapolis, IN 46250
(317) 845-8702

Accounting Careers Council
c/o American Institute of
Certified Public Accountants
1211 Avenue of the Americas
New York, NY 10036
(212) 575-6200

Accreditation Board for Engineering and Technology
345 East 47th Street
New York, NY 10017
(212) 705-7685

ADAPSO (Association of Data Processing Service Organizations, Inc.)
1300 North 17th Street, Suite 300
Arlington, VA 22209
(703) 522-5055

American Association for Career Education
P.O. Box 40720
Washington, DC 20016
(202) 724-4015

American Association of Engineering Societies
345 East 47th Street
New York, NY 10017
(212) 705-7840

American Council for Career Women
P.O. Box 50825
New Orleans, LA 70150
(504) 468-5665

American
Federation of
Information Processing Societies
1899 Preston White Drive
Reston, VA 22091
(703) 620-8900

The American Institute
for Professional Education
Carnegie Building
55 Main Street
Madison, NJ 07940
(201) 377-7400

American Institute
of Industrial Engineers
25 Technology Park/Atlanta
Norcross, GA 30092
(404) 499-0460

American Society for
Engineering Education
11 Dupont Circle, Suite 200
Washington, DC 20036
(202) 293-7080

American Society
for Information Science
1010 16th Street, NW
Washington, DC 20036
(202) 659-3644

American
Society of Certified
Engineering Technicians
Mark Twain Bank Building, 3rd floor
10401 Holmes Road
Kansas City, MO 64131
(816) 941-2838

American Society
of Computer Dealers
3500 Southland Center
Dallas, TX 75201
(214) 744-3500

American Society of
Mechanical Engineers
345 East 47th Street
New York, NY 10017
(212) 705-7375

American
Society of Professional
and Executive Women
1511 Walnut Street
Philadelphia, PA 19102
(215) 563-4415

American Vocational Association
2020 North 14th Street
Arlington, VA 22201
(703) 522-6121

American Vocational
Education Research Association
c/o Jay Smith
1960 Kenny Road
Columbus, OH 43214
(614) 486-3655

Association for
Computational Linguistics
c/o Dr. D.E. Walker, ACL
Bell Communications Research
445 South Street
Morristown, NJ 07960
(201) 829-4312

Association for
Computers and the Humanities
c/o Donald Ross
Department of English
University of Minneapolis
Minneapolis, MN 55455
(612) 373-2541

Association for
Computing Machinery, Inc.
11 West 42nd Street, 3rd floor
New York, NY 10036
(212) 869-7440

**Association for
Educational Data Systems**
1201 16th Street, NW
Washington, DC 20036
(202) 822-7845

**Association for
Systems Management**
24587 Bagley Road
Cleveland, OH 44138
(216) 243-6900

**Association for
Women in Computing**
407 Hillmoor Drive
Silver Spring, MD 20901

**Association of
Better Computer Dealers**
Suite 430, O'Hare Plaza
5725 East River Road
Chicago, IL 60631
(312) 693-2223

Association of Computer Users
P.O. Box 9003
Boulder, CO 80301
(303) 442-3600

**Association of Information
and Dissemination Centers**
P.O. Box 8105
Athena, GA 30603
(404) 542-3106

**Association of
Information Managers
for Saving Institutions**
111 East Wacker Drive, Suite 2221
Chicago, IL 60601
(312) 938-2576

**Association of
Information Systems Professionals**
1015 North York Road
Willow Grove, PA 19090
(215) 657-6300

**Association of Public
Data Users Princeton
University Computer Center**
87 Prospect Avenue
Princeton, NJ 08544
(609) 452-6025

**Association of Rehabilitation
Programs in Data Processing**
P.O. Box 2404
Gaithersburg, MD 20879
(301) 840-4980

**Association of the
Institute for Certification
of Computer Professionals**
2200 East Devon Avenue
Des Plaines, IL 60018
(312) 299-4270

Catalyst
250 Park Avenue South
New York, NY 10003
(212) 777-8900

**Computer Aided
Manufacturing International**
611 Ryan Plaza Drive
Suite 1107
Arlington, TX 76011
(817) 860-1654

**Computer and Automated
Systems Association of SME**
1 SME Drive
Box 930
Dearborn, MI 48121
(313) 271-1500

**Computer and
Communications Industry Association**
1500 Wilson Boulevard, Suite 512
Arlington, VA 22209
(703) 524-1360

**Computer Dealers
and Lessors Association**
1212 Potomac Street, NW
Georgetown
Washington, DC 20007
(202) 333-0102

**Coordinator
Special Interest Group for
Computer Science Education**
c/o ACM
11 West 42nd Street, 3rd floor
New York, NY 10036
(212) 869-7440

Council for Career Planning, Inc.
310 Madison Avenue
New York, NY 10017
(212) 758-2153

Council of Women in Business
c/o National Businesses League
4324 Georgia Avenue, NW
Washington, DC 20011
(202) 829-5900

Data Entry Management Association
P.O. Box 16711
Stamford, CT 06905
(203) 967-3500

**Data Processing
Management Association**
505 Busse Highway
Park Ridge, IL 60068
(312) 825-8124

EDP Auditors Association
373 South Schmale Road
Carol Stream, IL 60187
(312) 682-1200

EDP Auditors Foundation, Inc.
Administrative Office
373 South Schmale Road
Carol Stream, IL 60187
(312) 682-1200

GUIDE, International
111 East Wacker Drive
Chicago, IL 60601
(312) 644-6610

**Independent Computer
Consultants Association**
P.O. Box 27412
St. Louis, MO 63141
(314) 997-4633

Information Industry Association
316 Pennsylvania Avenue, SE
Suite 400
Washington, DC 20003
(202) 544-1969

**Information Management
and Processing Association**
P.O. Box 16267
Lansing, MI 48901
(517) 484-3480

**Institute for Certification
of Computer Professionals (ICCP)**

**Institute of Electrical
and Electronics Engineers**
345 East 47th Street
New York, NY 10017
(212) 705-7900

**Interuniversity
Communications Council (EDUCOM)**
P.O. Box 364
Princeton, NJ 08540
(609) 734-1915

**JETS, Inc., (Junior
Engineering Technical Society)**
United Engineering Center
345 East 47th Street
New York, NY 10017
(212) 705-7690

National Association of
Computer Stores
196 North Street
P.O. Box 1333
Stamford, CT 06904
(203) 323-3143

National Association
of Professional Word
Processing Technicians
110 West Byberry Road (E2)
Philadelphia, PA 19116
(215) 934-6448

National Association of
Trade and Technical Schools
2251 Wisconsin Avenue, NW
Washington, DC 20007
(202) 333-1021

National Association
of Working Women (9 to 5)
1224 Huron Road
Cleveland, OH 44115
(216) 566-9308

National Computer Association
1485 East Fremont Circle, South
Littleton, CO 80122
(303) 797-3559

National Council of Career Women
1133 15th Street, NW, Suite 1000
Washington, DC 20006
(202) 429-9440

National Federation of
Local Cable Programmers
906 Pennsylvania Avenue, SE
Washington, DC 20003
(202) 544-7272

North American
Computer Service Association
506 Georgetown Drive
Casselberry, FL 32707
(305) 422-2000

Office Technology
Management Association
9401 West Beloit Road, Suite 101
Milwaukee, WI 53227
(414) 321-0880

Office Technology Research Group
Box 65
Pasadena, CA 91102

Personal Computer
Management Association
11928 North Earlham
Orange, CA 92669

Recognition
Technologies Users Association
P.O. Box 2016
Manchester, VT 05255
(802) 362-4151

Robot Institute of America
P.O. Box 930
Dearborn, MI 48128
(313) 271-0778

Robotics International of SME
One SME Drive, P.O. Box 930
Dearborn, MI 48121
(313) 271-1500

Society for Computer
Application in Engineering,
Planning, and Architecture, Inc.
15713 Crabbs Branch Way
Rockville, MD 20855
(301) 926-7070

Society for Computer Simulation
P.O. Box 17900
San Diego, CA 92117
(617) 277-3888

Society for
Information Management
One Illinois Center
111 East Wacker Drive, Suite 600
Chicago, IL 60601
(312) 644-6610

**Society for
Technical Communication**
815 15th Street, NW, Suite 506
Washington, DC 20005
(202) 737-0035

**Society of
Manufacturing Engineers**
One SME Drive, P.O. Box 930
Dearborn, MI 48121
(313) 271-1500

**Society of Office
Automation Professionals**
233 Mountain Road
Ridgefield, CT 06877
(203) 431-0029

**Special Interest
Committee for Computers
& the Physically Handicapped**
c/o ACM
11 West 42nd Street
New York, NY 10036
(212) 869-7440

**Special Interest Group
for ADA Programming
Language (SIGADA of ACM)**
c/o ACM
11 West 42nd Street
New York, NY 10036
(212) 869-7440

**Special Interest Group
for Business Data Processing**
c/o ACM
11 West 42nd Street
New York, NY 10036
(212) 869-7440

**Special Interest Group for
Computer Personnel Research**
c/o Robert P. Bostrom
Indiana University
Bloomington, IN 47401
(812) 335-8449

**Special Interest Group on
Computer and Human Interaction**
Vagelback Computing Center
Northwestern University
Evanston, IL 60201

**Special Interest Group
on Programming Languages**
c/o ACM
11 West 42nd Street, 3rd floor
New York, NY 10036
(212) 869-7440

**Special Interest
Group on Small
Computing and Applications Systems**
c/o ACM
New York, NY 10036
(212) 869-7440

Women in Data Processing
P.O. Box 22818
San Diego, CA 92122
(619) 569-5615

Women in Information Processing
Lock Box 39173
Washington, DC 20016
(202) 328-6161

Working Women Education Fund
1224 Huron Road
Cleveland, OH 44115
(216) 566-1699

Appendix B

Publications

The following is a partial list of the major directories, periodicals, and publications in the computer area. For the most current information regarding price (which sometimes differs for members and non-members) and frequency of publication, either call or write to the publisher indicated.

ACM's Computing Surveys

The Administrative Directory (of Computer Science Departments and Computer Centers)
ACM
11 West 42nd Street
New York, NY 10036
(212) 869-7440

Administrative Directory of University and College Computer Science Data Processing Programs and Computer Facilities
Association for Computing Machinery (ACM)
11 West 42nd Street
New York, NY 10036
(212) 869-7440

Annals of the History of Computing
11 West 42nd Street
New York, NY 10036
(212) 869-7440

The AWC Source Association for Women in Computing
407 Hillmoor Drive
Silver Spring, MD 20901

A Better Channel (newsletter)
Association of Better
Computer Dealers
Suite 430, O'Hare Plaza
5725 East River Road
Chicago, IL 60631
(312) 693-2223

**Bibliography of
Robotic Technical Papers**
Robotics International of SME
One SME Drive
Post Office Box 930
Dearborn, MI 48121
(313) 271-1500

Byte
70 Main Street
Peterborough, NH 03458
(603) 924-9281

CEPA Newsletter
Society for Computer
Applications in Engineering,
Planning and Architecture, Inc.
15713 Crabbs Branch Way
Rockville, MD 20855
(301) 926-7070

**Challenging
Careers in Information**
American Society for
Information Science
1010 16th Street, Northwest
Washington, DC 20036
(202) 659-3644

Collected Algorithms from ACM
ACM
11 West 42nd Street
New York, NY 10036
(212) 869-7440

**Communications of
the ACM Association
for Computing Machinery, Inc.**
ACM
11 West 42nd Street
New York, NY 10036
(212) 869-7440

**Computational
Linguistics Association
for Computational Linguistics**
c/o Dr. D.E. Walker, ACL
Bell Communications Research
445 South Street
Morristown, NJ 07960

Computer World
375 Cochituate Road
Framingham, MA 01701
(617) 879-0700

Computing Reviews
ACM
11 West 42nd Street
New York, NY 10036
(212) 869-7440

**Database
SIGBDP**
ACM
11 West 42nd Street
New York, NY 10036
(212) 869-7440

Datamation
875 Third Avenue
New York, NY 10022
(212) 605-9400

DEMA Newsletter
Data Entry Management
Association
Post Office Box 16711
Stamford, CT 06905
(203) 967-3500

**Directory of
Engineering Societies**
AAES
415 2nd Street, Southeast, Suite 200
Washington, DC 20002
(202) 546-2237

**Directory of Robotics
Education and Training**
Education Dept.
Society of Manufacturing
Engineers
One SME Drive
Post Office Box 930
Dearborn, MI 48121
(313) 271-1500

**Engineers' Salaries:
Special Industry Report**
American Association of
Engineering Societies
415 Second Street, Southeast, Suite 200
Washington, DC 20002
(202) 546-2237

Executive Computing
Association of Computer Users
Post Office Box 9003
Boulder, CO 80301

**Graduate Assistantship
Directory in the Computer Sciences**

**Guide to
Computing Literature**
ACM
11 West 42nd Street
New York, NY 10036
(212) 869-7440

Information Sources
Information Industry
Association
316 Pennsylvania Avenue, Southeast
Suite 400
Washington, DC 20003
(202) 544-1969

Information Systems Curriculum
Recommendations for the 80's:
Undergraduate and Graduate
Programs
ACM
11 West 42nd Street
New York, NY 10036
(212) 869-7440

Infosystems
Geneva Road
Wheaton, IL 60187

Job Market
American Vocational Association
2020 North 14th Street
Arlington, VA 22201
(703) 522-6121

**Journal of the
Association for Computing Machinery**
ACM
11 West 42nd Street
New York, NY 10036
(212) 869-7440

Journal of Systems Management
Association for Systems
Management
24587 Bagley Road
Cleveland, OH 44138
(216) 243-6900

**Local Metropolitan
Computer Salary Survey**
Source edp
342 Madison Avenue
New York, NY 10017
(212) 557-8611

LOGOS (Newsletter)
Information Management and
Processing Association
Post Office Box 16267
Lansing, MI 48901

A Look at Computer Careers
American Federation of
Information Processing
Societies
AFIPS Press
1899 Preston White Drive
Reston, VA 22091
(703) 620-8937

OTMA Newsletter
Office Technology Management
Association, Inc.
9401 West Beloit Road
Milwaukee, WI 53227
(414) 321-0880

**Recommendations and
Guidelines for Vocational
Technical Career Programs for
Computer Personnel in Operations**

**Recommendations for a Two-Year
Associate Degree Career
Program in Computer
Programming**
ACM
11 West 42nd Street
New York, NY 10036
(212) 869-7440

Robotics Today
Robotics International of SME
One SME Drive
Post Office Box 930
Dearborn, MI 48121
(313) 271-1500

Recognition Technologies Today
Recognition Technologies Users
Association
Post Office Box 2016
Manchester Center, VT 05255
(802) 362-4151

Salary Survey
Office Technology Management
Association
9401 West Beloit Road
Milwaukee, WI 53227
(414) 321-0880

**SIGACT News (Automata and
Computability Theory)**

SIGADA Ada Letters (Ada)

SIGAPL Quote Quad (APL)

**SIGARCH Computer
Architecture News (Archi-
tecture of Computer Systems)**

**SIGART Newsletter
(Artificial Intelligence)**

**SIGBDP DATABASE
(Business Data Processing)**

**SIGBIO Newsletter
(Biomedical Computing)**

**SIGCAPH Newsletter (Computers
and the Physically
Handicapped), Print Edition or
Cassette**

**SIGCAS Newsletter
(Computer and Society)**

**SIGCHI Bulletin
(Computer and Human Interaction)**

**SIGCOMM Computer Communica-
tions Review (Data Communications)**

**SIGCPR Newsletter
(Computer Personnel Research)**

**SIGCSE Bulletin
(Computer Science Education)**

**SIGCUE Bulletin
(Computer Uses in Education)**

**SIGDA
Newsletter (Design Automation)**

**SIGDOC Newsletter
(Systems Documentation)**

SIGGRAPH Computer Graphics

SIGIR Forum
(Information Retrieval)

SIGMAP Newsletter
(Mathematical Programming)

SIGMETRICS
Performance Evaluation Review
(Measurement and Evaluation)

SIGMICRO
Newsletter (Microprogramming)

SIGMOD Record (Management of Data)

SIGNUM Newsletter
(Numerical Mathematics)

SIGOA Newsletter
(Office Automation)

SIGOPS Operating Systems Review

SIGPC Notes
Special Interest Group
on Personal Computing

SIGPLAN Notices
(Programming Languages)

SIGPLAN Fortran Forum

SIGSAC Newsletter
(Security, Audit and Control)

SIGSAM Bulletin (Symbolic
and Algebraic Manipulation)

SIGSIM Simuletter (Simulation)

SIGSMALL/PC
Newsletter (Small and Personal
Computing Systems and Applications)

SIGSOFT Software Engineering Notes

SIGUCCS Newsletter (University
and College Computing Services)
ACM
11 West 42nd Street
New York, NY 10036
(212) 869-7440

SME News
Society of Manufacturing Engineers
One SME Drive
Post Office Box 930
Dearborn, MI 48121
(313) 271-1500

SOAP Box
Society of Office Automation Professionals
233 Mountain Road
Ridgefield, CT 06877
(203) 431-0029

Software News
875 Third Avenue
New York, NY 10022
(212) 605-9400

STC Technical Communication
Waverly Press
c/o Patricia Morris
428 East Preston Street
Baltimore, MD 21202

Transactions on Computer Systems

Transactions on Database Systems

Transactions on Graphics

Transactions on Mathematical Software

Transactions on
Office Information Systems

Transactions on
Programming Languages and Systems
ACM
11 West 42nd Street
New York, NY 10036
(212) 869-7440

Who's Who in Engineering
AAES
415 2nd Street, Southeast, Suite 200
Washington, DC 20002
(202) 546-2237

WIP Survey '83:
Salary & Career Perceptions
Women in Information Processing
Lock Box 39173
4005 Wisconsin Avenue, Northwest
Washington, DC 20016

The Word
Office Technology Management
Association
9401 West Beloit Road
Milwaukee, WI 53227
(414) 321-0880

Your Computer Career
Data Processing Management
Association
505 Busse Highway
Park Ridge, IL 60068
(312) 825-8124

Index

Other Bestsellers From TAB

☐ **BECOMING SELF-EMPLOYED: HOW TO CREATE AN INDEPENDENT LIVELIHOOD—Susan Elliott**

If you've ever felt the urge to leave the corporate world to become your own boss, you'll want this book. It reveals what it's like to go out on your own, what it takes to become successful, and what mistakes to avoid. Includes case studies of twenty successful entrepreneurs—what they did right, what they did wrong, and what they plan for the future and why.

Paper $7.95   Book No. 30149

☐ **THE PERSONAL TAX ADVISOR: UNDERSTANDING THE NEW TAX LAW—Cliff Roberson, L.L.M., Ph.D.**

How will the new tax law affect your tax return this filing season? Any reform is certain to mean a change in the way your taxes are prepared. But you don't have to be an accountant or a lawyer to understand the new tax lawsuse this easy-to-read guide and learn how to reduce your income taxes under the new federal rules!

Paper $12.95   Book No. 30134

☐ **THE SMALL BUSINESS TAX ADVISOR: UNDERSTANDING THE NEW TAX LAW—Cliff Roberson, LLM, Ph.D**

The most extensive changes ever in the history of American tax laws were made in 1986. And to help you better understand these changes, Cliff Roberson has compiled the information every small business operator, corporate officer, director, or stockholder needs to know into a manageable and readily understandable new sourcebook. 176 pp., 6″ × 9″.

Paper $12.95   Book No. 30024

☐ **HARD DISK MANAGEMENT WITH MS-DOS® AND PC-DOS®—Dan Gookin and Andy Townsend**

Whether you're a novice struggling with your hard disk system, an intermediate user in need of advice, or an old hand looking for some expert tips . . . this sourcebook can give you a big boost in understanding hard disks and using them to their fullest advantage. And if you're trying to decide whether or not to purchase a hard disk system for your office or personal computer, this is an ideal book to buy before you invest! 320 pp., 42 illus.

Paper $18.95   Hard $26.95
Book No. 2897

☐ **FORMING CORPORATIONS AND PARTNERSHIPS—John C. Howell**

If you're considering offering a service out of your home, buying a franchise, incorporating your present business, or starting a business venture of any type you need this time- and money-saving guide. It explains the process of creating a corporation, gives information on franchising, the laws of partnership, and more.

Paper $9.95   Book No. 30143

☐ **THE ENTREPRENEUR'S GUIDE TO STARTING A SUCCESSFUL BUSINESS—James W. Halloran**

Here's a realistic approach to what it takes to start a small business, written by a successful entrepreneur and business owner. You'll learn step-by-step every phase of a business start-up from getting the initial idea to realizing a profit. Included is advice on: designing a store layout, pricing formulas and strategies, advertising and promotion, small business organization charts, an analysis of future small business opportunities, and more. 256 pp., Paperback.

Paper $15.95   Book No. 30049

☐ **INFORMATION FOR SALE: HOW TO START AND OPERATE YOUR OWN DATA RESEARCH COMPANY— John H. Everett and Elizabeth Powell Crowe**

For those who are considering careers as information specialists, this guide explains the business side of information brokering, defines the needs of the general user market, examines research as an academic and business discipline, discusses the necessary equipment, suggests marketing methods, tackles the difficult question of pricing your services, takes you through an online database re-search simulation, and warns of legal considerations that must be taken into account. 192 pp., 25 illus.

Paper $15.95   Book No. 3057

☐ **ENCYCLOPEDIA OF LOTUS® 1-2-3®: A COMPLETE CROSS-REFERENCE TO ALL MACROS, COMMANDS, FUNCTIONS, APPLICATIONS AND TROUBLESHOOTING—Robin Stark**

Now, at last, there is one single sourcebook that can answer *all* your questions about Lotus 1-2-3—from the basics, to advanced applications data; from a listing of commands and functions to the most efficient use of macros; and from user tips and shortcuts to troubleshooting techniques. 496 pp., 183 illus.

Paper $19.95   Hard $29.95
Book No. 2891

Other Bestsellers From TAB

☐ **MICROCOMPUTER APPLICATIONS DEVELOPMENT: TECHNIQUES FOR EVALUATION AND IMPLEMENTATION—Michael Simon Bodner and Pamela Kay Hutchins**

This comprehensive guide represents an overview of the process of application development in the microcomputer environment from BOTH a technical methodology and a business issues point of view. The authors introduce the steps involved in applications development as well as numerous shortcuts and development tips that they have learned over the years. You'll get invaluable insight into the various types of projects you may encounter. 256 pp., 69 illus.

Hard $24.95   **Book No. 2840**

☐ **ASSEMBLY LANGUAGE SUBROUTINES FOR MS-DOS®COMPUTERS—Leo J. Scanlon**

This collection of practical, easy-to-use subroutines is exactly what you need for performing high-precision math, converting code, manipulating strings and lists, sorting data, reading user commands and responses from the keyboard, and doing countless other jobs. If you consider your time a valuable asset, you won't want to miss this handy quick-reference to a gold mine of subroutines. 350 pp., 43 illus.

Paper $19.95   **Hard $27.95**

Book No. 2767

Send $1 for the new TAB Catalog describing over 1300 titles currently in print and receive a coupon worth $1 off on your next purchase from TAB.

*Prices subject to change without notice.

▬▬▬▬▬▬▬▬▬▬▬▬▬▬▬▬▬▬▬▬▬▬▬▬▬▬▬▬▬▬▬

To purchase these or any other books from TAB, visit your local bookstore, return this coupon, or call toll-free 1-800-233-1128 (In PA and AK call 1-717-794-2191).

Product No.	Hard or Paper	Title	Quantity	Price

☐ Check or money order enclosed made payable to TAB BOOKS Inc.

Charge my   ☐ VISA   ☐ MasterCard   ☐ American Express

Acct. No. _____ Exp. _____

Signature _____

Please Print
Name _____

Company _____

Address _____

City _____

State _____ Zip _____

Subtotal	
Postage/Handling ($5.00 outside U.S.A. and Canada)	$2.50
In PA add 6% sales tax	
TOTAL	

Mail coupon to:
TAB BOOKS Inc.
Blue Ridge Summit
PA 17294-0840   BC